THE
FERTILE
PRISON

THE FERTILE PRISON

FIDEL CASTRO IN BATISTA'S JAILS

Mario Mencía

OCEAN

The publisher gratefully acknowledges the assistance of the José Martí Foreign Languages Publishing House and UFO Services of Havana, Cuba, in the preparation of this book.

ISBN 1-875284-08-7

Cover design by David Spratt

First edition, 1993

Printed in Australia

Published by Ocean Press,
GPO Box 3279, Melbourne, Victoria 3001, Australia

Distributed in the USA by the Talman Company,
131 Spring Street, New York, NY 10012, USA
Distributed in Britain and Europe by Central Books,
99 Wallis Road, London E9 5LN, Britain
Distributed in Australia by Astam Books,
162-8 Parramatta Road, Stanmore, NSW 2048, Australia

Contents

Mario Mencía

Mario Mencía Cobas (Cuba, 1931-) Historian, journalist, essayist. Graduate in Political Science. Doctoral candidate in history. Associate Professor at the University of Havana. Member of the permanent board of examiners for history of the national commission of degrees in the sciences.

Mencía is a former member of the editorial boards of the following magazines: *OCLAE, El Caimán Barbudo, Bohemia,* and of the newspaper *Juventud Rebelde.* For several years he headed the historical department of the last two publications. He has won numerous prizes for poetry, essays, short stories, articles, chronicles and reporting. He obtained the National Journalists "July 26 Prize" 12 times.

Mencía has presented papers at various international conferences on politics and history held in Latin America, Cuba, Europe and Canada.

His book, *La Prisíon Fecunda* (The Fertile Prison), has sold more than 350,000 copies in Cuba with editions in a number of languages in several countries. *La Prisíon Fecunda* has been adopted as a text in the Cuban educational system. His other books, including *El Grito de Moncada* (The Cry of Moncada) and *Tiempos Precursores* (Preliminary Years), have also been widely recognized and distributed in Cuba.

In addition, Mencía is coauthor of the following books: *Jovenes de esta América* (Youth of this America), Colección La Honda, Ed. Casa, Havana (1978); *Antes de Moncada* (Before Moncada), Ed. Unión, Havana (1979); *México y Cuba: Dos Pueblos Unidos en la Historia* (Mexico and Cuba: Two Peoples United in History) Ed. Centro de Investigaciones Cientificas "Jorge L.Tamayo", Mexico (1983); *El Alma Visible de Cuba: José Martí y el Partido Revolucionario Cubano* (The Visible Soul of

Cuba: José Martí and the Cuban Revolutionary Party) Ed. Ciencias Sociales, Havana (1984); *Juventud de la Crisis* (Youth of the Crisis) Ed. Centro de Estudios Económicos y Sociales del Tercer Mundo, Ed. Nueva Imagen, Mexico (1985); *Cinco Analisis sobre "La Historia Me Absolverá"* (Five Studies of "History Will Absolve Me") Ed. Ciencias Sociales, Havana (1986).

Mencía is presently preparing three contributions for the *Enciclopedia de la Juventud "La Edad de Oro"* (The Golden Age Encyclopedia for Youth) Ed. Gente Nueva, Havana, and the new volume in his series on the insurrectional period of Cuban history, *Del Presidio al Exilio* (From Prison to Exile), Ed. Política, Havana.

Secretary of foreign relations of the Historians' Union of Cuba (UNHIC), Mencía is a member of the Artists' and Writers' Union of Cuba (UNEAC), of the Journalists' Union of Cuba (UPEC), and of the Association of Latin American and Caribbean Historians (ADHILAC).

He belongs to the advisory council of Editorial Abril and Editorial de Ciencias Sociales and to the executive secretariat of the Cuban committee of the Anti-Imperialist Tribunal of Our America (TANA).

Mencía currently works as a researcher and adviser on history for the Council of State of the Republic of Cuba.

Publisher's preface

I don't think we are wasting our time in prison. To the contrary, we are preparing the vanguard and the leaders of our Movement ideologically and intellectually. For us, this prison is our academy of struggle, and when the time comes, nothing will be able to stop us.
Fidel Castro, January 1, 1955,
National Men's Prison, Isle of Pines.

In the early hours of Sunday, July 26, 1953, a group of 131 young men and women launched an armed attack on the Moncada military garrison in Santiago de Cuba. A simultaneous assault was made by a smaller group on the army headquarters at Bayamo, also in Cuba's eastern province, Oriente. Their object was to rouse the people of Cuba against the dictator, Fulgencio Batista, who had seized power in a coup on March 10, 1952.

"We were just a small bunch of men," Fidel Castro recalled 13 years later, on July 26, 1966. "We didn't think that a group like ours could overthrow the Batista dictatorship and defeat his army. But we did think that our group could seize enough weapons to begin arming the people; we knew that while such a force would not be able to defeat the regime, it would be sufficient to unleash the enormous energy of the people who would be capable of overturning the government."

The young rebels had called themselves the "Centennial Youth" — 1953 being the centenary of the birth of another young Cuban national hero, José Martí, who was killed in the independence struggle against Spain in 1895.

Cuban historian Mario Mencía has commented, "To their

amazement, the Cuban people were witnessing the birth of a new revolutionary vanguard. The nation's youth stormed into history, arms in hand, in an action which was without precedent in the history of the republic."

The attack, although it failed, shook the dictatorship which responded with equally unprecedented brutality. Sixty-one of the young rebels were killed during the fighting or immediately afterwards. Some were forced to dig their own graves, while others were horribly tortured and mutilated, before being murdered by their military captors. Virtually the entire group led by Abel Santamaría, second-in-command to Fidel Castro, which occupied the Saturnino López Civilian Hospital was tortured and assassinated, including the rebel doctor, Mario Muñoz. Only Haydée Santamaría and Melba Hernández, the only women amongst the combatants, survived.

Fidel with 18 men managed to reach the Sierra Maestra mountains, from where they planned to launch a guerrilla war. However, weak from exhaustion, short of weapons, and with some of the combatants wounded, they were captured while sleeping on August 1.

The trial of the Moncada rebels became a major national political event, although the dictatorship tried to suppress its publicity. Following their conviction, the male prisoners were sent to the National Men's Prison, then known as the "Model Prison," on the Isle of Pines off Cuba's south coast.

The Fertile Prison describes the 22 months that followed — how the young rebels continued their struggle from inside the prison walls, rearming themselves through study and rigid self-discipline. This book sheds considerable light on both the nature and development of these young revolutionaries and the movement they sought to build. It presents a portrait of Fidel Castro, then 27 years of age, and already the central political leader.

Mario Mencía relates the remarkable circumstances of the reconstruction, publication and distribution of Fidel Castro's courtroom defense of the Moncada attack which became known as *History Will Absolve Me* — an historic document which has now been translated into most of the major languages of the world.

The Fertile Prison shows how the tide was rapidly turning against the Batista dictatorship, leaving no option but to amnesty the Moncada combatants, opening the way for the next phase of the Cuban revolution — the two months of organizing the movement in Cuba before the exile in Mexico; the preparation of the *Granma* expedition, culminating in the return of Fidel Castro and 81 others; and the commencement of the revolutionary war.

Mencía has emphasized the importance of understanding this historical background. "To see the Cuban revolution," he writes, "only through the amazing revolutionary military epic of the war that begins when the *Granma* expedition reaches Cuba on December 2, 1956 — although it is the principal factor that in the final analysis is decisive in the overthrow of the dictatorship and the liberation of the people — assigns to the victory of the revolution a magical, accidental character that does not correspond with reality."

"That war," Mencía continues, "could only be carried out with the support and participation — both a moral and a practical commitment — of the Cuban people. It could only be carried out with the extensive propaganda, financial and logistic support of the cadres of the July 26 Movement. The war was prepared over a long period of time, raising the consciousness of the people during the five years of constant, intelligent political work with the masses, work which builds on the results of the struggle of several generations of Cuban revolutionaries."

The Fertile Prison by Mario Mencía therefore makes an important contribution to correcting the misconception that the Cuban revolution was a "miracle" performed by a small band of heroic guerrillas in the Sierra Maestra.

Since it was first published in 1980, half a million copies of *The Fertile Prison* have been sold. Apart from being a best-seller in Cuba — where it has been incorporated as a text in the education system — the book has now been published in eight languages.

First published in Cuba under the title *Time Was On Our*

Side by Havana's Editora Politica in 1982, this edition includes a full revision of the translation. The author has also made numerous corrections and some additions to the text. Of greatest significance in this new edition are the glossary and chronology prepared by Mencía. They are of considerable value to both students of Cuba who have some prior knowledge of the period, as well as the reader who is entering for the first time the tumultuous years of pre-revolutionary Cuba.

What makes this book of exceptional interest is the extensive use of documents and letters from the period — most previously unpublished. Little wonder that the works of Mario Mencía are widely acknowledged both inside Cuba and abroad.

The Fertile Prison is part of a series being prepared by Mencía on the revolutionary movement in Cuba 1952-6 — a period of history largely unknown outside of Cuba. The series includes *The Cry of Moncada*, *The Fertile Prison*, *The Departure from Prison*, and *The Turbulent Exile*. While these volumes will constitute a whole when completed, *The Fertile Prison*, the second in the series, which covers the period Fidel and other revolutionary leaders spent in prison after the attack on the Moncada garrison, can easily be read independently — even more so now with the guides of the glossary and chronology that Mencía has included.

The publication of *The Fertile Prison*, more than a decade after it first appeared in Cuba, begins a commitment by Ocean Press to publish this series by one of the most reputable historians of the insurrectional period of the Cuban revolution. The first titles in the series have already been used extensively by biographers of Fidel Castro, for no other books published in Cuba or elsewhere can provide such an insight into this period of the life and political evolution of Cuba's foremost leader.

The preparation of this book would not have been possible without the constant willingness of Mencía to support the initiative. His meticulous attention to the facts made easier the tasks of the editors in preparing the text and its revisions.

The translation appearing in this edition is based on that prepared by the Cuban Center for Translation and Interpretation (ESTI), and in particular, Mary Todd. Further translation assistance was provided by the José Martí Foreign Languages Publishing House of Havana.

The publisher acknowledges the assistance provided by the José Martí Publishing House and Félix Sautié of UFO Services in the preparation of this book.

Photos were provided by Mario Mencía, the José Martí Publishing House, *Bohemia* magazine, and the Office of Historical Affairs of the Council of State of Cuba.

Finally, it is necessary to recognize the support and encouragement that we have received in the preparation of both this volume and those that follow from Jesús Montané, an actual participant in the events described in *The Fertile Prison*.

David Deutschmann

Introduction

This book is the product of research by Mario Mencía, focusing on the revolutionary work conducted by Fidel Castro and the other fighters who attacked the Moncada garrison during their nearly 20 months of imprisonment in the former Model Prison on the Isle of Pines (now the Isle of Youth).

Although the Cuban people are generally familiar with this subject, it has actually been studied very little. Mencía gives us a broader, fuller, and more detailed picture of that stage and its far-reaching importance for the development of the revolutionary movement begun on July 26, 1953. Although a great deal remains to be done before the analysis of this period is exhausted, the author has managed to present a work of historical accuracy written in a journalistic style that makes for easy reading.

The book originally appeared as a five-part series published in *Bohemia* magazine in 1980, on the 25th anniversary of the departure of Fidel and his comrades from prison. Some new materials were added following the favorable response from readers, when it was decided to publish the five articles in a single volume. The book is mainly aimed at Cuba's young people, although publishing houses in other countries have also expressed an interest in *The Fertile Prison*, a title that seems to capture the essence of the events described.

The Fertile Prison shows how Fidel set himself and carried out the task of converting the prison into a new battleground from which to advance toward his revolutionary objectives — just as he had done during the trial for the Moncada attack.

The Batista dictatorship tried to cover the July 26 prisoners in a cloak of silence, as it had done with the monstrous assassinations it committed in Santiago de Cuba and other parts of what was then Oriente Province. The bourgeois mass media used every weapon in its arsenal against Fidel and his comrades, ranging from the grossest lies by the Batista regime to paternalistic "advice" and appeals for a "sensible" approach by the opportunists and cowards of the pseudo-opposition. Prison itself — the rigors of being locked up, the enforced isolation from the life of the country and the rest of the world, and its tendency to sap men's strength and breed lethargy and discouragement — was another hurdle to be overcome by Fidel and the other Moncada rebels.

Then there was the no less difficult task of linking the small group of survivors with the still largely unknown group of *compañeros* [comrades] scattered throughout the country who were ready to start building the revolutionary movement all over again. Fidel confronted all these obstacles with an iron determination.

Now, more than 25 years later, as we recall those months in prison, we clearly see our group of Moncada combatants as a small, organized, and disciplined army united firmly around Fidel.

There was really no time for idleness or depression. The authorities subjected us to a severe prison regimen filled with arbitrary acts and absurdities, while we imposed on ourselves a work and study program that was even more demanding and conscious. The Abel Santamaría Ideological Academy and reading took up the greater part of our time. As Fidel himself pointed out, "The lads are all magnificent. They constitute an elite, because they have gone through a thousand trials. Those who learned how to handle weapons are now learning how to handle books, preparing for the great battles of the future. Discipline is Spartan, as is their way of life, education, and everything else. Their faith and unbreakable firmness are such that it may be said of them, too, 'With your shield or upon it.'"

Mario Mencía has accurately reconstructed prison life, with all its incidents, both large and small. One particularly valuable aspect of this work is the resurrection of Fidel's impressive reading list, ranging from the classics of world literature to the works of Martí, Marx, Engels, and Lenin, and his many comments on these books. Another valuable contribution is Mencía's inclusion of Fidel's prison letters — documents of exceptional revolutionary and human interest, often written from solitary confinement, where our commander in chief was isolated from the rest of his comrades. They are filled with his innermost thoughts, expressed in an impressive literary style.

These letters by Fidel, which are practically unknown to the Cuban people, are even more important from a political and historical point of view because they reflect our commander in chief's extraordinary sense of tactics: his orientation toward mobilizing public opinion in support of the Moncada rebels and their revolutionary program; and generating a mass movement, without which the revolution would not have been possible. In this regard, Mario Mencía's description of the vicissitudes involved in first getting the notes of *History Will Absolve Me* out of prison and then printing and distributing the first edition is of exceptional interest.

Another topic of obvious historical value is the people's movement demanding amnesty for the political prisoners, which culminated in our release on May 15, 1955. This has also been researched and presented here in its national context.

In short, these pages give us an idea of how, in solitary confinement, Fidel conceived, prepared, and organized the conditions that enabled him to go on to create the July 26 Movement, the *Granma* expedition, and the relaunching of armed struggle against the Batista dictatorship. They show how those nearly 20 months of imprisonment served to frustrate the regime's aim of burying us in oblivion, and how the new revolutionary vanguard, led by Fidel, won the trust of the Cuban people.

Thus, what the leader of the revolution himself had said in one of his letters was borne out: "There is nothing greater than the stubbornness of a man who believes in his ideas and his truth. He is invincible, and all the power on earth is of no avail against him."

During his recent trip to Nicaragua, Fidel commented favorably on these articles by Mencía published in *Bohemia*, saying they had helped even him, their main protagonist, to recall many details, documents, and situations he had nearly forgotten. That is the chief merit of this effort: to help people learn about and recognize that this chapter of struggle and sacrifice should never be forgotten or ignored.

Mario Mencía, who has already done an outstanding job of historical research on other aspects of the revolutionary struggle, deserves special recognition for this work.

The greatest recognition he can get, however, will come from the Cuban people — and especially our young people — in their reception of this book. We sincerely invite all of them to read *The Fertile Prison*.

Jesús Montané Oropesa
October 1980

Chronology

1952

March 10: Fulgencio Batista heads a military coup against the Authentic Party government of President Carlos Prío, 80 days before scheduled general elections in which Batista is trailing both the Orthodox and Authentic Party presidential candidates. Batista eliminates both houses of parliament and all other provincial and municipal governing bodies, establishing his dictatorial rule.

April 5: National Revolutionary Movement (MNR) attempts to take Camp Columbia, Batista's military headquarters in Havana.

June 2: Various moderate opposition leaders led by Carlos Prío and Emilio Ochoa meet in Canada to unite their forces against Batista. This accord becomes known as the Montreal Pact.

1953

July 26: With a force of 160 combatants, the young lawyer, Fidel Castro, leads an attack on the Moncada army garrison in Santiago de Cuba, together with a support action aimed at seizing the garrison in Bayamo. The goal of the action is to spark a popular uprising against the Batista regime, arguing that the violence of the dictatorship must be answered with revolutionary violence. Castro, then 26, had been organizing some 2,000 youth since the Batista coup. Both actions fail and dozens of the captured revolutionaries are tortured and murdered. A number of the rebels are able to escape, some of whom are captured subsequently. The government launches a wave of repression against its opponents.

August 1: Castro is captured while sleeping in a mountain hut. Despite an order to have him summarily executed, the officer in charge protects Castro's life and brings him safely to Santiago de Cuba. He is taken to the nearby provincial jail in Boniato, where the other surviving Moncada combatants are being held.

September 21: Case 37, the trial of the captured Moncada rebels, begins in the Santiago de Cuba Provisional Court. In addition to the imprisoned revolutionaries, the defendants include a number of the regime's opponents, along with dozens of other individuals having no connection with the attack. Castro is tried separately, along with Abelardo Crespo, and prevented from attending the trial of the other Moncada rebels.

October 6: Twenty-eight of the defendants are found guilty and sentenced to prison.

October 13: Twenty-six Moncada prisoners are sent to the National Men's Prison on the Isle of Pines, while Haydée Santamaría and Melba Hernández are sent to the National Women's Prison in Guanajay, 50 kilometers from Havana.

October 16: The Provisional Court in Santiago tries Castro and Crespo, who is wounded in the Saturnino Lora Hospital. Fidel defends himself, delivering a speech that he will later reconstruct and publish as *History Will Absolve Me*. Found guilty by the court, he is sentenced to 15 years' imprisonment. He is sent to the National Men's Prison on the Isle of Pines the next day.

October 26: Batista calls general elections for November 1, 1954.

November 13: Mario Aróstegui Recio, a young railroad worker and Orthodox Party member, is tortured and assassinated by the army in Camagüey.

November 19: A meeting of moderate opposition leaders takes place in Mexico City to ratify the Montreal Pact.

November 27: Mario Fortuny, one of the leaders of the AAA and an opponent of the Batista dictatorship is arrested and murdered by the police. A number of leading AAA members then leave for exile in Mexico.

December 12: Fidel Castro writes a letter denouncing the massacre of the captured Moncada rebels, which is subsequently published as the "Manifesto to the Nation."

December 14: Former President Ramón Grau announces his candidacy for president in Batista's scheduled elections for the following year.

December: The Supreme Electoral Tribunal rejects the application to register the National United Front Party, the name which the Marxists had sought to register the Popular Socialist Party.

1954

January 3: Antonio "Ñico" López and Ernesto "Che" Guevara first meet in Guatemala City. It is from this moment that the political link of Che Guevara with the Cuban revolution commences.

January 28: José "Pepito" Tey Saint-Blancard takes office as president of the Federation of University Students of Oriente (FEU-O).

January: A commission of U.S. congressmen visits Cuba. One of their main purposes is to force the Cuban government to open its markets to the import of more U.S. lard.

February 12: Batista visits the prison on the Isle of Pines. The Moncada prisoners confront the dictator by singing the July 26 March.

February 14: In reprisal for the defiant gesture toward Batista, Castro is placed in solitary confinement. Reprisals are also made against other prisoners, including Augustín Díaz Cartaya, the author of the march.

February 18: Abelardo Crespo is sent to prison on the Isle of Pines, despite his not being fully recovered from his wounds.

February 20: Haydée Santamaría and Melba Hernández are released from prison. One of their first acts is to place a wreath at the grave of Orthodox Party leader Eduardo Chibás. They denounce in *Diario Nacional* the treatment of the prisoners on the Isle of Pines.

February 23: José Antonio Echeverría is elected general secretary of the Federation of University Students at the University of Havana.

February: The Council of Ministers approves the "last straw decree," granting electoral recognition to all parties participating in the government's registration process.

Raúl Chibas takes on the presidency of the Orthodox Party stating that he will work for the unity of its divided membership.

March 3: The Cuban Guatemala Support Committee is set up at a meeting held at the University of Havana.

March 5: The press publishes the revolutionary manifesto of the FEU proposed by Echevarría.

March 10: On the second anniversary of Batista's coup, students at the University of Havana take to the streets in protest. The

Federation of University Students of Oriente declares March 10 to be a day of mourning for the Cuban people.

March 13: An act of solidarity with the independence struggle of the people of Puerto Rico is organized in the headquarters of the FEU.

March 19: The FEU issues a statement denouncing the measures taken in prison against Fidel Castro.

March 28: José Antonio Echeverría, Fructuoso Rodríguez and other leaders of the FEU are brutally beaten by the police after showing signs condemning the elections during the Havana carnival. Students at the University of Havana declare a 48 hour strike.

April 13: Echeverría and others arrested begin hunger strike in jail. They are sentenced on April 19 to a month of imprisonment. Their sentence is condemned by the FEU.

April 22: Judge Waldo Medina visits Castro in his cell, breaking his isolation for the first time.

May 1: The government bans all activities commemorating May Day, the international day of the workers, except those organized by the CTC. Students at the University of Oriente defy the ban.

May 7: The Third National Congress of Secondary Students condemns the Batsita dictatorship and issues a statement against imperialism. A portrait is also unveiled in the FEU headquarters of Raúl Gómez García, assassinated during the assault on the Moncada barracks.

May 19: Melba Hernández travels to Mexico to establish contact with Moncada veterans living in exile and to meet with opposition figures. Fidel had earlier warned against concluding alliances with leaders of the Montreal Pact.

May 25: Police raid house in the Country Club district of Havana where AAA leader Aureliano Sánchez was hiding. Sánchez takes asylum in the Uruguayan Embassy and on June 5 travels to Mexico, but a suitcase containing a list of AAA members is seized. Some of those on the list are captured while others are able to escape to exile.

June 2: The newspaper *Oriente* publishes a declaration condemning the Batista dictatorship and the electoral fraud, signed by Frank País, Pepito Tey and others.

June 4: The government grants a political amnesty to the regime's opponents, but excludes all those who participated in the Moncada attack. It is therefore dubbed the "false amnesty." Under this decree, Rafael García Bárcena, leader of the MNR, is freed from prison on June 5.

June 12: Police capture explosives arsenals in Havana of the group Liberator Action. Several of the group's members seek asylum in embassies and subsequently go into exile. Justo Carrillo, central leader of the group, escapes to the United States.

June 17: From Honduras, mercenary forces backed by the CIA invade Guatemala, then under the nationalist regime of Jacobo Arbenz. This provokes a wave of protest. Students at the University of Havana and Oriente volunteer to defend the Arbenz government. Police search the FEU headquarters and the School of Medicine in Havana for arms and the government accuses the students of being directed by communists.

June 27: Arbenz is betrayed by military leaders forced to resign and is replaced by a pro-U.S. regime, which carries out a massacre of its opponents.

After 134 days of solitary confinement, two other inmates are placed in Castro's cell.

June: Castro completes the reconstruction of his defense speech, *History Will Be Absolve Me*. The speech is smuggled out of the prison over the course of several months.

Echeverría goes to meet Prío in Miami. His appeal for arms is rejected.

The Popular Socialist Party launches its "vote against" slogan for the elections of November 1: a vote for Grau is a vote against Batista, although this is no solution to the crisis.

July 9: *Bohemia* publishes an interview with Castro by Raúl Martín in which he criticizes all the forces participating in Batista's electoral maneuver, while calling for unity in the struggle against the dictatorship.

July 12: An armed commando squad of the MNR rescues Gustavo Arcos from hospital, where he had been recovering from wounds received during the assault on the Moncada barracks. Arcos was subsequently recaptured July 29 and sent to prison on the Isle of Pines, condemned to 10 years' imprisonment.

July 14: Batista appoints Andrés Domingo Morales del Castillo as president. One of his first measures is to ban the Popular Socialist Party.

July 24: An armed commando unit led by Frank País attacks the police station in El Caney in the province of Oriente. Although the attack fails, they succeed in carrying off a Springfield rifle.

July 26: On the first anniversary of the Moncada attack, several commemorative activities are held. A demonstration led by Haydée Santamaría and Melba Hernández is broken up by the police at the Colón Cemetary. Thousands of leaflets are distributed denouncing the dictatorship's crimes against the Moncada combatants.

That same day the Federation of University Students holds a ceremony at the University of Havana, and a demonstration of Orthodox members is attacked by the police when it marches to Central Park in Havana.

Minister of the Interior Ramón O. Hermida visits Castro in his cell, provoking a controversy in government circles.

July: Raúl Castro is moved to a joint cell with Fidel. The two will be held together until their release.

August 29: Otto Parellada and three other members of Liberator Action are arrested when preparing an attempted explosive attack against Batista in Santiago de Cuba. They are sentenced to four years' imprisonment.

September 14: Lidia Castro, sister of Fidel and Raúl, publishes a statement in *Diario Nacional* rejecting the initiative of a group of Orthodox Party members to nominate Fidel Castro as an election candidate.

September 30: José Antonio Echeverría takes on the presidency of the FEU, and leads the call for a public boycott of the November elections.

October 12: Police capture in Havana a group of young members of the MNR, headed by Faustino Pérez, Pepé Prieto, Enriqué and Armando Hart, who, along with Frank País and Vilma Espín and other young activists from Oriente, were preparing sabotage actions against the elections. Faustino Pérez is sentenced to three years imprisonment. Even though he was not linked with these events, Rafael García Bárcena goes into exile once again.

October 26: Police capture an enormous arsenal of weapons in the basement of the house of Paquito Cairol in the Country Club. The weapons belonged to the AAA. A further group of its members went into exile.

October 28: During an election rally for Grau in Santiago de Cuba broadcast over national radio, the audience repeatedly chants the name of Fidel Castro.

October: *History Will Absolve Me* is published and circulated clandestinely throughout the country.

Frank País, Pepito Tey and other young militants in Oriente establish a new underground insurrectionary organization, Revolutionary Action of Oriente (ARO).

November 1: General elections are held throughout Cuba. Ramón Grau had withdrawn from the contest the day before, leaving Batista as the only candidate.

November 18: The FEU makes a public call for continuing the struggle against the Batista dictatorship, despite the legal disguise of its electoral "mandate."

December 1: The FEU calls for the release of all political prisoners, including the Moncada prisoners. The declaration provides a new impulse to the campaign for amnesty.

December 6: A law is announced granting private corporations the right to build a canal through Cuba. This is viewed as violating Cuba's sovereignty and a storm of protest leads to the eventual abandonment of the plan.

December: A committee of parents of the Moncada prisoners circulates postcards calling for a broad campaign aimed at winning amnesty.

1955

January 18: José Antonio Echeverría leads a group of students who travel to Costa Rica to fight against soldiers of the Nicaraguan dictator Somoza who had invaded Costa Rica. A week later they are arrested and deported to Cuba where student protests bring about their release.

January 23: President Andrés Domingo Morales signs a law prohibiting civil courts from trying any crime committed by military personnel.

January 27: A law is signed decreeing that any individual deemed a communist can be fired from any government or trade union post.

January 28: 500 young people commemorating the anniversary of José Martí's birth led by Frank País and Pepito Tey attempt to march to the cemetery in Santiago de Cuba where Martí is buried. The march is attacked by police and over 30 are wounded or arrested.

February 6: U.S. Vice-President Richard Nixon arrives in Cuba, apparently indicating U.S. support to Batista's regime.

February 8: In an underground statement the Popular Socialist Party condemned the many illegal acts of the dictatorship and called for popular support for amnesty for all political prisoners.

February 11: Carlos Prío and his followers in the United States send a letter to U.S. Vice-President Richard Nixon asking for the intervention of the U.S. government to pressure Batista to leave power.

February 13: Students organize a militant demonstration in the streets of Havana. Among the slogans taken up is one calling for the release of the Moncada prisoners. They are attacked by the police and José Antonio Echeverría is seriously wounded in the head.

February 24: Fulgencio Batista and Rafael Guas Inclán are formally proclaimed president and vice-president by Cuba's Senate and House of Representatives.

In a *Bohemia* interview, Batista states he is prepared to sign an amnesty law that would include the Moncada prisoners, if they agree not to participate in antigovernment activities.

A "Public Appeal" signed by prominent opposition leaders is circulated, calling for a general amnesty.

Two anti-Batista activists, Orlando León Lemus and José Angel "Mitico" Fernández are murdered by police.

March 10: Police break up a demonstration at the University of Havana protesting the third anniversary of Batista's coup.

March 27: *Bohemia* publishes a letter from Castro smuggled out of prison rejecting Batista's offer of conditional amnesty. Fidel and Raúl Castro are later punished by a 30-day suspension of communication and visits.

March: A shipment of arms belonging to the Authentic Party arrives in Pinar del Río from Mexico. Cándido de la Torre leads the operation which also secretly returns to Cuba a number of exiles.

A new legal organization emerges, the Radical Liberation Movement. Made up of young professionals and intellectuals, many of them religious activists, the new group is led by figures such as Amalio Fiallo, Andrés Valdespino, Nicolás Ríos and Mario Llerena.

April 1: Appearance of the first issue of the newspaper *La Calle*, published by Luis Orlando Rodríguez. Banned since 1952, the paper makes as its focus the call for amnesty for the Moncada prisoners.

April 9: The Movement of the Nation is formed by various representatives of the petty bourgeois opposition. It represents the formal departure from the Orthodox Party of Jorge Mañach and José Pardo Llada, as well as the dissolution of Liberator Action.

April 14: The police capture another arms cache of the Authentic Party, this time in the suburb of La Víbora in Havana.

April: The Batista government provides 10 million pesos to the Electricity Company of Cuba, a subsidiary of Electric Bond and Share which had a monopoly on power generation.

Allan Dulles, head of the CIA, arrives in Cuba to organize the Bureau for the Repression of Communist Activities (BRAC).

May 2: The House of Representatives approves a bill calling for amnesty for political prisoners, which includes the Moncada prisoners.

May 3: The Senate approves the Amnesty Law and sends it to the Council of Ministers for its official sanction.

May 4: The BRAC is established by presidential decree.

May 6: Batista signs the amnesty law.

May 8: José Antonio Echeverría, Fructuoso Rodríguez and José Venegas are brutally attacked and imprisoned by the police in Matanzas where they took part in an act to commemorate the 20th anniversary of the death of Antonio Guiteras.

May 15: Fidel Castro and the other Moncada prisoners are released under the amnesty law from the Isle of Pines.

June 12: Fidel Castro's revolutionary forces are reorganized as the

July 26 Revolutionary Movement.

July 7: With threats to his life, Fidel Castro leaves Cuba for exile in Mexico, where he begins preparations for relaunching the armed struggle against Batista.

1956

December 2: The yacht *Granma* lands in Cuba at Las Coloradas in the province of Oriente with 82 combatants to begin the war against Batista. Despite an initial reverse, some of the fighters succeed in reaching the Sierra Maestra mountains, where Castro reorganizes the Rebel Army forces.

1959

January 1: Batista flees Cuba. An attempt by the military leaders to form a government is thwarted by Fidel Castro's call from Santiago de Cuba for a national general strike. Units of the Rebel Army arrive in Havana.

CHAPTER 1

"For me, the happiest moment of 1953 and of all my life was when I went off to battle. The harshest was when I had to face the tremendous setback of defeat, with its aftermath of infamy, slander, ingratitude, misunderstanding, and envy," Fidel wrote from prison on December 31, 1953. The happiest moment was dawn on Sunday, July 26. The harshest was to begin six days later, on August 1, when he was taken prisoner, beginning a period that lasted 21 months and 15 days, until May 15, 1955 when he left prison. This was a period Fidel Castro himself described as one in which "I have rounded out my view of the world and determined the meaning of my life." This was the period that for him — and, therefore, for the triumphant development of the Cuban revolution — was the crucial time of...

The fertile prison

The communiqué was quite stark. The three-column headline — it did not even warrant top billing on the page — was mediocre. Nothing in the layout of the press dispatch in the *Diario de Cuba* indicated the deep-going significance of the news it contained:

"HAVANA, October 13 (By Prewi) — Dr. Ramón Hermida, minister of the interior, ordered yesterday that the 27 prisoners sentenced by the Provisional Court of Santiago de Cuba for the events surrounding the Moncada garrison be transferred to the national prison on the Isle of Pines."

The article then went on to print the text of the decree signed by the minister of the interior the day before, October 12, 1953.

In its second "whereas," the document stated: "The aforementioned Court has ordered that 27 of those sentenced serve their time at the prison of the La Cabaña fortress."

Nevertheless, in its first "be it resolved", the decree called for "the transfer of Ernesto Tizol Aguilera, Oscar Alcalde Valls, Pedro Miret Prieto, Raúl Castro Ruz, Andrés García Díaz, Enrique Cámara Pérez, Agustín Díaz Cartaya, René Bedia Morales, Eduardo Montano Benítez,[1] José Suárez Blanco, Mario Chanes de Armas,[2] Juan Almeida Bosque, Armando Mestre Martínez, Francisco González Hernández, Ciro Redondo García, José Ponce Díaz, Ramiro Valdés Menéndez, Rosendo Menéndez, Julio Díaz González, Israel Tápanes, Jesús Montané Oropesa, Reinaldo Benítez Nápoles, Fidel Labrador García, Gabriel Gil Alfonso, Orlando Cortés Gailardo, Eduardo Rodríguez Alemán, and Manuel Lorenzo Acosta,[3] now being held in the Oriente provincial prison, to the national prison for men at Nueva Gerona, on the Isle of Pines, where they will be held in special sections separated from the common prisoners until other instructions are issued."

In line with its usual practice since March 10, 1952,[4] the tyranny not only dictated the ruling of the court but also violated some of its specific orders. This was to be no exception.

When on the morning of Wednesday, October 13 the *Diario de Cuba* was being hawked through the streets of Santiago de Cuba, a group of prisoners composed of two women and 26 men was already being taken to Havana — at least that's where they thought they were going. This group included Melba Hernández and Haydée Santamaría, who had been sentenced to seven months in prison, and all the men named in the ministerial decree except Fidel Labrador, who was to be sent four days later.

During the flight, cooped up inside two military planes,

---

1. Later a traitor to the Cuban revolution.
2. Idem
3. He did not participate in the attack on the Moncada Garrison.
4. On March 10, 1952, Fulgencio Batista y Zaldívar headed a group of active and retired armed forces officers who occupied the general staff headquarters at Camp Columbia, seized military power, proclaimed Batista head of state, and forced President Carlos Prío Socarrás to resign. Known as the March 10 coup, this action initiated seven years of brutal dictatorship that ended with the triumph of the revolution on January 1, 1959.

staring at their guards' machine guns, there was almost no con-
versation — only the roar of the DC-3s as they left behind the
imposing mountains of Oriente, and with them a landmark in
history. Handcuffed in pairs and seated on benches with their
backs to the windows, those 26 men and two women embodied
an entire people's hopes for freedom.

Anxiety. Pain. Behind them in Santiago de Cuba, where José
Martí was buried after he had fallen fighting for his homeland's
independence, were their dead comrades. Behind them was Fidel,
still imprisoned in Santiago.

Ahead, the future and — or so they thought — Havana, which
165 of them had left three months earlier. Their sentence had
stipulated that they be sent as political prisoners to the La Cabaña
fortress, one of Havana's walled military bastions built during the
time of Spanish colonialism. Almost at the end of the trip, however, the two planes turned south over the Gulf of Batabanó and
circled over the tiny Sierra de Colombo.

Only one of the prisoners did not have to wonder where they
were being taken. Palmar Point, where the 12-kilometer long Las
Casas River flowed into the sea; the city blocks of Nueva Gerona;
the tiny El Abra Valley; the marble quarries; and finally the
swampy area on the other side of Guanábana Hill and its five
huge white buildings were all familiar landmarks to Jesús (Chuc-
ho) Montané. As a child he had left that smaller island to go to
the larger one and become an accountant. He had joined the
Orthodox Party and, alongside Abel Santamaría and Fidel, had
become a member of the Movement's leadership, one of those
who attacked the Moncada, and now...

"We touched down on a dusty landing strip," Israel Tápanes
recalled, "and, on descending from the plane, were met by
Lieutenant Perico.[5] Tall, thin, slightly stoop-shouldered, with a
hooked nose and a wrinkled face, he always wore huge, very
dark glasses that made it impossible to know where he was

---

5. Pedro Rodríguez Coto (Perico) was a police lieutenant in the Ministry of the
Interior. By December 1958 he had reached the rank of major in the repressive
forces of the dictatorship. He was shot following the triumph of the revolution.

looking. He had what was known as an ox-dick whip in his back pocket and a revolver of the kind issued to the Rural Guards in his belt," Tápanes recalled. "It was not a very friendly welcome. With an authoritarian tone he told us to get in line, counted us, and took us to a bus, where we were locked in and driven to the prison."

Valiant women
From there, Melba and Haydée were taken on to the airport at Camp Columbia, in Marianao, headquarters of the general staff of the dictatorship's armed forces, and then to the National Women's Prison in Guanajay, Pinar del Río Province.

The comrades, who had wanted to farewell Melba and Haydée with a last message of revolutionary encouragement did not even have time to see the plane carrying the two of them take off from Nueva Gerona for the capital. The women arrived at the Guanajay prison in a Military Investigation Service (SIM) car with a heavy escort.

The only other woman to have been jailed for revolutionary activities was Eva Jiménez. She was sentenced to six months for her participation in the Easter Sunday Conspiracy in April 1953, which was led by Rafael García Bárcena, who headed the Revolutionary Nationalist Movement.[6] Thus, Melba and Haydée were among the first women political prisoners in the history of the truncated republic.

The Guanajay prison consisted of four two-story rectangular buildings with a smaller, narrower administration building in front. The most troublesome prisoners were kept in Cellblock D, which had a punishment cell that was "really inhuman. It had a metal door with a hole at the bottom through which food was shoved to the inmate. It had no bed, no nothing. We slept on the

6. On Sunday, April 5, 1953, the Revolutionary National Movement (MNR) had planned an uprising to topple Batista by capturing Camp Columbia with the aid of sympathetic army officers. The leaders of the conspiracy were arrested several hours before the appointed time of the uprising after the government. Later many of key MNR activists joined the July 26 Movement.

floor," the heroines of the Moncada recalled years later.[7]

Cellblock B housed prisoners who had small children. Cellblock A was for those on good behavior. The first floor of Cellblock A also contained the kitchen and a small storage area. That area was fixed up as a cell for Melba and Haydée. Partitions were put up to divide it into four parts: a bedroom, kitchen (where they cooked for themselves), dining room and bathroom.

Friends were sometimes authorized to visit them, and they were allowed to receive all kinds of books. But they were always kept apart from the rest of the prisoners and were never allowed out in the yard to get any sun. They were able to enjoy this small privilege when relatives came to see them on visiting days.

Their intensely active previous life sharply contrasted the sedentary existence in Guanajay. There, behind the bars of a storeroom turned into a cell, time seemed to lose all meaning. Day after day dragged by: October, November...

November 27 brought memories of the year before, when together with Abel, Boris Luis,[8] Fidel and Montané they had gone to the steps of the university to attend the mass meeting on the 81st anniversary of the execution of the medical students.[9] That night, for the first time, the police halted the commemoration by cutting off the electricity in the area.

Now, behind the bars of their cell, how could they fail to think of Abel, Boris Luis, and all the other *compañeros* with whom they would never again share the enthusiasm of the struggle? This

---

7. Lechuga and B. Marqués: "Correr la misma suerte que nuestros compañeros" (Running the same risks as our comrades), *Bohemia*, July 26, 1974.
8. Abel Santamaria; Boris Luis Santa Coloma.
9. On November 27, 1871 — three years after the outbreak on October 10, 1968, of what was to be known as the Ten Years' War initiating Cuba's struggle for independence against Spanish colonialism — eight young medical students from the University of Havana were executed by firing squad. They were accused of having desecrated the tomb of ultrarightist Spanish journalist Gonzalo de Castañón, who had been killed in a duel with a Cuban patriot in Key West, Florida, at the beginning of the year. Even though the accusation was totally unfounded (it was shown that the cracks in the tomb's glass were caused by faulty construction) and the alleged perpetrators were arbitrarily selected (every 10th member of the student body was taken), a summary court-martial violating all norms of court procedure found them guilty and had them executed within a matter of hours.

time, the ceremony at the university was held without them. Its participants were on the alert as earlier that day Mario Fortuny, a fighter in the underground and a true representative of the sustained courage of the revolution of the 1930s, had been murdered — shot in the back by the henchmen of the regime.

When the two Moncada prisoners in Guanajay heard the news, they were so indignant that the head of the prison was called in to calm them down. This was useless, for they had such different ethics and ideas on how to react to the economic, political, and social problems of the country. How could there be any understanding?

Dr. Guanche de Cárdenas, the prison director, had been a feminist leader during the 1930s, but by middle age had lost the revolutionary spirit of her youth and had become a watchdog of a system that had once again sunk into a dehumanized satrapy. Her patronizing cynicism made no dent on the two Moncada rebels.

Moreover, this was not the first of these talks. The three or four hours' discussion they had had with her on the day of their arrival had been equally futile. Her kind gesture of phoning Haydée's and Melba's relatives to tell them they had arrived safely, did not temper the new prisoners' angry response to her description of the events at the Moncada as a romantic gesture by "crazy" young people. That was enough, and from that midday of October 13 on the women in the two opposing ideological camps were clearly divided by insurmountable differences.

Double punishment

At the same time, at midday on October 13, 1953, a bus with 26 new prisoners locked inside was hurtling along the palm-lined avenue in Nueva Gerona that led to what was then called the Model Prison of the Isle of Pines.[10]

Laid out symmetrically, its many buildings were surrounded by a double wire fence, with watchtowers both inside and out.

---

10. This was what it was called when it was opened by the Machado dictatorship in the 1930s. Later, it was called the National Men's Prison of the Isle of Pines. Following the triumph of the revolution, it was closed down as a prison, and in 1980 it was declared a national monument. It is now an historical museum.

The complex consisted of 10 large buildings, with a total capacity for 5,000 prisoners. Three rectangular buildings in front housed the administration, the offices for processing incoming prisoners, and the quarters for prisoners on good behavior. These were followed by four huge five-story circular buildings with 93 cells per tier, each with two bunks that could be folded back against the wall: a total of 465 cells, for 930 prisoners, in each building. Another circular building in the center, only two stories high, was the dining hall "of the 3,000 silent ones," as Pablo de la Torriente Brau described it in his time. Behind this were two square, one-story buildings containing four inner yards. One building was used as a hospital and the other was for mentally ill prisoners, who were kept in punishment cells.[11]

Work on the first circular cellblock began on February 17, 1928, and was completed in 1931. The building was intended for common prisoners sentenced to terms of more than 180 days. Soon, however, its bars clanked shut around the young fighters in the revolution of the 1930s who were sent there. One of them, Pablo de la Torriente Brau, writing with the pen of a cinematographer, vividly described the conditions there:

> Thousands of screams, cries of dying men drowning in the mud and putrifying matter of the swamps; cut down by the sabers of the soldiers; shot down like fleeing deer; dying of starvation, cold, and thirst in the cells; strangled in cold blood inside the circular cellblocks by older inmates; hurled like rag dolls from the top floors to crumple on the pavement; put to sleep forever on the operating table by a injection, with the terrified or accessory silence of the nurses.[12]

First Machado, then Batista. Tyranny is tyranny, no matter what

---

11. A detailed architectural description of each of the buildings, including a list of the materials used in their construction, furnishings, and ornamental and functional details may be found in *El gran suicida, apuntes de una época revolucionaria* (The great suicide: notes on a revolutionary era) by José E. Embade Neyra (Havana: Imprenta y Librería La Propagandística, Havana, 1934).

12. Pablo de la Torriente Brau, *Presidio Modelo* (Model Prison) (Havana: Editorial de Ciencias Sociales, 1969).

the tyrant's name. Its interests were the same, and it meted out the same treatment to its opponents whenever they escaped being murdered. Separated from the rest of the country by 56 miles of sea, the prison on the Isle of Pines carried a double punishment: imprisonment plus exile.

On the night of Wednesday, October 13, 1953, the first Moncada prisoners on the Isle of Pines got almost no sleep. After being processed, they were placed in one of the wards of the hospital — the one on the right, on the southern side of the building. In this ward blinding lights (five 500-watt bulbs) were kept on all night, every night during the next two years, while prisoners doing forced labor worked all night erecting a brick wall to isolate them from the rest of the prisoners.

At 5:00 in the morning, they were roused for the head count, which the night guard (on duty from 6:00 p.m. to 6:00 a.m.) made before turning over his post to the day guard (who was on duty the other 12 hours). The prisoners then cleaned their cells and made their beds — which they were not allowed to use again until midday, when a bell signaled the obligatory nap.

That was how it was at first, when they did not yet have any mosquito nets or places to put sheets and towels or pieces of cardboard to protect them from the light, and it had not occurred to them to make covers for their eyes. What with the bright light, the mosquitoes, their concern over their families — how they would make ends meet and the harassment to which the repressive forces would subject them in their own homes — the memory of their comrades who had been killed, and their sense of impotence triggered by the crushing of their revolutionary effort, it was nearly impossible to sleep.

Moreover, Fidel had not arrived, and they had no way of communicating with the outside world. Their only contact was with two prisoners and a guard. The prisoners brought in a sack of bread and a big can of milk for breakfast at 7:30 a.m. and returned at 11:00 with lunch and at 5:00 p.m. with dinner. The jailer, who drew his authority from his blue denim uniform, his 67-peso salary, his Springfield rifle, and his Colt .38 revolver, went near the political prisoners only to open the sole barred door to their cell in the morning. This permitted them to enter one of the walled, cement-floored inner yards, that offered them their only sight of sky, sun, and ever-changing clouds.

The yard — 12 white marble benches in a rectangle under a ledge — was locked again every evening at 6:00 p.m., when the prisoners' world was again reduced to the dormitory-style cell. The prison ward was quite luxurious: it had three showers, two toilets, and a sink jammed into a corner to the left, near the back. At 10:00 p.m., the hinges of the grate creaked, metal struck metal as the key turned in the lock, and the order for silence was given.

That was at first — before they put together the few pesos and scanty supplies sent them by friends and relatives and formed an equal-distribution cooperative, to "confront all individualistic traits," as Montané put it on May 15, 1975, the 20th anniversary of the Moncada prisoners' departure from the Isle of Pines:

> We set up a cooperative to improve the compañeros' diet, using the modest contributions of relatives and friends. This strengthened our sense of collectivity and solidarity, which was consolidated in meetings where we held frank discussions on all matters of common concern.

So they shared fruit and the food that they could prepare on the hot plate they were allowed to have — a pot of hot chocolate at night, for example, when they stayed up late reading the books that also began to arrive to stock their Raúl Gómez García Library.

This was even before they were granted one visiting day a month and the right to send and receive letters — which, it goes without saying, were read and strictly censored. This was long before they found ways to get around this control and the rigid isolation that was later imposed on them and it was shortly before they organized the Abel Santamaría Ideological Academy.

Some documents dated more than a year later show that in prison the Moncada fighters alternated their studies and discussions with recreational activities, which, because of their extreme confinement, were very limited: chess, table tennis, and volley-ball.[13] Everything seems to indicate that an attempt to send them a refrigerator, to make life a little more pleasant, was quashed by the director of the prison.[14]

Later, several months after their arrival, they took turns doing clean-up in pairs. Oscar Alcalde was placed in charge of purchases and individual accounts, Pepe Suárez distributed the cooperative's supplies, and others were assigned other permanent jobs. Regulations were drawn up, and all collective affairs were discussed in meetings that Miret presided over, in which Tápanes, as secretary, recorded the agreements.

The first agreement that appears in the book sets down the norms for holding these meetings, in 10 simple articles:

Article 1. Regular general assemblies will be held on the first day of each month, beginning at 7:00 p.m., unless the first falls on a Saturday, Sunday, or other holiday, in which case the assembly will be held either the next Monday or the following day.

Article 2. The group reading assigned for the day on which the regular assembly is to be held will be suspended.

Article 3. In every regular assembly, the secretary will read the minutes of the preceding session and the agenda, which he and the chairman have drawn up. The last item on the agenda will be general matters.

---

13. Volleyball was the best-suited sport for it required few material resources, and the space available in the inner yard was adequate. A report that First Lieutenant Pedro Rodríguez Coto, head of internal order in the prison, made to his supervisor on April 5, 1955, stated, "As a result of my investigation into how the prisoner Juan Almeida Bosque fractured the extremity of his right radius, I have learned that he slipped while playing volleyball in the yard of the building in which he is housed and fell to the pavement, hurting himself. I believe that it was an accident." The accident occurred on March 30.

14. The letter that Sergio Montané Soto, Jesús Montané's father, wrote to prison director Major Capote on February 20, 1955, contained the following: "As you will recall, the table tennis table has still not been brought to Nueva Gerona to be repaired. We would like you to repeat your order that the prison truck bring it to us so we can fix it, since it is no good as is.... Some of the boys' families want to chip in and get them a small refrigerator, but they don't know if you will authorize this or not. I therefore request your permission."

Article 4. A special assembly may be held whenever seven or more compañeros request it of the secretary in writing, explaining their reasons for doing so.

Article 5. The written request setting forth the reasons for holding the assembly should be presented before 6:00 p.m.

Article 6. No matters other than those listed in the request may be brought up in a special assembly.

Article 7. Special assemblies shall begin at 7:45 p.m., after the conclusion of the group reading.

Article 8. Insulting expressions may not be used in the debate, and it is absolutely prohibited to justify mistakes by claiming that the critic would have made the same, a similar, or any other kind of mistake.

Article 9. The chairman is empowered to take the floor away from any compañero he considers to be obstructing the progress of the assembly.

Article 10. The chairman is also invested with absolute power to conduct the assembly as he deems best to assure its success.
Signed:
Pedro Miret, Chairman
Israel Tápanes, Secretary

But all that was to come later.

It was now the morning of Saturday, October 16. Those in the building and the yard did not know that far off in a room in the Saturnino Lora Hospital in Santiago de Cuba, the next to the last part of Case 37, for "crimes against state powers" (the events of July 26) was coming to a close. The sentencing of the main defendant to 15 years' imprisonment came as an anticlimax to Fidel's last words in his two-hour defense speech: "Condemn me. It does not matter. History will absolve me."[15]

Those words, which closed the legal aspect of the Moncada history, simultaneously opened the most important chapter in the long history of the Cuban revolution.

A significant coincidence summed up the age-old class polariz-

<hr>

15. See the legal record of Fidel Castro's sentence, printed in appendix 3.

ation of antagonistic forces in Cuba. At the precise moment when Fidel Castro was making his accusation of the system and emerging as spokesman of the Cuban people and of the nation's basic rights to full independence and sovereignty, Batista was receiving the credentials of Arthur Gardner,[16] the new U.S. proconsul assigned to our country, in the Presidential Palace in sultry Havana.

A few hours later, on Sunday, October 17, 1953, Fidel entered Building 1 of the prison hospital in Nueva Gerona and embraced his comrades, trying to hug them all at once. That night, at the end of the room where his bed was,[17] nearly in front of the bathroom, he told them about everything that had happened since he had been separated from the group in the Boniato jail. The vanguard was reunited.

Because of their own wretched character, the officials of the regime assumed that others had the same petty reactions. They could not imagine the existence of a world that, unlike theirs, was

---

16. Named ambassador to Cuba by President Dwight D. Eisenhower, Gardner had been assistant-secretary of the treasury under U.S. President Harry S. Truman. Gardner was to become a close friend of Batista's. A little later, he considered himself to be the "father of BRAC" (Bureau for the Repression of Communist Activities), that was founded in Cuba in May 1955 and took its orders from Allen Dulles, director of the Central Intelligence Agency, and Lyman Kirkpatrick, its inspector-general. Replaced as ambassador to Cuba on May 14, 1957, by Earl T. Smith, Gardner told the U.S. Senate Internal Security Subcommitte years later that shortly before leaving Cuba, he had suggested to Batista that it would be a good idea for a CIA or FBI hit man to be sent to the Sierra Maestra to kill Fidel Castro. Gardner freely admitted to the members of the subcommittee that he did not think he had ever had a better friend than Batista and that it was a shame it had gotten out that, like all the other Latin American rulers, he got a kickback from everything that went on in the country. He added that he thought Batista had been doing a marvelous job.

17. The metal beds, typical of hospitals in that period, were in two rows, running the length of the rectangular ward. Their occupants were as follows: first row in this order: José Suárez, Fidel Castro, Jesús Montané, Julio Díaz, Ramiro Valdés, Oscar Alcalde — next came a bookcase — Ciro Redondo, Abelardo Crespo, Pedro Miret, Raúl Castro, Enrique Cámara, and Andrés García (then the two who later turned traitor, Eduardo Montano and Mario Chanes). Second row: Rosendo Menéndez, Reinaldo Benítez, Israel Tápanes, René Bedia, Armando Mestre, Juan Almeida — next came the door — Ernesto Tizol, Fidel Labrador, Eduardo Rodríguez, Orlando Cortés, Francisco González, Gabriel Gil, José Ponce, and Agustín Díaz Cartaya.

based on pure revolutionary values. Thus, when they took Fidel to Boniato, they imagined Fidel would be repudiated by the others. This did not — and could not possibly — have occurred to those who had generously joined together to fight and give their lives at the Moncada. They tried to humiliate Fidel; they forced him to sit on a bench at the entrance of the jail and made the rest of his imprisoned comrades file past.

"But just the opposite of what our enemies wanted to happen took place," Raúl Castro recalled 20 years later. "They did not succeed in humiliating or discouraging us, because all of us in that small group of survivors drew tremendous strength from Fidel's attitude. He was firm and indomitable, holding his head high and, with his glance, conveying his conviction that we were not defeated and that the struggle had only just begun."[18]

Two months later, on the Isle of Pines, something similar was feared. In view of what had happened at Boniato, some of the Moncada prisoners thought they would not be allowed to see Fidel and that he might be placed in another cell, separated from them by Major Juan M. Capote,[19] the head of the prison. This fear vanished immediately the morning he was reunited with his comrades.

Prior to the Moncada attack, innumerable graves enshrined the road toward achieving the dreams of freedom first voiced at Yara,[20] rising up as a clarion call to finish the battle. After

---

18. Raúl Castro, speech at the military ceremony commemorating the 20th anniversary of the attack on the Moncada garrison, *Granma*, July 23, 1973.

19. During the time Fidel and the Moncada combatants were imprisoned on the Isle of Pines, Capote — who commanded Squadron 57 of the Rural Guard on the Isle of Pines, a branch of the army — was also director of the prison. He had two lieutenants (Roger Pérez Díaz and Luis Montesinos Alfonso) to assist him, to whom he delegated some of his functions. In practice, they had the final word in running the prison, even though there was a lieutenant in charge of internal order (Pedro Rodríguez Coto), who, like the guards, belonged to the police force of the Ministry of the Interior. Major Capote was shot following the triumph of the revolution.

20. The Cry of Yara on October 10, 1868, launched the Cuban people's armed rebellion that marked the start of the first war of independence against Spanish colonialism. Yara was the first town the Cuban insurrectional forces attacked that day.

Moncada the survivors swore on the blood of their brothers killed in the heroic action of 1953 to take up arms and risk their lives as the vanguard of a powerful revolution that would win the right to proclaim the homeland finally free.

Now Fidel was with them, representing the unconquered determination that was to sustain them. He offered direction, leadership, determination, action, faith in the people, faith in the future — *faith*. In prison, there were no rifles for training, no stone fortresses from which to shoot. Behind those walls, their rifles were books. And through study, stone by stone, they built their fortress, the only one that is invincible: the fortress of ideas.[21]

Fortress of ideas
On December 17, 1953, Armando Mestre wrote from prison to his uncle:

> You realize that although the courts ordered that we be sent to the La Cabaña prison, the minister of the interior decided to send us to the Isle of Pines. Uncle, you know it's not the same being on the Isle of Pines — in exile — as it is being in La Cabaña, near home, where my mother is sick. However, you know that those of us who hold fast to our ideals do not complain; we wouldn't do so even if we were at the bottom of the sea.
>
> We have used the time to create a worthy life, studying eleven subjects for our own benefit and that of humanity. I am proud of my comrades and myself because, more than friends, we are brothers.
>
> We have founded a school named after one of our dead comrades, the Abel Santamaría Ideological Academy, and a library named after Raúl Gómez, also a dead brother. This library has more than 600 books sent by good friends, political figures, and university professors.

---

21. Among José Martí's fertile ideas was that "A fortress of ideas is worth more than a fortress of stone," a concept which was very important in educating Cuban revolutionaries.

In a letter signed by all the members of the group and sent to Baudilio Castellanos, their defense attorney at the Provisional Court of Santiago de Cuba, this description was amplified:

> Friend Bilito, we have organized an academy for the purpose of raising our educational level. We have named it after Abel Santamaría, in honor of that late compañero. Our subjects are philosophy, world history, political economy, mathematics, geography, and languages.
>
> We have also founded a modest library, which we have named in posthumous tribute to Compañero Raúl Gómez García. It is composed mainly of books generously and patriotically donated by numerous friends. Mainly they are on political, economic, and social subjects. It also contains classics of Spanish literature.
>
> We have a very rigid class schedule, and we are all really motivated to learn. We believe we should make the best possible use of the time we have to spend here.

The weapons were the library — two wooden book cases filled with books in the collective dormitory. The fortress was the academy, a small blackboard and the wooden tables on which they ate under the ledge in the yard.

Fidel described a typical day in a letter dated December 22, 1953:

> At 5:00 a.m. sharp, when you think you've just shut your eyes, a voice yells, "Line up!" accompanied by handclaps, and we remember — if we forgot it for a moment while we slept — that we're in prison. The lights, left on all night, glare more harshly than ever; our heads feel heavier than lead; and we have to get up! Naturally, I spend less than 30 seconds putting on my shoes, pants, and shirt. I won't sleep again until 11:00 at night, when sleep catches me reading Marx or Rolland — or, as today, when I finish writing.
>
> To sum up: 5:30, breakfast; 8:00 to 10:30 a.m., classes; 10:45, lunch; 2:00 to 3:00 p.m., classes again; recreation until 4:00; 4:45, dinner; 7:00 to 8:15, classes in political economy and

group reading; 9:30 p.m., silence.

Every morning on alternate days from 9:30 to 10:00 I explain philosophy or world history. Cuban history, grammar, arithmetic, geography, and English are taught by other compañeros. At night, I teach political economy and, twice a week, public speaking — that is, something like it.

Method: instead of classes on political economy, I read to them for half an hour — description of a battle, such as Napoleon Bonaparte's infantry attack on Hugomont, or an ideological topic such as Martí's plea to the Spanish republic or something similar. Immediately afterward, several fellows chosen at random or volunteers talk for three minutes on the topic in a contest with prizes, awarded by the judges we have chosen. On all patriotic dates, we have special talks on the topic.

On the 26th of every month, a party; on the 27th, mourning — commemorative meetings with reflection and oral presentations on the subject.[22] On the days of mourning, naturally, there is no recreation or diversion of any kind. Study days are from Monday through midday on Saturday.[23]

Following this self-imposed regimen inside prison, the members of the Moncada group were constantly asking for books. Guido García Inclán, who visited them several times, reported that when he asked what they wanted sent to them, Fidel always answered, "Books. Books. And don't forget those of Martí."

They asked for nothing else. An article by Raúl Roa[24] published in *Bohemia* magazine in November 1953 emphasizes this

22. The 26th of each month was celebrated with joy, in honor of the outbreak of the war against the dictatorship; the 27th was a day of mourning for the Moncada combatants who were taken prisoner on July 26 and murdered between then and July 29.

23. The originals of this and all the other letters that are quoted are in the archives of the Cuban Council of State's Office of Historical Affairs.

24. Raúl Roa, "Carta de Pedro Miret al rector Inclán" (Pedro Miret's letter to Rector Inclán), reprinted in *Retorno a la aborada* (Return to the dawn) (Santa Clara: Editora del Consejo Nacional de Universidades, Central University of Las Villas, 1964), vol. 2, pp. 205-6.

simple desire. Commenting on a letter the rector of the University of Havana had received from a prisoner, Roa wrote: "But this is not a prisoner punished for infringing the common penal code. This is a student temporarily deprived of his liberty for having sought the liberty of his people, even at the risk of his own life." Roa went on as follows:

Pedro Miret is a survivor of the terrible yet glorious events of the Moncada garrison. He wrote to Rector Inclán[25] not only to express his gratitude "for what you did on that occasion" (when he tried to save the lives of the participants in the action in the days following July 26) and what "you have always done for students," but also "to appeal to your kindness" and ask for help in setting up an "academy of study."

This desire to improve themselves in the midst of adversity reminds me of other, similar days spent at that same place. Like us 20 years earlier,[26] Pedro Miret and his comrades are concerned with taking maximum advantage of the "bitter hours" of prison, in which time seems to stop behind bars and the only thing that flourishes is the longing for open space. Their first step toward achieving this goal was to create a small library, which is why they wrote Dr. Inclán, asking him to send "practical teaching materials and readable illustrated reference books."

Specifically they requested *Elementary Physics* by Manuel F. Grant, *Geography* by Salvador Massip, *History of Cuba* by Ramiro Guerra, *The Philosophy of Art* by Hippolyte A. Taine, *The History of the Girondists* by Lamartine, and works by

---

25. Dr. Clemente Inclán y Costa was rector of the University of Havana from 1944 to 1961.

26. Roa is referring to the time he and other students were imprisoned on the Isle of Pines in the 1930s for having fought Gerardo Machado's dictatorship. His comrades included some — such as Roberto Lago Pereda, Rubén de León, and Aureliano Sánchez Arango — who, with the passing of time, were drawn into political intrigues and recanted their youthful ideals. Others — such as Isidoro Figueroa, Mario Fortuny, Pablo de la Torriente Brau (who was killed in 1937 while fighting for the Spanish republic in that country's civil war), and Ramiro Valdés Daussá (who was murdered when he opposed gangsterism at the University of Havana in 1940) — remained true to their principles.

Shakespeare, Lope de Vega, Ruiz de Alarcón, Tirso de Molina, and Calderón de la Barca. Pedro Miret and his comrades would have liked to leave the choice up to the rector but, since they were also addressing their appeal to other friends, they decided to suggest the titles and authors mentioned above.

Several of Fidel's letters during this period show the progress of his reading.

In November, it included several works by Shakespeare, A.J. Cronin's *The Keys of the Kingdom*, Axel Munthe's *The Story of San Michele*, Maurois' *Memoirs*, Rosie's *Memoirs*, Marías' *Philosophical Writings*, García Morente's *First Lessons in Philosophy*, Romain Rolland's *Jean-Christophe*, and Victor Hugo's *Les Misérables*, of which he made the following criticism four months later:

> It's impossible to express how much Victor Hugo stimulated me with *Les Misérables*. Nevertheless, as time goes on, I grow a little tired of his excessive romanticism, his verbosity, and the sometimes tedious and exaggerated heaviness of his erudition. On the same topic of Napoleon III, Karl Marx wrote a formidable work entitled *The Eighteenth Brumaire of Louis Bonaparte*. Placing these two works side by side, you can appreciate the tremendous difference between a scientific, realistic view of history and a purely romantic interpretation. Where Hugo sees no more than a lucky adventurer, Marx sees the inevitable result of social contradictions and the conflict of the prevailing interests of the time. For one, history is luck; for the other, it is a process governed by laws.

How far did the eagerness for knowledge go — so that their time in prison would be fruitfully spent? On December 8, Fidel wrote:

> When I read the work of a famous author, the history of a people, the doctrine of a thinker, the theories of an economist, or the preachings of a social reformer, I am filled with the desire to know everything that all authors have written, the doctrines of all the philosophers, the treatises of all the economists, and the preachings of all the apostles. I want to know

everything, and I even go through the bibliographies in each book, treasuring the hope of reading those books someday. Outside, I was restless because I did not have enough time; here, where there seems to be too much time, I am still restless.

On December 18, he mentioned William Thackeray's *Vanity Fair*, Ivan Turgenev's *A Nest of the Gentry*, Jorge Amado's *Luis Carlos Prestes: Champion of Hope*, the Dean of Canterbury's *The Secret of Soviet Strength*, Eric Knight's *Fugitives from Love*, Nikolai Ostrovsky's *How the Steel Was Tempered* ("a modern Russian novel that is a moving autobiography by a young man who participated in the revolution"), and A.J. Cronin's *The Citadel*. "I'm also studying Karl Marx's *Capital* in depth: five enormous volumes of economics, researched and set forth with the greatest scientific rigor. I have also begun studying Cuban authors: Félix Varela, Luz y Caballero, and so on."

Next, alternating with Lex Publishers' *Collected Works of José Martí* (his constant companion), he turned to Victor Hugo's *William Shakespeare*; Honoré de Balzac's *The Magic Skin*; Stefan Zweig's *Biography of Little Napoleon*; Rómulo Gallegos' *On Equal Footing*; A.J. Cronin's *The Stars Look Down*; Somerset Maugham's *The Razor's Edge*; four of the 18 volumes of the *Complete Works* of Sigmund Freud; and Dostoyevski's *The Brothers Karamazov*, *The Insulted and the Injured*, *Crime and Punishment*, *The Idiot*, *The House of the Dead*, *Poor Folk*, and the short story *Mr. Prokharchin*.

"My main attention, however, is on something else. I have rolled up my sleeves and taken on the study of world history and political doctrines," he wrote in a letter in March. Shortly afterward, when he had read Kant's *Critique of Pure Reason*, Mira y López's *Mass Psychology*, Cirilo Villaverde's *Cecilia Valdés*, and two biographies of Bolívar (Rourke's and Zweig's), he wrote, in a letter dated April 4:

It's 11:00 at night. Since 6:00, I have been reading one of Lenin's works nonstop — *The State and Revolution* — after having finished *The Eighteenth Brumaire of Louis Bonaparte* and *The Civil War in France*, both by Marx. All three of these books are interrelated and of immeasurable value.

He added,

> My ventures into the field of philosophy have served me well. After having knocked heads a good while with Kant, I find Marx easier than the "Pater nostrum." Both he and Lenin had a powerful polemical spirit, and I'm having a fine time with them, laughing and enjoying my reading. Implacable and formidable with the enemy, they were both truly model revolutionaries.

Some insightful notes resulted from his ventures into the field of philosophy, such as this letter dated March 18, 1954:

> I fell asleep finishing *The Transcendental Aesthetics of Space and Time*. Of course, space and time disappeared for a good while from my mind. Kant made me think of Einstein, with his theory of relativity of space and time and his famous formula for energy: $E = MC^2$ (mass times the speed of light squared); of what relation there could be between their perhaps opposing concepts; and of Kant's conviction that he had found definitive criteria that saved philosophy from being buried, beaten down by the experimental sciences and the tremendous results of its discoveries.
>
> Did Kant meet the same fate as Descartes, whose philosophy could not stand the test of events, because it went counter to the proven laws of Copernicus and Galileo? Kant, however, did not try to explain the nature of things — only the knowledge through which we arrived at it, whether or not it is possible to know the nature of things and, in line with this, when such knowledge is correct or erroneous. His was a philosophy of knowledge, not of the objects of knowledge. According to this, there should be no contradiction between him and Einstein. Yet there are his concepts of space and time, basic points for elaborating his philosophical system.
>
> Is there a contradiction? Obviously it will not be difficult to find out. But while I consider this and the many

other questions that constantly besiege me, I keep thinking how limited our knowledge is and how vast is the field that man has tackled with his intelligence and efforts throughout the centuries. Even the very relativity of this knowledge is saddening. How many theories and doctrines and beliefs, now outdated, used to be Bibles for science! How dearly man has had to pay for the progress of humanity!

In this period Fidel had already thoroughly assimilated and adopted the dialectical materialist conception of history as his method for analyzing social development. This is shown in his letter of January 27, 1954, in which he expresses his view on the role of the individual in history. In it, he established that a social being and his thinking are dependent on the social environment. However, especially in the field of art, he noted the relative independence of consciousness, which enables the artistic genius to forge ahead of his time. He backed up his explanations with a question about whether Romain Rolland would have been as great had he been born in the 17th century. Fidel answered this as follows:

Human thought is unfailingly conditioned by the circumstances of the era. In the case of a political genius, I venture to affirm that his genius depends exclusively on his era. Lenin during the time of Catherine, when the aristocracy was the ruling class, would necessarily have been a champion of the bourgeoisie — which was the revolutionary class at that time — or he would have been simply ignored by history. If Martí had lived when Havana was seized by the English, he would have defended the standard of Spain, alongside his father. What would Napoleon, Mirabeau, Danton, and Robespierre have been in the times of Charlemagne, if not humble serfs or anonymous inhabitants of some feudal castle?

Julius Caesar would never have crossed the Rubicon in the early years of the republic, before the intense class struggle that shook Rome was sharpened and the great plebeian party developed — for it was this situation that made his rise to power both possible and necessary. Julius Caesar was a true revolutionary, as was Catiline; while Cicero, so revered by history, embodied the genuine aristocrat of Rome.

This did not keep the French revolutionaries from cursing Caesar and deifying Brutus, who plunged the dagger of the aristocracy into his heart. Those men who struck the mortal blow against the French aristocracy lacked the historical perspective to understand that the Roman republic was the French monarchy of those times, that the plebs struggled against the republic just as the bourgeoisie fought against the monarchy. They were far from suspecting that a new Caesar was about to arise in Gaul and that this one would really and rightfully imitate the Roman emperor.

On this particular subject, I had always been intrigued by the question of where so much Roman influence on the French revolutionaries came from. Then one day, reading the history of French literature, I found that Amyot, a French writer of the 16th century, had translated Plutarch's *Lives* and *Morals* from Latin — and these memoirs of the great men and great scenes of Greece and Rome served, two centuries later, as a point of reference for the protagonists in the Great Revolution.

In the case of a literary, artistic, or philosophical genius, this is not so true. Rolland or Victor Hugo could have been born half a century earlier and been equally brilliant. Half a century earlier, they could have approached the caliber of Voltaire, although expounding very different ideas.

All ideas, even those of geniuses, are conditioned by the era. The philosophy of Aristotle in Greece was the culmination of the work of the philosophers who preceded him (Parmenides, Socrates, Plato), without which his work would not have been possible. Likewise, the doctrines of Marx, in the social field, was the climax of the efforts of the utopian socialists and, in the philosophical field, synthesized German materialism and idealism — although Marx, in addition to being a philosopher was also a political genius, and as such his role was entirely dependent on the era and circumstances in which he lived.

A genius creates universal values, such as the characters of Cervantes and Shakespeare. They, like Dostoyevski, were familiar with psychoanalysis before Freud — not through science, but by penetrating brilliantly into the psychological depths of the human spirit. At times, they made tremendous advances ahead of their time.

A literary, philosophical, or artistic genius has a considerably broader field in terms of time and history than that offered by the world of reality and action, which is the only arena where political geniuses emerge.

A universal education

Fidel's understanding of the breadth and depth of political, historical, literary, and general culture in this period is shown in several of his letters. These, we might add, were not written for publication and are therefore among the most legitimately authentic documents for the purposes of making a critical evaluation. But what they reveal can be measured fully only if we take into account certain factors of key importance:

1. Although the humanities course at the University of Havana displayed some diversity, the School of Law, of which Fidel was a graduate, was not exactly its best exponent. From the beginning it was stunted by the class affiliation of the vast majority of the professors — an affiliation which, it goes without saying, excluded Marxism-Leninism from the course of studies.

2. The young people in Cuba at that time did not, in general, have the all-encompassing thirst for culture that had characterized other periods in our history (the 19th century as a whole and the generations of the 1920s and 1930s). On the contrary, the interests of the more advanced young people centered almost exclusively on current political action without much concern for theory and even less for philosophy.

3. Fidel's background in the Orthodox Party did not give his principles any grounding in a revolutionary conception of society; rather, it grounded them in narrow populist measures designed to modify the system. With very few exceptions, the group of intellectuals in the leadership did not, ideologically, go beyond the liberal ideas of the end of the last century. Moreover, its members evidenced a strong dependency complex with respect to the

United States.

4. In addition, it should be recalled that Fidel Castro was then only 27 years old, and that his primary and secondary education had been obtained in religious schools. Furthermore, on graduating from the university in 1950, he had thrown himself into the practice of law and into political work in the Cuban People's (Orthodox) Party — and, after March 10, 1952, into the revolutionary tasks that led up to the people's armed insurrection, which consumed all of his time and tremendous work capacities.

We can deduce his main concerns in the field of social sciences from the books he requested and the letters he wrote during this period of imprisonment, even though he "devoured," one after another, works from the most dissimilar fields of culture. On March 24, 1954, he wrote:

In his biography of Shakespeare, Victor Hugo also has very beautiful and eloquent phrases, especially when he speaks of books: "The immense human Bible composed of all the prophets, all the poets, and all the philosophers is going to blaze forth in the hearth of this enormous, shining lens of compulsory education." His words have been prophetic where compulsory education has really taken root. At present, in many countries (including ours) it is compulsory only in theory. Other things are even more compulsory: poverty, incompetence, and anachronism.

On April 5, he made a request:

I have plenty of material for the study of the great contemporary political movements: socialism and fascism. I have nothing at all on Roosevelt's New Deal. I know of a one- or two-volume work in Spanish that contains a complete study of Roosevelt's program and what he did.

On April 15 he took up the same theme:

Roosevelt. I mainly want information on him: his policy of raising agricultural prices, the promotion and conservation of soil fertility, credit facilities, the debt moratorium, and the extension of markets at home and abroad in agriculture; in the social field, how he provided more jobs, shortened the work-day, raised wages, and pushed through social assistance to the unemployed, the old, and the disabled; and, in the field of the general economy, his reorganization of industry, new tax systems, regulation of the trusts, and banking and monetary reforms.

In those months, he studied the most diverse authors and topics. His prison file contains some lists of the books that the censor received in his name and then passed on to him after checking them.

Along with a *Latin Grammar*, a *Dictionary of Idiomatic Expressions*, and Demosthenes's *Oratory*, his bed was surrounded with José Ortega y Gasset's *The Revolt of the Masses* and *New Horizons: Fundamentals of Politics*; Curzio Malaparte's *The Techniques of Coups d'état*; Gustave Le Bon's *Mass Psychology*; *Naked Fascism*; *The Age of Religious Revolution: Reformation and Counterreformation*; and Thomas More's *Utopia*.

Side by side with the *Complete Works* of Homer, *The Rubaiyat*, and works by Cicero and Mirabeau were Rafael Rodríguez Delgado's *Introduction to a Philosophy for the Atomic Age*; Jorge Mañach's *For a Philosophy of Life*; *This Human Peace*; Paul Schmidt's *Europe Behind the Scenes*; José Ingenieros' *The Mediocre Man*; and José Enrique Rodó's *Ariel* and *Motives of Proteus*.

He read Raimundo Cabrera's *Cuba and Its Judges*; *Contribution to the Draft Penal Reform*; Guizot's *On the Death Penalty in Political Terms*; and the Constitution of the United States. He read Engels's *The Origin of the Family, Private Property and the State* and *The Condition of the Working Class in England*. He also read *100 Best Poems*; Margarita Ferrer's *Seven Songs*; Oscar Wilde's *The Nightingale and the Rose*; Honoré de Balzac's *Eugénie Grandet, The Lily of the Valley*, and *Ursule Mirouët*; *The Martyrdom of a Genius*; *Don Juan*; Anatole France's *At the Sign of the Reine Pédauque* and *The Amethyst Ring*; *The Patriot*; Antonio Zambrana's *Francisco the Black*; Sinclair Lewis's *Main Street*; Leo Tolstoy's *Anna Karenina*; Cirilo Villaverde's *Cecilia Valdés*; and Carlos Loveira's *Juan Criollo*.

The historic theme was constant, however: *Miguel Servet and His Times*; *Morelos*; *The Losing of America*; Herminio Portell Vilá's *Lives of American Unity*; Raimundo Cabrera's *The Autonomy Campaign*; and the 10 large volumes edited by Ramiro Guerra, *A History of the Cuban Nation*. There were many works by Martí, and he also read a lot on Bolívar: *Bonaparte and Bolívar*; Emeterio Santiago Santovenia's *Bolívar and the Spanish Antilles*; and Emil Ludwig's *Bolívar, Knight of Glory*.

Nothing seemed to escape him in the field of politics; he read everything he had ever heard of. When informed, mistakenly, that the censor had held back two books that should have reached him, he wrote a brilliant letter defending his right to direct investigation. In passing, this letter lets us appreciate the great tact employed in his correspondence with that prison official, which enabled him to establish an incredible tie that was to be of great importance in the future:

I have been informed that two books were confiscated. One of them is Trotsky's *Stalin*.

I suppose this was done because it is called *Stalin*, because I cannot conceive of any other reason for such an action. Even if it had been written by a supporter of Stalin's and were a defense of him, I sincerely do not believe that should be a reason for confiscating it. But the fact is that in this case we are not dealing with an impartial critical study. This book was written against Stalin by Leon Trotsky, his most irreconcilable enemy; far from being a defense, it is an implacable attack on him. As you can see, the reason that might be adduced for confiscating it does not exist.

I don't know what the other book is, but I suspect it is Curzio Malaparte's *The Techniques of Coups d'état*, because I seem to remember someone told me it was coming.

I know this book well and it is nothing but a fanciful version of fascist, Nazi, Falangist, and other coups d'état, which does not stick to historical truth, since its author is more a novelist than an historian. It has no practical value. Sometimes I am sent books that I have already read. But all right: because it has such a suggestive title I admit that objections might be raised. In any case, I'm not interested in this book, if it is the other one that was confiscated. But I am interested in the first one — and I assure you there is no reason at all for retaining it. It seems to me that a mistake has been made. Look into it and see for yourself.

I am not bringing this up out of caprice. This is something that worries me very much. I have enough tact and sense of responsibility not to ask for any book that would go against the norms of healthy moral or disciplinary standards. You know full well that I am interested only in serious books. You will never see me obtaining pornographic or obscene books or reading matter of any other kind that should not be admitted into a penal institution.

It is a great source of concern for me that a book I requested, such as this one by Trotsky, should be confiscated simply because of its title, without examining its contents. This business of censorship should be handled with a sense of justice. Everybody reads in accordance with his education and culture.

The study of economic, social, or philosophical questions requires books and authors with the most diverse viewpoints so one can analyze, compare, etc. Without the freedom to read one cannot study either religion or sociopolitical doctrines.

This problem arose once before, with other books, and Lieutenant Montesinos, to whom I explained the problem, settled it in a reasonable manner. I beg you to remember that I am a professional with more than one university degree — of which I do not like to speak often and which I mention in this case simply so you may understand that an incomprehensible limitation in this matter regarding books is quite humiliating and hard for me to take, because it interferes with something that is very personal to man: his desire for learning.

Shut up in this building, I spend all my time studying. In doing so, I am not hurting or bothering anyone, nor does this damage the prison or the state. I am not asking for improvements of any kind or changes in the prison regulations.

I have not asked for anything — only that no harm be done to me that is useless, senseless, and benefits no one. We have not had any difficulties for some time, and it may really be said that I am spending my days here as if I did not exist. I hardly ever write, so even the slightest difficulties with letters have completely disappeared, and I do not believe there is any intention to injure us without reason — at least, there shouldn't be.

I have set forth my reasons. Look into them, and you will see they are well founded. If you consulted with your superiors regarding the seizure of these books, I beg you to set forth my reasons, confident that they will listen to them. I repeat that I am only interested in the book by Trotsky. The other, if it is Malaparte's, does not interest me. Above all, I would like an assurance that there will be no unnecessary difficulties concerning the question of books, which are cultural works authorized by the laws of the country. I await your response.

Fidel received not only a quick reply from the censor but also the books, which had just arrived at the prison. As a result, he immediately wrote the following note to the official:

I am not to blame for the report that I received regarding the two missing books; Lieutenant Perico passed on the news to my guard.

In any case, I am glad the mistake occurred, because I have had another opportunity to see how invariably kind you are; I am not sorry I sent you a reasoned, cordial letter, even though I was very annoyed by what I thought was an injustice, because I can write you only with the greatest consideration and courtesy.

I know that if you do not solve a problem, it is simply because you cannot. I received the books with much joy, and this showed me once again that when people talk things over they understand each other, and that what men need is goodwill.

In this case, you may rest assured I am very pleased

and that all my concern has evaporated.

Once more, I repeat my warmest thanks.

Fidel

One aspect that cannot be overlooked when examining the details of Fidel's correspondence during this period is his obvious consciousness of history. This consciousness, already part of his earlier life, was to become a constant feature of his fundamental documents in the future. In this sense, he totally identified with the greatest figures in our history: Céspedes, Agramonte, Maceo, Máximo Gómez, and all the rest of our 19th-century leaders, culminating in José Martí; and with Julio Antonio Mella — who, mortally wounded, exclaimed, "I die for the revolution." All the representatives of the Cuban revolution have shown a clear awareness of having participated in the unfolding of our nation's history, and this was also true of Fidel. But there is something more: a deep passion and love for our history; a healthy pride and a legitimate desire to belong to it and be a worthy heir of the tradition of rebellion, dignity, and honor bequeathed us by our forebears.

In March 1954, Fidel received the *War Chronicles* of José Miró Argenter, chief of the general staff of Lt. Gen. Antonio Maceo of the Liberation Army. Fidel and many of the other Moncada veterans had read this book constantly in the months leading up to the attack. In his letter of March 3, Fidel commented:

His book was a veritable Bible for all of us (I speak both of those who were killed on July 26 and those who are imprisoned or in exile). The immortal march of the Invading Army has come to mind very often. We have lived each battle with emotion and tried to cull as many tactical and strategic details as we could from that useful experience. Even though times have changed — and, with them, the art of war — all these events came out of the same sentiment, the only one that makes the impossible possible and that compels posterity to believe what seemed incredible to many contemporaries.

The pages of the *War Chronicles* overflow with this feeling. When you read it your blood will boil with the desire to emulate our ancestors, if you believe in them, and you will blush with the shame of their disgrace, if you have an ounce of fighting spirit.

Homer's *Iliad* contains no events more heroic, and our *Mambís*[27] seem more legendary than they, Achilles less invincible than Maceo. Why must we live in ignorance of our great feat? I am ashamed to think that this book is not to be found in all homes. It was our firm intention to make it compulsory reading in all the schools. If children were to grow up exposed to such examples and inspired by those great souls, who could ever subjugate them?

This constant awareness of history is also shown in his references to his comrades' stubborn dedication to study. Thus, on December 22, 1953, he wrote:

The lads are all magnificent. They constitute an elite, because they have gone through a thousand trials. Those who learned how to handle weapons are now learning how to handle books, preparing for the great battles of the future. Discipline is Spartan, as is their way of life, education, and everything else. Their faith and unbreakable firmness are such that it may be said of them, too, "With your shield or upon it."

They were of the same revolutionary stock as those who had given their lives and, though no longer present, would always remain alive in the hearts of the people. And while he was unfalteringly aware of the need to train the survivors, he was also concerned with setting down for posterity the facts about those who had been killed — to whom he never referred as if they were absent.

On December 16, 1954, he wrote a beautiful letter to René Guitart, the father of Renato Guitart, one of the Moncada martyrs. In it, with great tact, he respectfully took into consideration the beliefs of the addressee. Fidel wrote:

---

27. Cuban independence fighters in the wars against Spain were known as *Mambís*.

It is difficult for me to begin this, to address you in some way, and to find the words with which to express my gratitude, my emotion, and my deep appreciation for your kind and so heartfelt letter, filled with paternal affection. You address me as "my very dear Fidel." How should I address you? Few times in my life have I felt so honored as I did on receiving those lines from you, or so stimulated to be good, worthy, and loyal to my last breath.

That long embrace of which you speak and which I will give you someday, with all my heart — how I would have wished it were in other circumstances, without the cruel physical absence of Renato, without the bitter gall of adversity in which everything turns against you, and you have nothing but conviction and faith to sustain you. The fact that in such circumstances you have approached me and generously flung open the doors of your affection brings out all the goodness and nobility of that gesture, in which I recognize a worthy father of an equally worthy son.

I will not speak to you of him as if he were absent — which he has not been and never will be. These are not mere words of consolation. Only those of us who really and permanently feel this in the depths of our hearts can understand it. Physical life is ephemeral and inexorably passes — as it has for so many generations of men and soon will for each one of us. The truth that the immortal values of the spirit are more important than life should be taught to all human beings. What meaning does life have without these values? How could those who, because they understand this, generously give their lives for goodness and justice possibly die? God is the supreme idea of goodness and justice. Those who, for one reason or another, die for their homeland must necessarily go to God.

I admire the courage, resignation, and nobility of character with which you have sacrificed so much — in tribute to the ideals for which he gave his life. Your courage in the face of sorrow is just as heroic and generous as his in the face of death. He must be proud of you, as you have more than enough reason to be eternally proud of him. From the depths of my heart, I would voice a hope for Cuba: that it may always have men like you and him.

I will never give you reason to repent of those beautiful lines you sent me — for which I am infinitely grateful and which I will always treasure. I hope that you and your wife will find relief for your sorrow in our affection and especially in our conduct. I know that she is a Spartan mother, filled like you with resignation, goodness, and faith. "The son who leaves the earth lives on in the heart of his mother." Please convey our devoted, warm affection to her and to your daughter — who has many brothers in us.

Words are not needed when our feelings wish to speak; we must divine what we feel but cannot express, even if we wanted to. You will understand my feelings, as I sense and understand yours. Renato is and will always be present among us, and he will be ever more so in the hearts of all Cubans. He was all ideals, courage, dignity, character, and lasting example — and he knew that those who fall as he did never die.

The first fruits

Outside prison, the final months of 1953 passed without much change. October closed with a new disgrace. Batista presented the Carlos Manuel de Céspedes Order to Héctor Trujillo, puppet president of the Dominican Republic and brother of satrap Rafael Leónidas Trujillo, and to Peruvian dictator Manuel Odría. Gorged with blood, the beasts doubtless made a spectacle of their mutual flattery and indulgences — made possible by the enslavement of their peoples.

As in every year during those times, the period just before and right at the start of the sugarcane harvest saw an increase in clashes between sugar workers and the large landowners. The workers organized protests, partial work stoppages, and strikes against the landowners' efforts to minimize repairs in the sugar mills, shorten the grinding period, fire workers, cut wages, cheat on production bonuses and the sugar differential,[28] and ship sugar out in bulk.

Carlos Prío, Guillermo Alonso Pujol, Millo Ochoa, and other photogenic actors in the Montreal Pact[29] met in November in Monterrey, Mexico — as always, without agreeing on a single concrete action against Batista's regime. The opportunist José Pardo Llada made the most of the occasion to announce his readiness to "take it to the ballot box, in a real election" — a decision that effectively wiped out his alignment with the Montreal group. It therefore came as no surprise when, two weeks later, he publicly resigned from the Orthodox Party.

On November 23, the repressive forces attacked the University of Havana, Calixto García Hospital, and the university stadium and pool searching for arms, but found nothing.

Prío's September genuflection did not help him in December when — amazingly! — the government in Washington compelled him to register as an "agent of a foreign power," a fascist-like measure previously applied only to members of the Communist Party in the United States. Prío swallowed the humiliation so as not to have to leave the country and immediately held a press

---

28. The sugar differential was the additional sum Cuba received based on how much the price of sugar had risen above the average 3.675 cents per pound paid in 1945. A portion of this price differential was to be used to subsidize the foodstuffs imported from the United States, so their increased prices would not have to be absorbed by Cuban consumers. Another portion was to be applied to projects that would benefit the people and help the country's economic development. The remainder was to go to the sugarcane workers in the form of increased wages.

29. The Montreal Pact of June, 1953 was signed in Montreal, Canada by Carlos Prío and Emilio Ochoa, agreeing to support the struggle against the Batista regime. Emilio Ochoa headed the Orthodox Party, in which Eduardo Chibás's principle of no pacts with any other political party or force reigned. His participation in the pact created the first split within the Orthodox leadership — Prío's Authentic Party had been the main enemy against which Chibás had struggled and for which he had lost his life. The pact consisted of two agreements: a public one, which stated the need for unity in the struggle against Batista, and a secret one, in which Prío agreed to provide the funds for the struggle. It hinged on getting support from military men within the dictatorial regime and obtaining the backing of the United States government. Tony Varona and José Pardo Llada were other well-known political figures of the time who signed the Pact on behalf of the Cuban Revolutionary (Authentic) Party and the Cuban People's (Orthodox) Party, respectively.

conference — to blast the Soviet Union and the Cuban Communists! In December, however, Prío was arrested in Miami and charged with violating the Neutrality Act. He had to put up $50,000 in bail. He was photographed and fingerprinted like a common criminal, and was to be sent for trial. Even though the matter went no further and he continued kissing his master's hand, the Cuban people viewed the humiliation as indicative of the U.S. rulers' satisfaction with the continuing reign of Fulgencio Batista, who was assiduous in looking after their interests in Cuba.

In an article published in *Bohemia* on November 1, 1953, former member of the ABC, Jorge Mañach,[30] let his reactionary nature show through the threads of his tattered liberal trappings by ceremoniously pontificating:

In late July, an attack was made on the Moncada garrison. For many, very evident reasons, this will go down in history as a youthful blunder, but it was also a demonstration of rash courage and of something even more noble and encouraging: the fact that there are still young people in Cuba who are ready to sacrifice everything for an ideal. As I would not like to see them take those tragic paths again, I call on them to learn to wait.

This was the same attitude displayed by the director of the Guanajay prison and others who had been absorbed by the system. This viewpoint, so popular among the ideologues of the bourgeoisie to justify their lack of action, may have been what Fidel was referring to in this powerful paragraph from a letter dated December 19:

---

30.   The ABC was founded in Cuba early in the 1930s as a terrorist organization that opposed the Gerardo Machado dictatorship. It was composed of very dissimilar elements, with intellectuals and students predominating in its leadership. Its program was permeated with fascist-like tendencies. After Machado's fall, it became a political party and began to play a counterrevolutionary role in collaboration with the U.S. Embassy in Cuba and the rightist forces that put down the revolutionary upsurge of the 1930s.

What a tremendous school this prison is! Here, I have rounded out my view of the world and determined the meaning of my life. I don't know if it will be long or short, fruitful or in vain, but my dedication to sacrifice and struggle has been reaffirmed. I abhor being tied to petty trifles of comfort and self-interest. I think a man should not live beyond that moment when his life begins to decline and the flame that illuminated the brightest moment of his existence is snuffed out, when the force that guided his steps during his worthy period fades away.

Then you see dejection and repentance bearing that vile renegade off into the depths of degradation. He becomes ashamed of the only noble things in his life: his years of selflessness and generosity. This is the tendency of those who do the opposite of what they once preached. From then on, they look back on their own youth as a period of naiveté, rashness, inexperience, and dreaming. They do not realize that in reality they are entering a period of impotence, frustration, deceit, and submissiveness; a miserable and ridiculous retreat; the sad spectacle of man abandoning the path he has traveled, never to find it again.

In the first week of December a manifesto was issued denouncing the despot for having "taken a new step toward open tyranny, approving a legislative decree to persecute Communists — and, under that pretext, all who oppose his regime." Its effect, however, was diminished by the identity of its author, as the empty grandiloquence of Max Lesnick, general secretary of the Orthodox Youth, no longer convinced anyone. The Orthodox (and non-Orthodox) young people increasingly came to acknowledge those behind the iron bars of a cell on the Isle of Pines as their real leaders.

There, those 27 men (Fidel Labrador had arrived with Fidel Castro) turned down the special Christmas Eve dinner offered them by officials of the dictatorship. As Montané explained many years after those initial months in prison:[31]

> How could we accept even a plate of food from those who had
> just murdered hapless workers who had nothing to do with
> the events and so many of our comrades, whose only crime
> was to treat their enemies as gentlemen during a heroic battle
> in which we defended our homeland's sacred right to be free?

At the same time, in a quite different manner, they also turned
down funds that supporters outside had collected for them. In a
gesture showing tremendous sensitivity in the midst of that
selfish society, Fidel wrote on December 12:

> Except for the expenses already incurred, spend all the funds
> collected to help the widows and other relatives of those who
> were killed. We do not need or want anything. It goes without
> saying that we will not celebrate Christmas. We intend to fast
> and not even drink water that day, as a sign of mourning. Let
> this be known, because I think that our objective will be more
> noble and humane this way. It is senseless for prisoners such
> as us to aspire to the joys of Christmas. We prefer that those
> who have lost their loved ones and breadwinners not be
> evicted or go hungry.

On December 21, he wrote:

> Christmas Eve is almost upon us. I will not celebrate it. I am
> so filled with sad memories that even Christmas music grates
> on me.

Why was this? The opening paragraphs of another letter, written
in the first few minutes of the new year, reveals his thoughts and
show a clear class perspective. After listening to the Cuban
national anthem at midnight, Fidel wrote:

---

31. Jesús Montané Oropesa, speech on the 20th anniversary of the freeing of Fidel
and his comrades from the Model Prison on the Isle of Pines, *Granma*, May 16,
1975.

It is right that my first and purest memory of this day be of the valiant men who died for our homeland because they chose this eternal life rather than resign themselves to a miserable existence chained to disgrace and dishonor.

How many of them are being remembered right now? I have the cruel feeling that the answer is very few. Instead, many people enjoy themselves and laugh. What do our homeland's pain and the people's mourning matter to the rich and fatuous who fill the dance halls? For them, we are unthinking young people, disturbers of the existing social paradise. There will be no lack of idiots who think we envy them and aspire to the same miserable idle and reptilian existence they enjoy today.

Perhaps in many poor homes, especially there in indomitable Oriente, our national anthem will have led the noble, good sons of this land to spare a thought for our dead.

The rest of this letter expressed a reaffirmation, certainty, conviction, and commitment to the future. The tremendous task of the people's liberation still lay ahead:

I have just heard two beautiful speeches over the radio. How impressive is the human word in such circumstances — above all, for one who listens in a distant prison, fired by a double striving for freedom. The strong invocation they made of my beloved brothers is a spark of justice. At last I can glimpse the first rays of the light with which glory must forge halos for 80 martyred heads — the martyrs of the Centennial![32]

---

32. January 28, 1953 (the year in which the Moncada garrison was attacked), was the 100th anniversary of the birth of José Martí. In Cuba 1953 was called the Year of the Centennial. The revolutionary movement Fidel Castro organized to struggle against the Batista dictatorship had around 2,000 members prior to the attack on the Moncada. The vast majority of these were young people who called themselves members or representatives of the Centennial Youth. In signing their manifesto, containing their program and the reasons for the July 26, 1953 actions, they used the name Centennial Youth. The expression "martyrs of the Centennial" refers to those who lost their lives in those actions.

For me, the happiest moment of 1953 and of all my life was when I went off to battle. The harshest was when I had to face the tremendous setback of defeat, with its aftermath of infamy, slander, ingratitude, misunderstanding, and envy.

I still do not understand where man gets the unshakable strength to affirm his convictions and his faith under the most inconceivably adverse circumstances, and be so encouraged during the most bitter hours of pain, general confusion, uncertainty, and fog. I understood the real situation right from the start; I formulated my obligations and carried them out, never doubting for a second — not even on those occasions when I seemed to be absolutely alone.

There is nothing greater than the stubbornness of a man who believes in his ideas and his truth. He is invincible, and all the power on earth is of no avail against him. With a kind of joy, I see the first fruits in the form of truths that have no possible reply.

Such were Fidel's first thoughts in the new year, as dawn broke beyond the prison bars, symbolizing the future. Before his fallen comrades he vowed to continue the struggle for which they had given their lives.

So ended 1953, the year of the attack on the Moncada garrison — an enduring call to the full dignity of humanity — in this account of our history.

CHAPTER 2

It was not just the frustration of the first major attempt to overthrow the dictatorship. Deep inside, even more saddening and painful was the memory of the compañeros who had died. Exasperation grew during those months when the revolution was imprisoned, the unfinished battle postponed.

In prison, where duty is the only compelling force, the vanguard of the vanguard must conduct itself with firmness. No matter how miserably the enemy behaves, decadence must be answered with honor, with the courage to throw a battle hymn in the face of an oppressive tyrant.

Contrasting the dignity of those who were supposedly conquered, the insecure victors acted despicably, making stupid, petty, and infamous efforts to break the will of a man who, although only 27 years of age, already embodied the hopes of a people.

His prison comrades were beaten and brutally vilified in the face of frightened, complicit, or guilty silence. Fidel Castro was held in solitary confinement, in a dark cell where during those months of tyrannical cruelty, he was not allowed to see a "single human being, dead or alive...that would be too magnanimous"...

Not even a corpse

Juan Manuel Martínez Tinguao's large, green Buick stopped beside the gate to the prison. Charles Varona, Luis Conte Agüero, and Martínez Tinguao got out. The parents of Melba and Haydée and Haydée's brother Aldo Santamaría were already waiting.

A number of young revolutionaries from Guanajay were also

there. A photo shows Angel Eros, Pedro Esperón, and Evelio Prieto[1] among them. By mid-morning the greetings were mixed with tears that could not be held back — and then they all went to carry out the plan agreed upon some days earlier: to lay flowers on the grave of Eduardo Chibás in the Colón Cemetery.

It was February 20, 1954.

As Melba and Haydée walked down the 100-meter drive from the door of the National Women's Prison in Guanajay to the outer gate, they left behind an experience they would never forget. Since July 1953, they had spent seven months in three different jails, with only one happy time during those 198 days: on January 6, 1954.

That was a day that brought laughter and surprises to the faces of the children of the women prisoners, when toys sent by the Martí Women's Civic Front arrived. Under the pretext of covering the scene for the press, journalist Marta Rojas was able to penetrate the prison that day and snapped a picture of the two Moncada combatants behind bars.

Many years later, Melba recalled "the heart-wrenching situation of the women prisoners' children. There were more than 20 children under five serving the same terms as their mothers. Some of them were born in prison, punished by society without having committed any crime — like the children of slaves who were born slaves. Some of them were terrified when we gave them the toys. They had never seen anything like them before. The little girls were frightened by the dolls. It took us several days to get them used to the toys, on those rare occasions when any of them were allowed to see us."

As the car sped toward Havana, no one looked back at the receding buildings. Melba Hernández could not have imagined that five years later, after the triumph of the revolution — then only a distant dream — she would return to the prison as director, to humanize prison treatment in the name of that revolution for whose triumph she had suffered so much behind bars.

---

1 These three later took part in the March 13, 1957, attack on the Presidential Palace, in which Pedro Esperón Delgado and Evelio Prieto Guillaume were killed.

The anguish of imprisonment while dreams remain unfulfilled is the harshest sentence for any revolutionary. But prison also forges an iron will for future battles. For those two women, their first battle began the same day they left prison, for they wasted no time in launching a political struggle to free their brothers imprisoned on the Isle of Pines.

That afternoon, Melba replied to the despot's miserable statement of the day before, as he was leaving for Camagüey. In a clear allusion to the Moncada group Batista had said, "No proposal that seeks to turn into political prisoners those who massacred the sick and took the lives of trusted agents of order can be seriously considered." Melba's reply was heard on all the news broadcasts:

We went to the Moncada moved by a sacred love for freedom, and we are ready to give our lives for its principles. We are governed by humanitarian feelings — proved by the fact that we did not so much as leave a scratch on any of the soldiers we held. This attitude of ours has been repaid with hatred — Abelardo Crespo Arias is in the Model Prison with a bullet in his lung, and the rest of the compañeros there are badly treated, too.

What was the treatment Melba was referring to?

Vileness against dignity

Behind the last two buildings of the Isle of Pines prison are three sheds, each divided into three sections. One is a warehouse for materials and the shops of the shoemaker, tailor, blacksmith, mechanic, repairman, carpenter, tile setter, and printer. In the center, circled by the prison road, is the power plant. The ward where the members of the Moncada group were imprisoned is around 20 meters away.

Corporal Ramos, known as *Pistolita* (Little Gunman) because of his buffoonish, provocative poses, came very early one morning to tell them they would have to remain in the ward and could not go out in the yard.

This unusual security measure and the sounds outside alerted the men that something was going on. One of them stood on another's shoulders to reach one of the nine barred windows up high. He saw that someone had just arrived to attend the formal inauguration of the power plant, surrounded by a sizable claque of gesturing followers wearing laughable military decorations that had nothing to do with honor. It was Fulgencio Batista himself.

The news spread through the ward. Striding up and down in an already characteristic manner when he was engrossed in thought, Fidel made a few turns, stopped suddenly, and called everyone together. They gathered around and, after a brief discussion, unanimously accepted his idea. Almeida, who was glued to a window to determine the precise moment when Batista started to leave after the pompous ceremony, finally shouted, "Now!" Twenty-six[2] voices rose in unison with the accumulated strength of an entire people's rebellion, filling the morning air of February 12, 1954, with the defiant words and music of a battle hymn that would later be known throughout the world as the *July 26 March.* Perhaps no other martial tune was ever sung with such vigor as when that temporarily imprisoned vanguard of a revolution struck out at the tyrant.

Shortly before the attack on the Moncada garrison, Fidel had learned that a member of one cell of the Movement in Marianao sang and wrote songs, and he asked him to compose something of an epic nature.

Twenty-seven years later, Agustín Díaz Cartaya told us, "I began to work on that musical composition during target practice at the Los Palos farm, and I finished it two weeks later. It was originally called the *Freedom March.* One day, when Fidel was visiting Mercedes Valdés, Hugo Camejo's mother, in Marianao, he asked me if I had managed to come up with anything, so I sang it

---

2 Ciro Redondo and Abelardo Crespo were not there. Ciro had been temporarily transferred to a prison in Pinar del Río to testify in a court hearing as the defendant in Case 125 of 1953. This case, filed in Artemisa, concerned the discovery in Pijirigua of one of the farms that had been used for military training prior to the attack on the Moncada. He returned to the Isle of Pines on March 2, 1954. Abelardo, who had not yet recovered from a serious bullet wound in one of his lungs, was still in Santiago de Cuba. He rejoined his prison comrades on February 18, six days after the incident.

to him. He liked and approved it."

The original words to the Freedom March consisted of four stanzas, the third one different from the one we know today.

Marching onward toward an ideal,
we're certain to carry the day;
in furtherance of peace and prosperity
we'll struggle so freedom will win.

Forward, all Cubans,
may Cuba ever prize our heroism;
we're soldiers united, fighting so our country may be free,
our weapons destroying the evil that has plagued our troubled
    land
of errant, unwanted rulers and of cruel insatiable tyrants
who have dragged us down in the mire.

For us, death means victory and glory, too —
an epic that the future will know well.

Our flaming torch, through a clouded sky,
lights up a horizon of full liberty.

The people of Cuba,
bowed down by endless suffering and pain,
have decided to struggle until they find a real solution
to serve as an example for all who have no compassion,
and we are determined to risk even our lives for this cause.

Long live the Revolution!

While imprisoned in Boniato, the Moncada combatants received a message from Fidel suggesting that the words of the march reflect what had just taken place in Bayamo and Santiago de Cuba, and that the memory of the brothers who had died serve as a sacred force for unity in the ongoing struggle. Thus, a new stanza was written in the Boniato prison to complete the anthem:

Our comrades in Oriente have died;
their sacrifice must not be in vain.
United we all must remain
to honor their memory and fight on to win.

There, in the Boniato jail, the Moncada rebels learned the march and enraged their jailers by singing it. It was first sung in public when they were being taken to the Provisional Court for sentencing.

These were the words sung that February 12, 1954, on the Isle of Pines. The only change made since then was to replace the word "Oriente" with "Cuba" in the new stanza and call it the *July 26 March.*

They say that Batista smiled when the singing started — perhaps thinking it was some added homage from the prison administration. But as soon as he began to listen and clearly heard the words, his face fell, his smile disappeared, and his mouth tightened shut, opened only to demand to know who was singing. Then he left in a huff, followed by his infuriated cohorts.

"I'll kill them; I'll kill them," *Pistolita* was heard angrily shouting inside the prison building, but that's as far as his boast went just then. Neither the pompous voice of a local politician presenting the "General" with a scroll declaring him "an adopted and beloved son" nor the savory food and fine liquor served at a banquet given in his honor by a local landowner were enough to banish the displeasure from the dictator's face. It was still there hours later when he boarded the luxurious yacht he had arrived in and left Nueva Gerona on his return trip to Batabanó, escorted by units of the navy.

In the prison, the Moncada combatants remained tense for the rest of that Friday, awaiting some kind of reprisal. But nothing happened that day or the following morning. Then, after lunch on Sunday, February 14, Lieutenant Perico came in and read from a list: "Ramiro Valdés, Oscar Alcalde, Ernesto Tizol, Israel Tápanes."

As it was a Sunday, and that was the usual method of calling those who had visitors, nobody was suspicious.

Oscar Alcalde was lying on his bed reading when he heard his name called. He quickly shaved and changed his clothes. The men followed the officer. Outside the door, the usual thing was to turn right, toward the administration building. But this time the lieutenant signaled them to follow him to the entrance of Building 2.

Building 2, alongside the hospital in Building 1, was used for mental patients. Its 11 individual punishment cells were 2 x 1 x 1.5-meter cubicles in which the prisoner had to stoop when he tried to stand up. Their metal cell doors were completely sealed except for a small opening near the floor, just large enough for the daily ration of slop. A bare cot of dirty rusted metal was fastened to the wall; a stench-filled hole in the damp floor, covered with filth, served as a toilet. But even the vermin and disgusting bugs that inhabited the place were less revolting than the grim figure of *Cebolla* (Onion), a cretin serving a term of over a 100 years for murders committed outside and inside the penitentiary.[3] *Cebolla* was head of that nightmare-building, that hellhole in which sleep was possible only if you could shut out the screams of the demented as they were given the only treatment provided there: buckets of cold water and cruel beatings.

That was where Ramiro, Oscar, Ernesto, and Israel were locked up.

Then the lieutenant returned to the ward and called out, "Fidel Castro."

None of them returned that day. Twenty years later Tápanes recalled what happened:

Many hours passed before I received my first visitor. He was a strange type, a common prisoner who had committed several murders. In spite of that, he enjoyed the confidence of the prison authorities — so the prisoners thoroughly despised him. He was short, chubby, and big-bellied, completely bald, and had small round eyes that were almost lost in his pudgy face.

---

3 The designation of individuals such as *Cebolla* was one of the many criminal irregularities in the prison. Article 32 of the Regulations for Penal Establishments in the Republic — established by Decree 3688 of November 6, 1950, and in force at the time — stipulated that prisoners could be chosen for these auxiliary functions "only when their record shows they are not dangerous."

He looked like a pig.

He offered me a tin dish of milk with some lumpy mush and, in a strident voice, said merely, "Eat." I told him I wasn't hungry — in reality, I had completely lost what little appetite I'd had. He replied "If you haven't eaten this in 15 minutes, I'll make you eat it. I'm *Cebolla*, the head of this cellblock, and what I say goes." With that, he went out, slamming the door shut behind him.

Once again, I was alone with my thoughts — and with that dish of mush that I had absolutely no desire to eat. I thought about the situation and noted that there were several holes in each corner of the cell. I came up with what seemed like a brilliant idea: stuffing the food into the holes — all except the sweet potato, which I would eat — so I could return the dish empty to that repulsive character. That night, when I finally fell asleep, I was awakened by huge rats climbing all over me. My "brilliant" idea of filling the holes with food had attracted a pack of them.

The following day, Monday, Agustín Díaz Cartaya was called and locked up in the building for mental patients. As he recalled,

Montesinos, Perico and *Cebolla* called me in and said, "So you're the author of that piece of shit. Well, now you're going to sing it for us." Of course, I refused to sing, so *Cebolla* came over to me and said, "What are you, a wise guy?" In jail I was too aggressive for my own good and I told him, "If you come any closer, I'll punch you." *Cebolla* pulled back, but sometime after midnight the three of them came back with Sergeant Rojas and two others — six of them in all. They opened the door to my cell and jumped me. They stripped me, beat me with ox-dick whips, kicked me, and pummeled me all over.

Early on the morning of February 16, they left the composer of the march unconscious on the floor of cell number nine.[4] Ramiro Valdés, Oscar Alcalde, Ernesto Tizol, Israel Tápanes, and Agustín Díaz Cartaya spent two weeks in the punishment cells.

Meanwhile, the authorities punished the compañeros who remained in the ward by taking away their radio, denying them newspapers, and holding up their mail — both incoming and outgoing. Visits were prohibited and no one knew what had happened to Fidel.[5]

Duty, the only strength
Fidel was put in a solitary confinement cell to the left of the entrance of the hospital building.[6] While he was with his comrades, the powerful lights kept on all night had been a source of constant annoyance. Now it was just the opposite; high barred windows let in some daylight. But at night the cell was pitch black, with no light at all.

Anticipating all this in his October 16, 1953 defense, Fidel had told the judges,

> I know that prison will be harder for me than it has ever been for anyone, filled with cowardly threats and hideous cruelty. But I do not fear prison, as I do not fear the fury of the miserable tyrant who took the lives of 70 of my comrades.

---

4 In the case of Agustín Díaz Cartaya, not only was there a violation of Article 8 of the regulations, which specifically prohibited "any type of violence or maltreatment" of prisoners, but common crimes listed in that article as punishable under the Social Defense Code were committed against him.

5 All prisoners had the inalienable right to communicate with the outside world — including the right to have visitors. This was set forth in the regulations and therefore could not be restricted by the prison authorities. In the case of the Moncada group, the infraction was even more criminal, since even those restrictive measures included in the regulation should not have been applied to them. Section A of Article 7 of Decree 3688, based on constitutional provisions 26 and 27, stated, "Political detainees or prisoners will be held in areas separate from those provided for common criminals and will not be subjected to any kind of work or other penal regulations applied to common prisoners."

6 Section B of Article 7 of Decree 3688 expressly prohibited the solitary confinement of any prisoner.

He first referred to his new situation near the end of February, stating, "For the past two weeks I have been confined to a small solitary cell."

On March 1, the same day the other five were returned to the collective ward and before he learned how brutally they had been treated, Fidel gave a succinct and moving description of his own situation.

> I still have no light, after 17 days here, and they will not allow any candles. But last night, it was not just the darkness and solitude but also the rain. Darkness had just fallen when there was a rumble of thunder. Lightning flashed, cutting the darkness and illuminating the cell through the high windows, casting the shadows of the bars into the corners.
>
> Then came the storm, accompanied by a strong wind that blew the rain in, soaking everything. I did what I could to protect my books by putting them inside the suitcase and covering it with a blanket. Meanwhile, the bed got soaked; the floor was flooded; and the cold, wet air penetrated everywhere. Wet and chilled to the bone, I waited in a corner with infinite patience until the gale subsided. It was Sunday night!

The Isle of Pines was famed for its mineral soil (ideal for citrus orchards) and its turbulent electrical storms, which always seemed about to sink the entire island. Imagine what it must have been like inside that small prison cell during such a storm, thinking that you might well spend 15 years there, and while the anxiety of a revolution to be made rages inside your chest.

Even the simplest aspects of normal life assume gigantic importance under such aggravating circumstances. Fidel's almost childish joy, followed by sharp irritability, were understandable given the degrading situation he had been forced to endure for six weeks. His letter of March 22 reflects this:

> Now I have light. I lived without it for 40 days and learned to understand its value. I'll never forget that, just as I'll never forget the terrible humiliation of being engulfed in darkness. I fought against it and managed to ward it off for nearly 200

hours, using a tiny oil lamp with a dim and wavering flame, my eyes burning, my heart beating with indignation. Of all human barbarities, the least bearable is the absurd.

The absurd, however, was a constant factor during the nearly 22 months in which the revolution was imprisoned. With a people to free, they were subjected to the desolation of being kept behind bars. Constant self-control was needed to prevent possible abuses by some imbecile with a modicum of power. It was an absurd kingdom of the absurd, in which any idiot could become a big shot just because he was in a position to supply a tray of food, yell "On your feet!" and be obeyed, prevent their writing, read other people's mail, interrupt their thinking, or stop them from reading.

What an absurd kingdom of the absurd, in which every detail of daily routine occupied the thoughts of a person forced into physical idleness by confinement in that flat landscape — a room no more than five meters in length, enclosed by four too-smooth and all-too-identical white walls inducing lethargy, day after day. Books are the only escape, the isolated manifestation of life; and thinking the only freedom. On March 28, Fidel wrote:

I turn on the light about 7:00 p.m., and then I begin to fight the mosquitoes. If I'm writing, I scare them by blowing cigarette smoke. Then I get under the mosquito net and start chasing one by one those that have managed to get in with me.

But that's not all. As soon as I start to read, I realize that I've left my colored pencil outside. I go get it and open the book — and it turns out to be the wrong volume! I go out again to get the dictionary, or my glasses. What a problem! So now I've made a little pile to the right of the bed and another pile on the bed itself, of which I take very good care. I read as long as I can, usually 10, 12, or 14 hours a day.

The cell is also inhabited by ants that eat everything: cheese, grease, bread. Strangely, the only thing they don't touch is the condensed milk. There's a constant battle among the animal life. The flies fight the mosquitoes; the frogs hunt the flies; and the ants, like tiny vultures, carry away whatever's left. The prison that I find so confining is a huge world for them.

Every once in a while a small, bright bird flies up to one of the high windows, happy and free. Then I understand more clearly than ever what a crime it is to cage these birds, and I'm reminded of *The Story of San Michele*. In the late afternoon, the sun shines obliquely through the windows, and the shadows of the bars fall across the floor for several minutes.

Something new broadens the possibilities for amusement, at times ironically pointing to the bitterness of confinement.

On April 4, after reading Lenin's *State and Revolution*, Fidel wrote:

Now I am allowed outside several hours every afternoon, as well as Tuesday, Thursday, and Sunday mornings, in a big, empty enclosed yard with a gallery all around. I enjoy it very much, although I will come out mute....

I fixed up my cell Friday. I scrubbed the granite floor first with soap and water and then with scouring powder, then washed it down with detergent. Finally, I rinsed it with a disinfectant, aromatic solution. I put everything in perfect order. The rooms at the Hotel Nacional are not as clean....

I'm going to dine on spaghetti with squid, Italian bonbons for dessert with fresh coffee, and then smoke a four-inch H. Upmann cigar. Aren't you jealous? They look after me and they take pretty good care of me. They pay no attention to what I say; I try to keep them from sending in things. When I go out in the morning in my shorts and breathe the sea air, I feel like I'm at the beach, and that there's a little restaurant here. They're going to make me think I'm on vacation. What would Karl Marx say about such revolutionaries?

But these were fleeting moments. The harsh reality filtered through in other letters — along with the ever-present attitude of struggle. On April 11, he wrote:

Some days ago, they took me to court. It had been a long time since I had seen fields and distant horizons. The landscape here is beautiful, full of light and radiant sun. I stood a while talking to the employees in the trial court — very nice people — about national affairs. When I returned to my cell, I felt strange, uncomfortable. I thought about what I had said to them. It was quick and precise, but I realized I had spoken mechanically. I had the feeling that the light, the landscape, the horizon — everything — had affected me, as if I had entered a strange, distant, and forgotten world.

Battle in solitude

Those trips to court were the only break from the rigid prison regimen. They were the only chance the prisoners had, alone or in groups, to leave the prison for a few hours and see what life was like outside its walls. Because of the testimony given during the hearings on Case 37 concerning the crimes committed by the repressive forces in Oriente following the Moncada attack, the Trial Court of Northern Santiago de Cuba was hearing three new criminal suits brought by the survivors of the attack. These were Cases 938, 1073, and 1083 of 1953. Between October 1953 and January 1954, almost all the Moncada rebels imprisoned on the Isle of Pines had been summoned before the Nueva Gerona trial judge at least five times to testify concerning these charges.

In June and October 1954, Cases 284 and 303, filed for homicide, were transferred from the Bayamo Trial Court and consolidated with the other cases.

Other trips to court, however, involved charges against the Moncada prisoners. For example, the Fifth Section Correctional Court of Havana summoned Montané five times between February 8 and July 10, 1954, in Case 12,868 of 1953, concerning "illicit" revolutionary propaganda activities. The prison authorities, however, refused to send him to Havana until the sixth summons was issued, after 11 months. Then, on January 4, 1955, he was taken to the capital, stood trial, was acquitted, and on January 27 returned to prison on the Isle of Pines.

Ciro Redondo was taken to Havana and then back to Pinar del Río as a defendant in Case 125 of 1953 at the Pinar del Río Court (January 29 - March 2, 1954), while Julito Díaz, José Ponce, and

Fidel Labrador had hearings there September 6-24, 1954. Pepe Suárez, who went with them, was held in the Havana jail to testify in Case 938 of 1953.[7] Later, he was sent back to Havana and held there over two months — from November 19, 1954, to January 27, 1955 — for hearings in the same case.

On 10 different occasions the administration of the National Men's Prison received telegrams signed by Ramón O. Hermida, Minister of the Interior, ordering prisoner Raúl Castro to be transferred to Havana for a hearing in the Provisional Court as defendant in Case 412 of 1953, in which he was charged with a crime against public order. Each time, the prison director gave excuses for not complying with the order. Sometimes he lied and said the prisoner was ill; at other times he claimed there was no escort to take the prisoner to Havana or no tickets for the trip — whatever occurred to him.

The same thing happened when Fidel was ordered to appear with Raúl before the Provisional Court of Santiago de Cuba in Case 1104 of 1953, in which they were charged with making threats; when he was ordered to appear alone in Case 559 of 1951, before the Trial Court of Colón; and when he was ordered to appear before the Provisional Court of Havana in Case 719 of 1953, for contempt and violation of Legislative Decree 997 of 1953. Immediately after the incident involving Batista, every conceivable objection was raised to prevent Fidel from being moved and to keep him in total solitary confinement. One week after the incident, on February 19, 1954, Director Capote sent a sharply worded telegram to Minister Hermida that illustrated the worsening situation:

---

7 "Guess who headed the group of guards that took us from Havana to Pinar del Río?" Pepe Ponce asked during the course of a talk in August 1980. "A sergeant named Esteban Ventura Novo." The name would not mean much except when one recalls that Ventura Novo's "career" had a meteoric rise during the Batista years, reaching the highest levels of the police hierarchy, where he made a name for himself as one of the dictatorship's most brutal murderers and torturers. He managed to leave the country with Batista at dawn on January 1, 1959, fleeing first to Trujillo's satrapy in the Dominican Republic and then to the United States — as a "refugee."

I respectfully submit impossibility of transferring prisoner Fidel Castro Ruz for hearing before Havana Provisional Court today in Case 719 of 1953 (Case 37/953, Provisional Court of Santiago de Cuba), due to total lack of custody to make this transfer with the required precautions and in view of escape possibilities from this penitentiary STOP I herewith communicate this for your information and whatever effect it may have STOP

In spite of frequent requests, Fidel was permitted to make only five quick visits to the Nueva Gerona Court after he was placed in solitary confinement. The rest of the letter Fidel wrote on April 11, eight days after his first court hearing following the February incident, is more easily understood knowing this background. It reflects sadness but not discouragement. No matter how hard he was hit, his morale — based on what motivated him to fight — remained high:

It has been only eight and a half months, but how much I have had to suffer in every way! I've spent most of the time alone; to a certain extent, that has been my fate. There's a law of inertia in the moral as well as the physical world, and both worlds also have their laws of gravitation; a thousand forces tend to slow you down, and sometimes you have to combat them with every ounce of psychic and spiritual energy.

Your confidence in my determination to resist is not unfounded. It is true that I am bearing up firmly. But this is not a normal life I am leading; and it goes against the grain in every way. It's as if a body, which has its own shape, were being pressed into a different mold.

The strange thing is that I have no personal ambitions; all my motives are moral ones — a sense of honor, dignity, and duty. The reasons others have for valuing life mean nothing to me. The greatest contradiction in my situation is that I am totally indifferent to physical or material punishment, to biological existence; I could mock all that with a smile. The only prison, chain, or force I recognize is that of duty. Physically, I feel powerful, confident that no force on earth can harm me — simply because I do not fear it. Nevertheless, the physical must submit to the moral, the innate rebel ever at war with calm, cold reason, which in turn is based on strong moral feelings.

Later, his thoughts and the treatment given him were to become public knowledge. But at that time — the last half of February 1954 — a heavy curtain had been drawn to keep the outside world from knowing what was really taking place inside the prison.

The press remained paralyzed by the fascist-like application of the so-called 'Law of Public Order.' It was more than mere coincidence that Legislative Decree 997 — aimed at preventing the release of any statement or any information against the dictatorship and its ability to rule, its officials, and the prevailing status quo — had been signed on July 26, 1953.

One section of that decree provided for a series of monstrous changes in the Social Defense Code regarding criminal penalties for contempt, libel, slander, and other charges of this kind. For instance contempt — defined as provocation or as personal or written threats against "any official exercising his prerogatives" or any "head of a foreign state or its agents" (the reference could not be more obvious) — was made punishable by up to two years in prison and a fine of 700 quotas (an elastic measure). Libel was defined as a "true [sic] or false imputation, through publicity, of a crime, vice, or lack of morality that might damage the reputation or the social or economic standing of the aggrieved party." It was made punishable by up to a year in prison and a fine of 1,000 quotas.

In either case, the newspaper that had published the information had to publish a retraction, and could be shut down for up to 60 days and fined 1,000 pesos. It was clear that those who would be determining guilt or innocence would be those who made the laws.

The most significant section of the law was Chapter 1, which left the dictatorship free to decide what would be considered attacks on "public confidence, peace, or tranquility, the stability of state powers, the value of money, or the issuance of legal currency or bearer's bonds and other valuables." When propogated, published, or transmitted (Article 1), such acts would carry a sentence of up to two years in prison and a fine of 1,000 quotas. This was also applicable (Article 2) to "those who, openly or clandestinely, issue propaganda aimed at producing or favoring the attainment of any of the following goals:

1. Violently subverting or destroying the political, social, economic, or legal structure of the state as presently constituted.
2. Promoting discord or antagonisms within the various state, provincial, or municipal bodies; within institutes and agencies — both civilian and military — or their components; or inciting citizens or classes of society to hatred or armed struggle or causing alarm or affecting the public confidence, peace, or tranquility in any other way.
3. Injuring national dignity or disparaging state powers and agencies, the Constitution,[8] laws, or actions taken by the authorities.
4. Disobeying the Constitutional Law, laws, decrees issued by the authorities, or judgements made by the courts."

As for the newspaper that published this "propaganda," it would be closed down for a period of three months to a year and fined up to 1,000 pesos. This coercive law, backed by the repressive

---

8 The Constitutional Law, as it was pompously called in the officious language of the dictatorship, was nothing more than the so-called constitutional statutes published April 4, 1952, 25 days after the overthrow of Carlos Prío Socarrás. The statutes transgressed the principles of popular sovereignty and the functional organization of the state as set forth in the 1940 constitution of the republic. Legally null and void because they were issued by those who had committed various crimes listed in the Social Defense and Military Penal Codes, the statutes were a monstrous parody of legality. They were nonetheless validated by the Court of Constitutional Guarantees, thus providing a "legal" basis for the de facto regime that had emerged from the reactionary coup of March 10, 1952. The statutes empowered Fulgencio Batista and his Council of Ministers to exercise executive and legislative powers and gave them jurisdiction over the courts. They also authorized them to suspend, annul, or modify any statutory provisions, giving them a free hand to "juridically" exercise power with impunity.

forces, succeeded in its goal of using terror to cut off all information about what was going on.

Meanwhile, what was happening to the group of prisoners who had attacked the Moncada?

Concern outside the prison mounted as the silence over their fate deepened, visitors were turned back, relatives were denied entry, and mail was prevented from leaving the prison. Rumors of foul play increased this concern, and people began to fear for the lives of the prisoners. Had they killed Fidel and the others? Who were the victims?

Recalling those days 27 years later, Juan Almeida's father said:

Sergio, Montané's father, asked me to go with him, and I went right away, with Rubén Eugenio, my 11-year-old son. It wasn't easy to enter the prison. Sergio had tried a number of times before the day Lieutenant Roger Pérez Díaz finally let us through.

First we went to see the boys, and they begged us to let them know if we saw Fidel, because they didn't know whether he was dead or alive. They had been told he'd been murdered.

Well, we managed to see Fidel in his cell. While we were talking to him, along came Montesinos, very angry because we were there. You should have seen how Fidel grabbed him by the lapels of his jacket and rebuked him. "You're all alike, all alike," Fidel told him. "Not one of you is any better." He told him to his face that they were beating and killing men in the building next door.

As we left, we managed to send the group a message saying that Fidel was alive.

Only one other visitor succeeded in breaking through the wall of solitude that surrounded Fidel: Judge Waldo Medina, who was to get to know him personally. In a situation permeated with fear and political opportunism, very few dared extend a hand to the "conquered." With a conspiracy of almost total silence surrounding the Moncada events and those who had taken part in them — a silence heightened by the regime's censorship and terrorizing of the press — this unusual gesture stands out.

Judge Medina's background helps explain the "eccentricity" of his visit to Fidel on Sunday, April 22, 1954. Here was a man who still bore the scars of bullets fired at him years earlier by a big landowner who could not bribe him to change an adverse ruling, a man who had taken dozens of cases on behalf of poor tenants threatened with eviction, as well as cases of low-income families who could not meet installment payments on furniture or electrical appliances, who had written hundreds of newspaper articles denouncing social problems and pointing out that their underlying cause was economic inequality and other types of injustice. Medina's concern for these problems led him, in 1947, to write *La prisión que estorba* (How prison blocks progress), a sharp attack on the deforming penal system existing in Cuba at that time, with special emphasis on the horrors of the prison on the Isle of Pines, which it described as "a hell blazing with layer upon layer of human beings, lives rotting away in the worst of all the dung heaps of society."

While Fidel was still a university student, Medina was a member of a committee (to which Sergio Montané also belonged) that undertook to build an airport in Nueva Gerona and a library in Santa Fe, and to restore the El Abra farm, where Martí began his exile. Even more significant was his role as a judge in Nueva Gerona, where with the sparkle of exceptional dignity he sentenced Captain Angel Pedro Pérez, the all-powerful prison director in Carlos Prío's administration, to six months' imprisonment for misappropriating public funds and abusing prisoners — and made him serve it — an action unequalled in the history of the mutilated republic.

The idea for the visit had arisen several days earlier, when a group of students from Institute No. 1 visited Medina in his office in the Municipal Court of Northern Havana, on Lealtad Street. They asked for his help — as a former judge on the Isle of Pines for several years, with possible connections there — in meeting the imprisoned Moncada group.

Medina agreed and went with them to Nueva Gerona that same week. Luckily, Major Capote, the prison director, was not there that day, for he had had nothing to do with Medina since the time the judge had courageously sentenced Captain Pérez.

It was not easy to convince Lieutenant Montesinos, either. He was afraid he might be reprimanded for going against the order denying Fidel visitors, but Medina kept appealing to him until he finally gave in. The students were authorized to talk to the other Moncada prisoners, but only the judge was allowed to see Fidel — and then for just a few minutes.

Waldo Medina later recalled:

All the men were outside in the yard when we arrived. The students went right over and greeted them and began talking. I followed Montesinos to a small area that had once been a dentist's office, with toilet facilities. The lieutenant unlocked the chain on the heavy barred door, and we went in. Fidel was in shorts and shirtless. He did not know who I was, but he immediately rose and shook my hand. Montesinos, who kept trying to rush me, stayed in the background, leaning against the door. There was a cot in the middle of the room, looking like an island, surrounded by books.

"Fidel, I'm Waldo Medina, judge for Northern Havana," I said, and explained that I had come with a group of students. I told him about our trip, and we talked about his books and his health, not saying anything about the Moncada. Then he said, "So you're a judge in Havana. Well, they're going to kick you out for having come here."

Years later, when I was director of the Legal Department of the National Institute of Agrarian Reform, Fidel reminded me, "Didn't I tell you they would kick you out?" And it's true that in 1956, after many years as a judge, I was fired and left without a job. Fidel had been right, but it wasn't just because of that visit. Although the arbitrary verdict by the so-called Supreme Court of Justice upheld charges lodged against me by several profiteers whose interests I had managed to hurt, the real reason was that Andrés Domingo Morales del Castillo had pressured the court and the judges to take measures against me because I had written articles attacking the regime. Besides, I was the only Electoral Board chairman who petitioned to have the illegal election of November 1954 declared null and void.

When I visited Fidel in prison, I must have interrupted his reading and writing — I was impressed by how many books he had piled up at his side. Nevertheless, he greeted me most courteously and did not seem a bit upset, even though I noticed that he looked at me with an expression that asked, "What's this man here for?" That was to be expected. After all, why should I, a judge, who did not even know Fidel, suddenly appear in his cell? You must remember that I represented "order" in that society.

Attack without respite

The bars closed behind the unexpected visitor, and solitude descended once more. Two months later, still in solitary confinement — shortly before two midshipmen were put in his cell, apparently as a new method of keeping him under constant surveillance — Fidel wrote a letter to Haydée and Melba dated June 18. In it he mentioned that "in addition to three months in solitary in Santiago de Cuba," he had spent more than 3,000 hours completely alone on the Isle of Pines:

They have kept me locked up in this solitary cell for four months and one week now. At first, they said it was for four months, but they really intend to leave me here indefinitely. I will not waste time giving you my opinion of these people; Castells[9] and his gang of assassins were little angels compared to the intransigent, soulless, stupid band that runs this prison.

The situation really could not be any worse. I'm not sure whether it is so much the mental torture and the unnaturalness of the situation, as the thought that these things can take place in Cuba with absolute impunity, in the midst of a horrifying indifference on the part of the press. The more you learn about the moral degradation from which the republic is suffering, the harder it is to stomach.

But aside from the efforts of three or four individuals —

---

9 Captain Castells, first director of the Model Prison on the Isle of Pines, was notorious for the crimes he himself committed, ordered, or condoned against the prisoners held there during the Machado tyranny, in the early 1930s.

you, first of all — there is absolutely no opposition to the regime. Suffice it to recall the battle that was waged against Prío's 200-million-peso loan and then see how calmly Batista is negotiating one now for 350 million. This loan, together with the others he has gotten recently, will bring the total to over 500 million pesos, all this obtained through violations of the law, secret negotiations, and mysterious visits by Martínez Sáenz to the United States. Everything is completely chaotic, without plan or program, so Batista can spend the money any way he likes, mortgaging the country for more than a quarter of a century. Except for Cepero Bonilla, I don't see the slightest resistance to this in the press — nothing but a total indifference.

The picture is thoroughly distressing. Don't think I am discouraged or that I plan to give vent to my feelings — that would take at least 30 pages — but it is not very easy to console oneself when there is no one with whom you can exchange a word of encouragement. Still, when I think about it, I come to the conclusion that this national crisis was inevitable and necessary and that the greater the crisis, the greater the hope that we can conceive of a different future. At this time, for those of us whose ideals are sincere, Cuba is like the Mount of Olives, on which we must sweat blood.

The letter went on to display the same wisdom he was to show during the subsequent years of struggle against the dictatorship and, later, in permanent confrontation with Yankee imperialism:

Here I spend the day reading and practicing self-control. It's true I feel better when I do not read the newspapers. The political deals and submissiveness I see everywhere make me furious. If anybody's patience has ever been put to the test, it is mine. Sometimes I spend hours fighting a desire to explode or declare a hunger strike and refuse to eat anything until they take me out of this cell or kill me — which would not be unlikely. I'm convinced they are really trying to provoke me, but they won't succeed. Why have they kept me in isolation beyond the four months? I'm not sure how long I will have the strength to control myself.

Somehow he found the strength, and he did resist. Defeatism was never a part of his temperament. He had a special ability to fight back, even under the most unfavorable circumstances, maneuvering to change the situation and turn it into a defeat for his enemies.

Proof of this was the fact that despite the exasperating situation, he managed to send instructions to Havana for drawing up a detailed campaign to wear the dictatorship down, based precisely on the unique situation in which it had placed him. He realized that this was the moment to use the so-called "democratic opening" the regime had been forced to proclaim prior to the November 1954 election. Outlining his ideas, he wrote on June 18:

> Certainly this is the greatest contradiction that could be hurled at the government, coming in the midst of an electoral campaign and following the pseudo-amnesty decree, it offers a great opportunity to put the politicians on the spot.
>
> As for the authorities here, one of the most serious mistakes they made was to beat up Cartaya early on the morning of February 15. Lieutenant Perico, Sergeant Rojas, a certain *Cebolla*, and others under the orders of Major Capote were in on it. It's a point on which we should attack them without respite. I consider it the most important and effective point we can make.

At the same time, although the dictatorship was the main enemy and had to be the target of their greatest efforts, there was no reason to leave any flank unguarded against other enemies every bit as dangerous — or even more so from a strategic point of view. Fidel continued to explain this orientation to the leading cadres of the Movement, so that useless, disruptive efforts might be avoided. In this regard, the "strictly confidential" message he sent Melba on May 12, a few days before she left on a delicate mission abroad, is quite clear:

> I have a tremendous lack of confidence and a pretty low opinion of the Montreal group. Their behavior toward me and the Movement has been as follows: before July 26, they refused to recognize us, excluded us, sabotaged us, and poisoned

people against us by filling their heads with rumors, lies, and predictions and by bragging about the advantages they had because of the millions they had stolen.

At the time of July 26 and in the days that followed, they showed how envious they were by criticizing and slandering us, even going so far as to say we had carried out the attack as part of an agreement with Batista.

Then came the trial. They kept quiet and left us alone to fight the slander, crimes, and indignities that were heaped on us. They were not even smart about it, because, fearing to enhance the heroism of our cause, they failed to denounce Batista's crimes.

We have had to fight alone before, during, and after July 26. We now represent a lofty and unblemished ideal, and we have the right to be the standard-bearers of the future. We must not sell our souls for a mess of pottage. What position do these gentlemen take now? They have not changed, except to add a little word of praise to deceive us and then do as bad or worse to us as they did to the Orthodox Party — which they led into a dead-end, discredited, and then booted out like an unwanted mistress.

I know it is hard to stand firm when the whole world is saying it's zero hour. I know all too well that everyone is desperate to get hold of a gun and that the only resource the Montreal group has to gain followers is by offering weapons. But I have had enough of desperate men. They are always the most demanding and impatient ones before the struggle begins, and then the ones least interested in fighting when the time comes. For them, the revolution is nothing but a fine adventure.

We must realize that rather than a real force we are still an idea, a symbol, a great potential force. It will be to Cuba's benefit if we can follow a line. We are ready to give the last drop of our blood for freedom. But if the struggle means we must be humiliated and forced to put up with the arrogance and conceit of those who lead simply because they have stolen millions and are now pontificating what they're going to do later, it's not worth a single drop of blood. Their only goal is power, while ours is a true revolution. They are leading the struggle now because they have millions. Tomorrow, they will steal millions on the pretext that it's for the struggle. No agreement can be reached with them unless they first accept our program — not because it's ours, but because it points the way toward the only possible revolution. This program does not, of course, exclude confiscating the property of all the crooks in all the administrations. That should certainly hit pretty close to home.

This is what I really feel. I want you to tell this to the people in Mexico, for I'm sure they will see it the same way. I repeat that we will accept whatever you finally decide, because you are in a better position to judge. The only thing I ask is that you weigh each step intelligently and in all its magnitude. It does not matter how few we are, for there's a long road ahead. If we can uphold our principles, they will one day become the banner of a real and possible revolution.

In spite of all the coercive measures employed against him, by June 1954 Fidel had worked tirelessly, carefully, and in strict secrecy on another vitally important plan that would deal a powerful blow against the enemy. Very soon he would break through the conspiracy of silence surrounding the Moncada events, whose first anniversary was only six weeks away.

With indomitable determination, he gathered his strength for a battle to be waged from the most adverse, most indefensible position possible. On June 12, Fidel described the dictatorship's unchanging brutality:

For several months, ever since we sang the patriotic march during the dictator's visit to the prison, I have not been allowed to see my brother, who is just 50 meters away from my cell, or even write him a few lines....

The only time there's anyone nearby is when the corpse of a prisoner — perhaps mysteriously hanged, beaten, or otherwise tortured to death — is laid out in the small funeral parlor opposite my cell. However, a six-foot high partition has been erected in front of the only entrance to my cell to keep me from seeing a single human being, dead or alive. It would be too magnanimous to permit me even the company of a corpse!

CHAPTER 3

The dictatorship was not as solid as it claimed to be — nor was its repressive apparatus as clever. Fidel found ways, even in his solitary cell, to elude his jailers' constant surveillance and secretly make contact with his comrades in the collective ward and those outside the prison. He smuggled out messages, directives, and — most important of all — a fragment by fragment reconstruction of his defense speech during the trial for the events of July 26, 1953. It is "our revolutionary program," as he called it in a letter dated May 12, 1954, "a document on which the struggle is to be based."

At the same time, Fidel denounced as fraudulent the regime's plans for elections in November of that year; attended to the reorganization of the revolutionary movement inside Cuba and abroad, explaining that unity must be based on principles, and that the Movement's purity must be kept untarnished by any compromise with the discredited bourgeois politicians. His real attention, however, was focused on one aspect of the ideological struggle that, with his extraordinary gift for tactics, had been part of his political thinking ever since his days as a student leader and that he saw as a key to the struggle: "I believe," he wrote on June 18, 1954, "that at the present time propaganda is vital. Without propaganda, there can be no mass movement, and...

Without a mass movement there can be no revolution

"I write this document with the blood of my dead brothers. They alone inspire me. We demand justice for them even more than our own freedom and lives. Justice that is not, in this case, a monument to the heroes and martyrs killed in battle or murdered afterwards. Justice — not simply a grave so they may rest in peace together instead of being scattered over the fields of Oriente, many in places known only to their killers — for it is not possible to speak of peace for the dead in this oppressed land. Posterity, which is always more generous to the just, will erect those symbols in their memory, and the generations of tomorrow will pay due respect to those who vindicated the nation's honor in this hour of infinite shame."

Fidel wrote these lines on December 12, 1953, in response to the criminal indifference of those who were trying to grab easy headlines for their verbal opposition to the Batista regime without a word about the crimes the dictator had committed against the brave young men who stormed the Moncada garrison in July. Fidel continued:

Why has no one had the courage to denounce the atrocious tortures and the barbarous, senseless mass murder of 70 young prisoners on July 26, 27, 28, and 29? This is indeed an unavoidable duty, and those who shirk it will be forever shamed. No other such massacre has ever occurred in the history of Cuba, either as a colony or a republic. I realize that terror has had a paralyzing effect for a long time, but it is no longer possible to permit a cowardly cloak of silence to cover up those appalling crimes — that response of base and brutal hatred by a tyrant who took on Cuba's purest, most generous, and most idealistic young people for their natural rebelliousness as enslaved sons of our heroic people. This silence is shameful complicity, as repulsive as the crime itself. The tyrant must be licking his lips with satisfaction at the ferocity of his henchmen and the terror this inspires in his enemies.

But the truth cannot be hidden. Everybody in Oriente knows it and talks about it behind closed doors. They know that the vicious accusations that we were cruel to the soldiers we captured are a pack of lies. The government could not prove any of its charges in court. Depositions were taken from 20 soldiers who were captured by us at the outset and 30 who were wounded in battle — and all of them agreed that our men had not even spoken harshly to them. The court doctors, experts, and even witnesses for the prosecution itself spoke up and demolished the government's claims in statements that were often commendably honest. It was also proven that the arms had been acquired in Cuba, that there was no connection with the old-style politicians, that no one had been stabbed, and that only one patient in the Military Hospital had been wounded when he leaned out the window. The prosecutor himself[1] — which is unusual — had to admit in his summary to "the honorable and humane behavior of the attackers."

Meanwhile, where were our wounded? There were only five in all. Ninety dead and five wounded. Can anyone imagine such a ratio in any war? What about the others? Where were the fighters who were arrested on July 26, 27, 28, and 29? Santiago de Cuba knows the answer. The wounded were snatched from the private hospitals, even from the operating tables, and killed immediately, in some cases on the premises. Two wounded prisoners who entered an elevator with their captors were taken out dead. Those interned in the Military Hospital had air and camphor injected into their veins. Pedro

---

1. Dr. Francisco Mendieta Hechavarría, prosecutor in Case 37 (1953) in the Provisional Court of Santiago de Cuba, who was familiar with the events surrounding the July 26 attacks on the Moncada and Bayamo garrisons.

Miret, an engineering student, survived this deadly procedure and told the whole story.

Only five lived, I repeat. Two — José Ponce and Gustavo Arcos — were protected by Dr. Posada, who refused to let them be taken away by the soldiers in the Spanish Colony Hospital. The other three owe their lives to Captain Tamayo, an army physician and worthy professional who, in a courageous act, pistol in hand, transferred the wounded Pedro Miret, Abelardo Crespo, and Fidel Labrador from the Military hospital to the Civilian hospital. The assassins did not want to let even these five live. The numbers speak eloquently for themselves.

This statement was not published by any of the newspapers. But it was typed up and circulated clandestinely as the *Manifesto to the Nation*, with a brief introductory note that stated, "The Cuban Patriotic League issues the following manifesto because of its great historical significance. Copy and distribute it among your friends and try to have them do the same." In the document, Fidel added:

As far as the prisoners were concerned, the entrance to the Moncada garrison could well have borne the legend posted at the entrance to Dante's Inferno: "Abandon all hope, ye who enter here!" Thirty were murdered the first night. Gen. Martín Díaz Tamayo arrived at 3:00 p.m. and gave the order because, he said, the army should be ashamed at having three times as many casualties in battle as the attackers — so 10 should be put to death for each soldier killed.

This order was the product of a meeting attended by Batista, Tabernilla, Ugalde Carrillo, and other officials. To avoid legal difficulties, that same Sunday the Council of Ministers suspended Article 26 of the statutes establishing the responsibility of guards for the lives of prisoners. The order was applied with horrible cruelty. When the dead were interred they had no eyes, no teeth, and no testicles; even their valuables were taken by their murderers, who later showed them off without batting an eye.

Indescribable courage was shown in confronting the torturers. Two young women, our heroic comrades Melba Hernández and Haydée Santamaría, were arrested in the Civilian hospital — where they were stationed to nurse the wounded. They were taken to the Moncada; at nightfall, Sgt. Eulalio González (the "Tiger"), who had just gouged out Abel Santamaría's eyes, brought them in to show Haydée. Later that night, they told her that her fiancée, also a prisoner, had been killed. Full of indignation she faced the murderers and told them, "He is not dead. To die for one's homeland is to live." The women were spared — the fiends did not dare go so far as to kill them — and are exceptional witnesses to all that happened in that hellhole.

On the outskirts of Santiago de Cuba, forces under the command of Major Pérez Chaumont murdered 21 unarmed men scattered over the area. Many were forced to dig their own graves; one of them bravely turned his spade against his killers and hit one of them in the face.

The only fighters who still had their guns were those who were with me when we took to the mountains. The army did not catch up with us until six days later, when exhaustion and hunger won out over our resolve not to let ourselves be caught sleeping. The bloody orgy was already over, in the face of the immense popular outcry. Even so, only the miracle that a decent officer found us and that I was not recognized until we were registered at the police station kept us from being killed, as well.

On July 27, at midnight, at km. 39 of the Manzanillo-Bayamo road, the captain in charge of the Manzanillo area had Pedro Véliz, Hugo Camejo and Andrés García[2] dragged along

---

2. Hugo Camejo Valdés (born on May 7, 1918), had been head of one of the cells of the Movement in Marianao, Havana, which included José Testa Zaragoza (born April 15, 1924), Rolando San Román de las Llamas (born June 1, 1929), Rafael Freyre Torres (born February 25, 1931), Angelo de la Guardia Guerra Díaz (born March 31, 1931), Luciano González Camejo (born December 18, 1913), Lázaro Hernández Arroyo (born December 7, 1934), Andrés García, Agustín Díaz Cartalaya, Adalberto Ruanes, and Orestes Abad Lorenzo. Together, they all participated in the attack on the Bayamo garrison. Only the last four survived. The others were

the ground with nooses around their necks until he thought they were dead, and left them there.

García survived and has since told the story, through the good offices of Monsignor Pérez Serantes.[3] In the early morning of July 28, near the Cauto River, on the road to Palma, several young men, including Raúl de Aguiar and Andrés Valdés,[4] were finished off by Sergeant Montes de Oca, acting chief of the Alto Cedro post, and Corporal Maceo, who threw the bodies into a well on the river bank, near Bananea. Raúl and Andrés had been in touch with friends of mine who had helped them[5] and later learned about their deaths. All these crimes were committed with the prior knowledge of the regimental command.

It is absolutely false that the Fingerprint Department has identified all the corpses recovered — it has done so with less than half the total. In every case, the victim's name and general data were recorded before he was killed, and then the names were released in dribs and drabs — never the complete list. Only some of those killed in battle were identified by their fingerprints; the rest remained unidentified. These procedures have caused indescribable suffering and uncertainty among the fighters' relatives. I denounced these and other facts and gave all the details at the hearing, in the presence of soldiers armed with machine guns and rifles who filled the courtroom in an

---

captured and murdered. Orestes Abad later betrayed the principles he had defended on July 26, 1953, by becoming a soldier for the Batista dictatorship.

3. Monsignor Enrique Pérez Serantes, archbishop of Santiago de Cuba.

4. Raúl de Aguiar Fernández (born September 18, 1922) was cell leader in Havana's Cayo Hueso district. Cell members Andrés Valdés Fuentes (born February 24, 1929), Armando Valle López (born October 27, 1929), and José de Jesús Maderas Fernández (born October 15, 1935) also participated in the July 26 events. All were captured and murdered.

5. Fidel wrote about this with understandable discretion. Raúl de Aguiar, who had accompanied Fidel on a visit to the Castros' farm in Birán, northern Oriente, some months earlier, managed to make his way back to the farm after July 26 with his comrades Armando Valle and Andrés Valdés. There, they were fed and hidden by Ramón Castro, older brother of Fidel and Raúl, who advised them to stay under cover. They insisted on going back to Havana, however, and Ramón gave them money for the trip. They were captured and murdered on the way, although their bodies were never found.

obvious attempt to intimidate. They themselves were affected when they heard what barbarities had been committed.

I was excluded from the third session of the trial, in flagrant violation of all the rules of procedure. This was done to prevent me, as my own attorney, from examining the witnesses and thus throwing light on what really happened. They were especially fearful that my questioning of the prosecution witnesses would disclose the horrendous crimes that were committed, without making any attempt to keep up appearances. In spite of everything they could not prevent the scandal — other lawyers saw to that.

From our testimony denouncing these crimes, Cases 938, 1073, and 1083 of 1953 have been filed in the Trial Court of Northern Santiago de Cuba, charging murder and torture — in addition to many other cases for continued violation of human rights.[6] We have filed all of them in the Trial Court of Nueva Gerona. We have accused Batista, Tabernilla, Ugalde Carrillo, and Díaz Tamayo of issuing the order to kill the prisoners and we know beyond a shadow of a doubt that the charge is true. We have also brought charges against Colonel Alberto del Río Chaviano and all the officers, noncommissioned officers, and privates who so distinguished themselves in carrying out that bloodbath.

Under existing law, the civil courts are responsible for trying those charged, except for Batista; and so far the Court of Santiago de Cuba has been quite firm about this. There is no doubt whatsoever that the silence surrounding this trial is the greatest favor that could be done for the criminals and simply gives them the green light to go on killing without any restraint. Of course, I have not the slightest hope of a legal conviction. That would be too much to expect of a regime in which murderers and torturers enjoy freedom, wear uniforms, and represent authority while honorable men are sent to jail

---

6. On the basis of the Moncada rebels' charges at the hearing on Case 37, homicide charges were filed in the Bayamo Trial Court in Cases 284 and 303 of 1953, scheduled to be heard in June and October 1954. Thus, Fidel could not refer to them in this document, dated December 12, 1953.

for the crime of defending a constitution that granted the people rights and freedoms. The real criminals will not be jailed, sentenced, or even tried. In fact, they will enjoy absolute moral impunity — after so many have generously given their lives fighting them, and while so many are suffering the ignominy of imprisonment.

Onward to freedom

After Haydée and Melba were released from prison, the document was printed in a pamphlet entitled *Message to Suffering Cuba*, with a picture of José Martí on the cover and a quote from him on the back: "The southern sea will join the northern one before I give up trying to make my country free and prosperous." In this pamphlet Fidel defined, exposed, appealed, and anticipated:

Those gallant men who marched to their deaths with smiles of supreme happiness on their lips, responding to the call of duty, did well in dying; because they were not born to resign themselves to the hypocritical, wretched life of these times. When all is said and done, that is really why they died — because they could not adapt themselves to the contemptible, repugnant reality. If our revolutionary action triumphed, we would have put the most fervent idealists in power.

The reestablishment of the 1940 constitution — adapted, of course, to an abnormal situation — was the first point in our proclamation to the people. Once we held the capital of Oriente, six basic, deeply revolutionary laws were to be issued. These laws would have given definitive title to the land to the small sugarcane growers, tenant farmers, sharecroppers, and squatters[7] while providing state compensation for the expropri-

---

7. The small sugarcane plantations were called colonies, and the growers were therefore also known as *colonos*. The tenant farmers — some of whom had subtenants — paid the landowners rent in order to work the land. There was also sharecropping, a semifeudal economic relationship in which the peasant paid the landowner a half, a third, or a quarter of what he harvested for permission to work the land. The squatters were those who took over land without any deed or contract to protect them. The agricultural census of 1946, twelve years before the revolution,

ated owners. The right of workers to a share of the company's profits would have been established. The small sugarcane growers would receive a 55 percent share in the cane yield. These measures would naturally have been part of a dynamic, vigorous state policy to promote new industries by the mobilization of the vast reserves of national capital, and cracking down on the organized resistance of powerful interests.

All municipal, provincial, and national judicial and administrative officials who had betrayed the constitution by endorsing the statutes would be removed. The properties of all who embezzled public funds over the course of the various administrations would be confiscated following speedy investigatory procedures, since the government has seen to it that all the documentary evidence has disappeared.

The people knew nothing of these measures, however, because in order to avoid the possibility of a general massacre, we had decided not to seize the radio stations until the garrison was firmly in our hands. Once we took the stations, we had planned to broadcast a continuous recording of Chibás'[8] last speech, to let people know immediately that this was a revolutionary uprising completely independent of the personalities of the past.

Timid souls will say we were wrong, using the legal *juris et de jure* argument of success vs. failure. The failure was due

---

showed "the existence of 53,035 peasants who paid cash rent to landowners, 33,064 sharecroppers who paid in kind, and 13,718 squatters who lived mainly on state land." *Las luchas campesinas en Cuba* (Peasant struggles in Cuba), by Antero Regalado.

8. Eduardo Chibás was the founder and leader of the Cuban People's (Orthodox) Party. It became a powerful contender in the 1948 elections, attracting Fidel Castro and most of those who became involved in the attack on the Moncada garrison. Chibás became an ardent advocate for a strong and deeply rooted mass movement for civic and moral reform. On August 5, 1951, in his usual Sunday night radio program, he delivered his final speech, known as the "last warning," in which he wound up by saying, "Forward, compañeros of the Orthodox Party, for economic independence, political freedom, and social justice! Out with the thieves in office! People of Cuba, arise and go forward! People of Cuba, wake up! This is my last warning!" Then, still sitting in front of the microphone, he shot himself in the stomach. On August 16, less than a year before the presidential election he had been expected to win, and after 11 days of agony, Chibás died in Havana.

to painful last-minute details, so simple that it is maddening to think of them. The possibility of success was directly related to our resources; if these been available to us, we would surely have gone into the battle with a 90 percent chance of winning.

These considerations bring to mind the strength and concerns of those who had rebelled in anger against the prevailing mediocrity, gross complacency, and repugnant selfishness of the vested interests. These men wanted to set an example by doing something great for their homeland. Each day that passes provides more justification of the cause for which they sacrificed themselves.

The anniversary of November 27 was commemorated a few days ago. All those who wrote and spoke about the event spouted wrathful, fiery phrases filled with high-sounding epithets and sham indignation against the soldiers who killed those eight students. Yet no one uttered even a single word denouncing the murder of 70 young men who were equally sterling, decent, honest, and idealistic....

Innocents... whose hot blood still burns the soul of Cuba. Let history curse the names of the hypocrites! The students of 1871 were not tortured; they were given what passed for a trial; they were buried in marked graves; and those who perpetrated that abominable deed, although relying on beliefs that mankind now rejects, felt they had a divine, four-century-old, legitimate, inviolable, eternal right to do as they did.

Nine times over, eight young men were killed by torture and bullets in Santiago de Cuba — without trial — killed in the name of a hated, godless, lawless, illegitimate dictatorship that usurped power 16 months ago. This regime violated the noblest Cuban traditions and the most sacred human principles, scattered the remains of its victims in unknown places in the same republic that our liberators founded for the dignity and honor of man, and in the very year of the Apostle's Centennial!

What was their crime? To have carried out Martí's teaching: "Whereas there are many men without honor, there are other men who carry inside them the honor of many. These are the ones who rise up in terrible wrath against those who rob the peoples of their freedom, which is to rob men of their dignity."

Whose interests were affected? The boundless ambitions of a gang of Cains who exploit and enslave our people solely for their own selfish gain. If the hatred that inspired the slaughter of November 27, "emerged, foaming at the mouth, from the belly of man," as Martí said, then what was the source of the massacres of July 26, 27, 28, and 29? Yet, I know of no Cuban army officer who has broken his sword and turned in his uniform.[9] Rather, that army's only honor was to "Kill 10 young men for every soldier killed in battle." That was the honor sought by the general staff.

No one should have been engaged in sterile, inappropriate debates about putsch vs. revolution when their duty was to denounce the monstrous crimes the government had committed by murdering more Cubans in four days than in the previous 11 years. Who in Cuba has given proof of greater faith in the masses, of their love of liberty, of their repudiation of the dictatorship, of their desperate poverty, and of their mature consciousness? Could the people's efforts to keep the Maceo Regiment fighting on the morning of March 10 in opposition to the coup be called a putsch, even though all the other regiments had accepted it?[10] Is there less awareness of freedom today than there was on the dawn of October 10, 1868?

When the time comes to begin the battle for liberty, it is not the number of the enemy's weapons that counts, but the virtues of the people. If 100 young men died bravely in Santiago, this means there are 100,000 in our country who are ready to die. Look for them and they will be found; show

9. A tacit reference to Captain Nicolás Estévanez of the Spanish colonial army, who, on hearing the soldiers fire the volley that killed eight innocent medical students in 1871, unsheathed his sword and publicly broke it as a protest against the crime. He then resigned as an officer of the colonial armed forces in Cuba. Cuban history records Estévanez's gallant action as a symbol of military dignity.
10. The Antonio Maceo Regiment based at the Moncada garrison in Santiago de Cuba initially opposed Batista's March 10, 1952 coup. In protest to the coup, the people of Santiago marched on the Moncada, demanding weapons. However, pro-Batista officers quickly took control of the garrison.

them the way and they will move forward, no matter how difficult the road. The masses are ready — they need only to be shown the true course.

Denounce the crimes: that is a duty and a powerful weapon, a formidable and revolutionary step. The lawsuits have been filed and the charges pressed. Demand that the murderers be punished and imprisoned; if necessary, find a private prosecutor. Do everything possible to keep these cases from being arbitrarily transferred to a military court. The time is ripe for such a campaign. Simply publishing our charges will be a tremendous blow to the government.

I repeat: failure to do this would be an unforgivable dereliction of duty. I hope that someday, in a free country, the fields of indomitable Oriente will be searched for the remains of our heroic comrades so they may be buried together in one great tomb next to the Apostle's, as martyrs of the Centennial, with an epitaph taken from Martí: "No martyr dies in vain; no idea is lost in the torrents of the wind; it simply moves closer or farther away, always leaving traces of its passing."

There are still 27 Cubans with the strength to fight and the courage to die.

Onward to freedom!

Fidel Castro Ruz

Days passed, and the silence concerning the July 1953 events in Oriente continued, due to official censorship and from fear of reprisal. It was also the product of the wretched political hacks who were manueuvering to make a deal with the March 10 clique in order to protect thier economic, political and social interests. This would help the regime consolidate its dictatorial power. Thus there was silence on the unprecedented massacres committed by the repressive forces in Santiago de Cuba and Bayamo during the middle of the year.

It was therefore only logical for the fearless fighter who had confronted and denounced not only all the excesses of the Batista regime but also the license, scandals, and immoralities of the last Authentic Party government, overthrown by Batista's coup, to expect the rapid exposure of these crimes — the most recent, brutal, and monstrous crimes in the nation's history. The people were also waiting to hear more than the rumors and the few details — some true and others distorted — that had leaked out.

But the days and weeks passed. Five months after the events, the politicians were still silent and the press had said nothing. What could be done? Fidel wrote constantly, appealing to everyone with access to the media to denounce the crimes. But the silence continued. On December 19, he wrote from prison:

In adversity one understands better the absurd evolution of the human drama. I have an infinite number of complaints against its actors. I'm referring principally to those who play an important role, and those who affect us most directly. Their principles are totally false, their conduct is wretched, their words are all hypocritical. Nonsense and the absurd prevail.

I can make these judgments calmly, because my existence has been reduced to the narrowest limits of privation and sacrifice. My soul has been indescribably mutilated by the affection and memory of so many good men who died. My heart has been tempered by the cruelest blows of adversity. My mind has not been bothered by petty sentiments of any kind. My spirit is free of impurities. And in sorrow I have learned to despise the vanity and selfishness that reduce men in stature.

To assail such an ignominious farce would be a major crime that cannot be forgiven. Such a terrible crime must be forgotten and silenced, buried under a crushing pile of lies and slander.

Magazines, newspapers, politicians, columnists — How pathetic they are, how revolting! Yet how they are feared! Many, like Don Quixote, see powerful armies where there are only flocks of sheep. But there are men who will rise from the ashes like the Phoenix, and the loud beating of their wings will be heard in the skies over our homeland.

As the silence continued, Fidel's letter of December 12 became the document to be circulated as the *Manifesto to the Nation*, with its penetrating message of protest. But even with all its strength, the manifesto was not enough; it reached too few people to break through the silence.

The crimes had to be denounced, but something more was needed. The people were unaware of the cause or objectives for which the first martyrs of the Centennial Youth had given their lives on July 26, 1953, the dawn of the revolution. They had not only tried to destroy the hated dictatorship but also to make sure it would never reappear. They sought the end of social injustice once and for all. Very few knew this, however: the surviving rebels and perhaps 50 others who had heard Fidel speak on October 16, 1953.

This was a revolution, a revolution with a program, which met the aspirations and interests of the people and reflecting their level of consciousness at the time. But it was a program of which the people had yet to learn. Prior to the Moncada attack, the task had been to raise the level of consciousness of a few thousand in order to move the entire people. Now it was a question of preparing the entire people at the same time. Denounce the crimes, yes, but in a way that would make it clear that the struggle was against the tyranny and the system that had engendered it — against March 9 as well as March 10.

This had to be the main task — an extremely difficult one to accomplish in the following months from a dark and solitary prison cell.

Outside the prison
Outside, the de facto government advanced step by step in its strategic mission of implementing the Truslow Plan.[11] This meant

---

11. The Truslow Plan was named for the banker Francis Adam Truslow, who headed a U.S. delegation from the Bank for Reconstruction and Development that visited Cuba in 1949 to "study" the economic situation and make recommendations. The Truslow mission's proposals centered around a number of measures designed to increase the exploitation of Cuban workers and, as a result, greatly enlarge corporate profits. It proposed wiping out the chief gains the proletariat had made during decades of struggle, permitting the arbitrary firing of workers, lengthening the workday, cutting wages and increasing productivity by introducing machinery and cutting the number of workers. Enforcing these reactionary measures, the report stated, would require a tough government that could impose them on the people. In spite of its own anti-working-class character, the Prío

raising the capitalist profits of the U.S. imperialist corporations; decapitalizing the country; increasing the public debt and the country's economic distortion, dependency, and underdevelopment — all based on the superexploitation of the workers and growing repression against the masses.

In April 1954, a plenary meeting of the Popular Socialist Party called for amnesty for political and social prisoners and accurately stated: "The perspectives are for a sharpening of the class struggle and conflicts between the exploited and exploiters. Imperialism, the ruling classes, and the government not only will not, and cannot, take steps to remedy the situation, but will constantly exacerbate it because their policy and plans are aimed at maintaining the imperialists' profits and the exploiters' many benefits, at the cost of greater poverty for the masses and the ruin of Cuba."

The conclusions from that meeting, issued in a mimeographed pamphlet entitled *La clase obrera y la nación ante la zafra* (The working class, the nation and the sugarcane harvest), went on to state,

This perspective conditions the entire situation, pointing to an increase in struggle and to the sharpening and politicalization of conflicts, with economic and political struggles merging, becoming more violent, explosive and bloody. The government, with its machinery of persecution and abuse, fully backs the plan of the wealthy, the exploiters, the foreign and domestic famine-makers, as it continues to oppose the demands and aspirations of the masses.

A number of strikes marked the first months of 1954. Meanwhile, Batista's wife was given a royal welcome in Washington and, in January, the red carpet was rolled out for a U.S. congressional delegation that arrived in Havana. The apparently tourist nature of the visit was dispelled by a United Press International dispatch

---

government did not dare try to put the Truslow Plan's recommendations into effect. Implementation of the plan was one of the main motivations behind the March 10, 1952, military coup.

linking the group's presence in Cuba to a statement made by the president of the American Meat Institute. The director of that trust told the press that the congressmen were there to impress on the Cuban government "the need to drop its protectionist measures favoring Cuban lard, so that the United States can maintain its level of lard exports to Cuba." As always, the most telling argument was a threat to reduce the sugar quota.

It was then up to Ambassador Arthur Gardner to smooth over the discontent caused by the incident. He did so by belittling its importance compared to the great benefits Cuba would obtain from a big project that was about to be launched, involving an investment of $43 million in the Nicaro Nickel Company as "a demonstration of United States goodwill toward Cuba."

"Not goodwill but cynicism," the first Cuban Marxist-Leninist party replied in the January 25, 1954, issue of its underground *Carta Semanal* (Weekly Newsletter):

Because those 'investments' will benefit not Cuba but the United States — or rather, the Yankee millionaires. Neither at Nicaro nor at Moa does the mining benefit Cuba. Cuba is plundered, which is hardly the same thing.... Because the final processsing is not done at Nicaro or at Moa. It is as if the molasses extracted from the sugarcane planted in Cuba were sent to the United States to be refined into sugar over there.

Two weeks later, in its February 6 issue, the paper returned to this theme:

The Yankees continue with their plan to "help" us. General Batista and his associates have joyfully proclaimed that the General Services Administration, a U.S. government agency in charge of state-run industries, will invest 43 million pesos in Nicaro and get the plant working at full capacity. The news was released as an example of U.S. "aid" to Cuba and Latin America, but lies don't go very far. *Time* magazine has discovered what is behind this "generosity." That conservative Yankee publication reported that nickel was a very scarce raw material and that the United States had been unable to meet its

civilian, military, and reserve nickel needs either from Canada
— which produces 85 percent of the annual "free" world's
supply — or from domestic sources.

Thus, to bridge this gap, the General Services Administration announced last week that it would spend $43 million to
expand its only defense plant outside the United States.

Four months later, at the beginning of June, Batista decreed a
political amnesty that included Carlos Prío and the rest of the
globe-trotting Montreal group but specifically excluded "those
who took part in the attack on the Moncada garrison."

The real meaning of the U.S. anticommunist maneuvering in
Latin American countries during those weeks was becoming
apparent. On March 14, the 10th Regional Conference of the
Organization of American States met in Caracas, Venzuela. There
it adopted Resolution 93, an imperial diktat imposed on the
foreign ministers (only Mexico and Argentina failed to go along)
by U.S. Secretary of State John Foster Dulles. Like his brother
Allen, Dulles was a lawyer for the United Fruit Company, whose
vast plantations in Guatemala had just been expropriated under
the agrarian reform law passed by the government of President
Jacobo Arbenz.

Resolution 93 nullified the principle of nonintervention and
paved the way for the imperialist aggression against the Guatemalan people. Economically, politically, and diplomatically be-
sieged and isolated, Guatemala was finally invaded on June 17 by
mercenary forces organized, financed, trained, and armed by the
United States, with the collaboration of the dictatorships of Gálvez
in Honduras and Somoza in Nicaragua. Ten days later, on June
27, the Arbenz government was overthrown.

This action against Guatemala clearly showed Yankee imperialism's rapacious, immoral, and criminal nature, while also high-
lighting the submissive, dependent relations that most of the
governments in the region had with the United States. Guatemala
was therefore to become a rallying point for anti-imperialist forces
in Latin America, especially those in Cuba.

From November 1953, the Popular Socialist Party steadily
worked towards "organizing mass protests in defense of

Guatemala and against Yankee imperialist intervention" and "urging the adoption of statements and resolutions along these lines in factories, trade unions, schools, etc."

As the unequal confrontation in Central America sharpened, the Guatemalan cause won ever greater support among the Cuban people, expressed in solidarity activities such as the huge meeting held at the University of Havana in March 1954. That same month, the Cuban Guatemala Support Committee was formed to denounce the shameful Resolution 93. Orthodox Party member Eduardo Corona served as chairman of the committee, whose members included Juan Marinello, Carlos Rafael Rodríguez, Flavio Bravo and thousands of students and workers.

When the mercenary invasion of Guatemala took place, a number of recruiting centers opened immediately to process volunteers to go defend the Guatemalan people. Two of these centers were especially active: the one opened at the University of Havana by the Federation of University Students (FEU), led by José Antonio Echeverría, and the one opened at the University of Oriente by the FEU of Oriente (FEU-O), in which Frank País and Pepito Tey were student leaders.

Two young Latin Americans were already in Guatemala where they had formed a fast friendship, sharing the same commitment to popular revolution. Two and a half years later, both would travel from Mexico to Cuba aboard the tiny yacht *Granma*. One of them was a Cuban worker who was in exile following his participation in that first revolutionary effort on July 26, 1953: Antonio "Ñico" López. The other was a studious Argentine doctor traveling through Latin America in search of a revolution: Ernesto "Che" Guevara.

The group of men imprisoned in Cuba for trying to liberate their people had no doubt as to which side they were on. They were on the side of reason, justice, history, and the Guatemalan people's right to freedom. They studied and debated the issue. René Bedia, a manual worker who was later to die as a member of the *Granma* expeditionary force, wrote at the time:

Guatemala has had a history of dictatorship and pseudo-democratic governments, which have handed over the

country's wealth to the largest Yankee imperialist monopoly in
Latin America (United Fruit). This huge company, protected
by the big Wall Street interests, has been plundering the poor,
illiterate Indians, who are paid a minimum wage of 30 to 40
cents a day while the company reaps millions.

Compañeros, this is U.S. democracy's policy for Latin
America. This is the famous Monroe Doctrine. This is the
Good Neighbor Policy! If Guatemala is finally defeated, she
will go down with dignity, having fulfilled her duty, and as an
example for all the peoples of our continent. If she triumphs in
her titanic struggle, she will become a beacon guiding us to
true freedom, equality among peoples, and social justice.

On one side were those who, for infamous reasons, were linked to
imperialism's interests and those of its lackeys; on the other were
those who came together for other reasons and whom history
would unite in revolutionary activity.

In June 1954, the dark forces of reaction snuffed out freedom
in Guatemala and enchained its people. In that same month, a
document containing the revolutionary program that would lead
a people to freedom was drawn up in a Cuban prison cell.

Resourcefulness and tenacity

A little ball fell at their feet. It had come from the adjacent yard,
tracing a parabola over the roof. Not a real ball, it was the kind
the poorest children made, weaving strips of cardboard from
packs of cigarettes over a central core of wadded paper.

Orlando Cortés Gallardo recalled that Miret picked up the ball
in surprise and, not attaching any importance to it, kept on talking while he nonchalantly took it apart. When the stuffing came
out, they saw it consisted of pages of paper covered with tiny
handwriting — not the pieces of old newspaper usually used for
this purpose. Curiosity led to surprise: the pages contained a
message from Fidel.

This was how the first rudimentary yet effective means of
communication was set up between Fidel and the rest of the
Moncada prisoners on the Isle of Pines. Paper or rubber balls
containing messages were thrown back and forth between the

enclosed prison yards. It is said that sometimes an obliging guard helped out in this original form of correspondence, returning the balls when they fell short and landed on the roof.

Other means of communication were also found to link those inside the prison with each other and with the outside world. On visiting days, messages were slipped in between the layers of the bottoms of matchboxes. Despite the restrictions, freedom could not be muzzled. Messages were inserted in clothes, cigars, and food. Common prisoners cooperated. Guards took messages, and even someone in the director's office helped out. Both brief notes and longer messages circulated in these ways.

Even the ordinary mail was used, outwitting the prison censor. Between the lines of ordinary letters to relatives and friends, Fidel wrote with invisible ink — lemon juice, from lemons sent along with other foods, not arousing the slightest suspicion. Heat applied to the white paper brought forth the brown tracing of Fidel's precise instructions to compañeros along with damning denunciations. They ran rings around the regime during that period.

The first mention of this system appeared in a letter to Melba Hernández dated April 17, 1954, in which Fidel referred to "a means for you to get in touch with me every day if you want," but warned, "Keep this under your hat; only let Yeyé[12] know when she returns." The letter continued as follows: "Propaganda cannot be neglected even for a minute, for it is the heart of every struggle. Ours should have its own style and be adapted to circumstances."

This was obviously a direct reference to the project of reconstructing and publishing his defense speech at his trial for the July 26 events. Fidel mentioned "a pamphlet of decisive importance because of its ideological content and powerful accusations, which I want you to read with the greatest attention."

In view of the generalized silence — and, what was worse, the attempt to distort the revolutionary character and program of the Moncada action — it was necessary to openly denounce the

---

12 . Haydée Santamaría Cuadrado.

dictatorship, publicize the revolution's program, and rally the masses around it in action. The conspiracy of silence had to be challenged, and the opportunism and counterrevolution masquerading as revolution had to be exposed.

The gravity of the situation may be clearly seen several months later in the following letter, dated October 3, 1954:

The conspiracy of the vested interests raised its ugly head against the July 26 action because it was something that didn't fit any conventional pattern. It was an effort unprecedented in the annals of the republic, a feat created by the faith and courage of a handful of young people without any political background or resources of any kind. They did not rob, attack, or kidnap anyone to raise funds; they cleverly eluded the dictatorship's notice; they stormed bastions so powerful while so overwhelmingly outnumbered by the armed forces that not even the wars of emancipation had witnessed such a deed. They had a well worked-out plan of struggle and a broad revolutionary program.

This awakening of a new revolutionary generation obviously threatened all social privileges and political heirarchies. Never before had established political interests reacted so unanimously to obliterate the memory of such an outstanding act of heroism, idealism, self-sacrifice, and patriotism. Even when they seem to be lauding it, they have tried to deny the most worthy essence of that deed.

"It has been said that the attack on the Moncada garrison was a rash crazy action not based on a coherent plan. *Yet this reproach contains its greatest strength.* They did not go there to seize power. They went there to die." (Aracelio Azcuy, speech in the Spanish Athenaeum) That is, what many say is not denied; it is accepted, and they claim to see merit in it. Thus, we are denied our true merit of having gone to die for a great revolutionary objective — which means denying everything.

That was the situation. There could be no more waiting.

Therefore a plan was skilfully and tenaciously put into operation — a plan which, a few months later, was to culminate in a masterpiece of clandestine work, carried out under the most difficult conditions: from a solitary cell.

Lidia Castro, Fidel's ever-active sister who was ready to run all kinds of risks, was to coordinate the work of producing the long document. Fidel reconstructed his defense speech in bits and pieces, written in ink or pencil or with lemon juice. Many letters which left the jail containing simple greetings to friends or acquaintances were immediately retrieved. Lidia, Melba, or Haydée ironed the letters, and the heat brought out the fragments of the defense speech that Fidel had written with lemon juice between the lines.

Several people were in charge of retrieving the letters, and four or five did the typing. All rules of secrecy and need-to-know were followed in this work. At 107 Jovellar Street, Melba's home, she and Manuel Hernández, her father, typed many of the fragments. All typewritten pages were delivered to Lidia Castro, who was responsible for keeping and hiding the manuscripts.

In June, the iron produced a paragraph containing a warning to the regime:

I know that prison will be harder for me than it has ever been for anyone, filled with cowardly threats and hideous cruelty. But I do not fear prison, as I do not fear the fury of the miserable tyrant who took the lives of 70[13] of my comrades. Condemn me. It does not matter. History will absolve me.

With incredible tenacity and resourcefulness, the drafting of the document was completed. On June 18, 1954, in a letter to Haydée and Melba, Fidel issued instructions regarding aspects of the next phase of the plan:

---

13. In the clandestine editions that followed, the whereabouts of some of the compañeros were not known, so the figure was raised from 70 to 80. Only after victory could it be determined exactly how many — 61 — fighters had died in the action that started the war against the tyranny, how many had stayed in Cuba, how many had gone into exile, and how many — nine — of those murdered by the repressive forces were innocent victims totally unconnected with the Moncada group. The 61 martyrs are listed in appendix 1.

Meanwhile, I want you to pay special attention to the following:

1. The speech. At least 100,000 copies should be distributed within a period of four months. This must be done following a well organized plan covering the whole island. Copies should be mailed to all journalists, lawyers' and doctors' offices, and teachers' and other professional groups.... Precaution should be taken so the copies are not discovered and no one is arrested. The same care and discretion should be employed as if dealing with weapons. It must be printed in at least two different printshops, at the lowest price. A batch of 10,000 should not cost more than $300.00.... You must work on this strictly according to plan.

The document is of decisive importance. It contains our program and our ideology — without which nothing of significance can be attained — and a denunciation of the dictatorship's crimes. These have not been publicized enough, and that is our first duty to those who died. It also tells of the role you two played, which should be made known to make your work easier. Having done this there are a series of organizational and propaganda tasks that I am working on now.

2. Questions of finances should be handled according to a plan.... This is one of the aspects to which you must give the greatest care, order, and coordination, as we did. Priority must now be given to publishing the defense. I'm sure many will help to defray the costs, for it is the most devastating attack that could possibly be published against the government.

Further on in this letter he expressed his view in the form of an axiom: "I believe that at this time propaganda is vital. Without propaganda, there can be no mass movement, and without a mass movement, there can be no revolution."

The next day, June 19, he elaborated on this idea in another letter to Melba and Haydée:

Our immediate task — and I want you to be fully convinced of this — is not to organize revolutionary cells to build our ranks. That would be a grievous error. Our task now is to mobilize public opinion in our favor, to spread our ideas and win the backing of the masses of the people. Our revolutionary program is the most complete, our line of action the clearest, and our history the most self-sacrificing. We have a right to the people's faith — without which, I repeat a thousand times, there can be no revolution.

Moving toward history

The next stage was not easy, either, for it involved financing, printing, and distributing the pamphlet. José Valmaña Mujica's work proved extremely valuable in the task of financing. Valmaña was a public accountant who had completed everything but his thesis for a doctorate in commercial sciences at the University of Havana. He was never able to return to his studies after 1939 when he became involved in a political strike, and had not changed his views since then.

When Haydée and Melba were released from prison, Valmaña joined the revolutionary nucleus they led, carrying out instructions from Fidel, to reorganize the Movement's scattered forces in Havana, Matanzas, and Pinar del Río.

Valmaña described the process as follows: "Centavo by centavo and peso by peso, hundreds of pesos were collected to print the pamphlet. But first a decision had to be made on how to print it and who would do the work. This was not a simple leaflet or a three- or four-page bulletin, but a 100-page manuscript written on legal-size paper that was to have a run of at least 20,000 to 30,000 copies. And it all had to be done clandestinely!"[14]

Valmaña became treasurer of the publication. The fund-raisers included Pedro Celestino Aguilera and Orbeín Hernández (participants in the July 26 events), Calixto Morales and René Reiné (who were later to join the *Granma* expeditionary group — Reiné was killed shortly after landing), Elda Pérez, Ondina Matheu (sister of Moncada martyrs Wilfredo and Horacio Matheu Orihuela), Humberto Grillo, and Julio Martínez (who fought as a

---

14. J. Petinaud, "El primer editor" (The first publisher), *Moncada* magazine, May 1976.

guerrilla in the July 26 Movement's front in the Escambray mountains and died later).

Some donors contributed more than had been expected. But many who it had been hoped would be major contributors (top leaders in the Orthodox Party, for example) flatly refused to give anything at all. After exhausting and often risky efforts that endangered the success of the mission, it became clear that the funds, meticulously controlled by Valmaña, were insufficient to pay for 100,000 copies, as Fidel had suggested, or even a much more modest run.

It was then, as Melba Hernández described it, that they resorted to the popular practice of holding a raffle. Numbered tickets were printed for a supposed raffle for two TV sets and sold for a peso each. But the buyers were told there were no prizes this time, for the money was to be used in the struggle against the dictatorship. Since the amount involved was small, the "non-raffle" was effective in broadening the base of contributors. So, in fact, the first edition of *History Will Absolve Me* was financed chiefly by anonymous individuals from the poorest classes of society.[15]

Nearly 2,000 pesos was collected. A small part of this was used for a trip to Mexico by Melba that Fidel had suggested, where she was able to contact the Moncada veterans in exile. She found them in a rather precarious economic situation and gave them $100 to tide them over.[16]

---

15. The author has since learned that a much smaller edition may have been issued prior to this one, in Pinar del Río, but this has not yet been confirmed.

16. A statement of funds dated July 18, 1954, shows that 50 pesos were used to print the pamphlet *Message to Suffering Cuba*; 30 pesos to pay for a leaflet on the first anniversary of July 26; and 548 pesos, for the initial expenses in the printing of *History Will Absolve Me*, with 652 pesos still due, meaning that it cost 1,200 pesos to print the 27,500 copies. However, the figure may have been higher by October 1954, when the printing was completed. We know, for example, that the original lead type had to be replaced when it turned out to be inadequate for the job; the linotypist was paid 300 pesos; additional coated paper for the cover had to be purchased, due to an error in the title in the first printing; additional paper had to be ordered for use in the rest of the pamphlet, since the printer used the original paper for another job; and several stitchers had to be bought for the binding.

Almost all the rest of the money was used to defray the cost of the first edition, only 27,500 copies. Nor was it easy to find a totally reliable printer who could guarantee a secure location for such a delicate job. The revolutionaries themselves had neither the space, the machinery, nor the technical resources to do the printing themselves.

They finally chose a small printshop at 65 Desagüe Street near the corner of Ayestarán, in Havana, and arranged for the work to be done on alternate days, avoiding night work so as not to arouse the suspicions of the police as they made their rounds. As a security measure, Lidia gave the typed originals to someone else to deliver to the printer. At the height of the political campaign preceding the November 1954 election, the printshop had accepted orders to print propaganda material for a couple of candidates, who visited the shop occasionally.

One day, one of these politicians dropped in unexpectedly. In order to hide what was on the press and to justify the delay in delivering the politician's materials, the printer claimed that the machine had broken down. As this was the second time this excuse had been used, the annoyed politician replied, "Look, buddy, I'm fed up with this business of the machine being out of whack. Want me to find you a good mechanic right away?"

More than just an anecdote, this incident demonstrates the risks involved in getting out that first edition and explains why it took so much longer than had been expected. Some of Fidel's letters from prison during these months show how anxious he was to have the document printed and distributed.

A group of compañeros was assigned to assist the printers in order to speed up the job. This group included Gustavo Ameijeiras (who was later killed in the urban armed struggle), Santiago Terry, Angel Pla and Tony García. They folded, collated (a tricky job since the pages were not numbered), stitched, counted and packed the pamphlets.

On October 11, Aguilera gave Valmaña evidence he had just obtained that the police had learned of the printshop and the network. Although the material had already left the shop, the other compañeros had to be warned. Valmaña managed to get rid of a few compromising documents and hid two packages containing 600 copies of the pamphlet, which he was to distribute himself.

A few days earlier, Angel and Gustavo Ameijeiras, Pla, Aguilera, Reiné, and others had loaded most of the packages on a truck and delivered those for distribution in Havana to Ondina Matheu, who also stored the lead type.

When the police raided the shop, the only evidence they could find was a copy of the cover that had been thrown out because of errors. The printer was arrested, and the same day agents of the sinister Bureau of Investigations searched Valmaña's house. Even though they found nothing, they went to his office in Old Havana to pick him up, harass him, book him, and lock him in Príncipe Fortress. He and the printer were both acquitted for lack of evidence.

The final stage was distribution of the pamphlet throughout the country, which was so difficult and involved so many people that it would be impossible to give an adequate account of what happened.

A contact with access to a commercial trucking firm arranged to send the pamphlets to the provinces. In Havana, Melba and Haydée directed the distribution, with the invaluable assistance of Humberto Grillo, Valmaña and many other compañeros.

Aguilera was in charge of Pinar del Río, with Angel Eros assisting. Gustavo Ameijeiras handled Matanzas with the help of Leonel Guedes. The shipment to Santa Clara remained at the express company warehouse until Gustavo and Santiago Terry made a special trip to retrieve it.

Cándido González (later a member of the *Granma* expeditionary force who was killed in action shortly after the landing) delivered most of the material for Camagüey in his car.

Oriente Province was assigned the largest shipment, as Fidel had instructed, but a special trip had to be made in order to guarantee and verify that risky and complicated distribution.

Melba later related:

Gustavo and Angel ("Machaco") Ameijeiras got hold of a rundown car which nevertheless they were confident could make the trip. But they had no money — not even for the gas!

We were all racking our brains, trying to figure out how to help them. We got together to discuss the situation and find out how much the Ameijeiras brothers would need for the trip. Gustavo surprised us all by saying that five pesos would be enough to make the trip to Oriente. Five pesos was barely enough to fill the tank!

We all protested, but Gustavo assured us they would manage once they were on their way. Of course, there really was no alternative, so his proposal was accepted, and the Ameijeirases loaded the car and took off.

It was later learned that they knocked on many a door, seeking out the most radical members of the Orthodox Party, who were always good for a tank of gas, a meal, or even a bed — although there were times they fell asleep in the car on an empty stomach.

History Will Absolve Me has now been translated into most languages and is one of the most widely read documents of the second half of the 20th century. This is the story of how it first began to raise the consciousness of the people, who would participate actively in the conclusive phase of their liberation.

History Will Absolve Me thus first appeared under these conditions of bitter struggle against adversity. But courage, tenacity, hope, the will to fight, humility, and heroism helped it on its way into political history.

CHAPTER 4

In the face of the dictatorship, which continued to unleash repression while the ineffective, splintered and generally erratic, ambitious, timid and subservient opposition stood by and did nothing...

In the face of those who, through error or opportunism, held up to the people the utopian mirage of elections as the only path to a possible national solution...

In the face of those who sought personal gain from the blood of July 26 and the revolutionary authority of its imprisoned vanguard; and others who claimed they represented the insurrection while actually leading the people farther and farther from that road, and became, in fact, a counterrevolutionary force blocking all attempts at revolution...

In the face of all those forces who either consciously or unconsciously insulted or denied the unparalleled Moncada action — the only immediate option for revolution at that time...

In the face of all these, from a prison cell came an accusing finger, a clarifying analysis, a talent for giving the people wise, rapid and accurate leadership. This was the remarkable period of...

Infallible tactics from prison

With the revolution imprisoned, that solitary cell became the source of a network that called on the people to remain alert while keeping the dictatorship off guard. Day-to-day activity helped define political positions and prepared the conditions for reviving a strong revolutionary movement deeply rooted in the masses.

Several of Fidel's letters from prison show the priority he gave to various questions at different times. For example, on December 12, 1953, at a time when he was concentrating on the cultural and ideological education of his imprisoned comrades, he issued the following instructions to his comrades on the outside:

1. Denounce "the atrocious tortures and barbaric, criminal mass murder" of nearly half the young people who took part in the July 26 actions.
2. Show the people the "honorable, humane behavior of the attackers" — described as such even by the prosecutor during the trial — to expose the lies propogated and spread by the regime.
3. Clarify to the Leadership Council and the masses of the Orthodox Party the popular, revolutionary — and not putsch-ist — character of July 26 and the political program it would have carried out had it succeeded.

In April 1954, isolated and incommunicado, Fidel was immersed in the task of reconstructing his defense speech, so its publication could break through the conspiracy of silence surrounding the events of July 26, 1953, as well as publicize the Movement's program and revolutionary aims.

He also suggested that a campaign be launched protesting the abuses committed against them in prison. In a letter to Melba dated April 12, after emphasizing the need for revolutionary propaganda as an indispensable weapon of struggle, Fidel noted:

Moreover, it is absolutely necessary to commemorate July 26 in a fitting manner. A ceremony must be held on the university steps. That will deal the government a telling blow. Careful preparations should begin right now, and meetings should also be held in the secondary schools, in Santiago de Cuba, and abroad. The Orthodox committees in New York, Mexico, and Costa Rica should be in charge of this.

The work of our people here and abroad has to be coordinated. Make preparations as soon as possible to go to Mexico to meet with Raúl Martínez and Léster Rodríguez.[1] After a careful study of the situation, together you should decide what line to follow. Any proposal to coordinate actions with other forces should be evaluated with extreme caution, to prevent them from simply using our name, as Pardo Llada and Co. did. That is, we have to keep their bad reputation from tainting any group they are associated with. Don't let them underestimate us. Don't come to any agreement except on firm, clear foundations with a good possibility of success and of positive benefit for Cuba. Otherwise, it would be better for us to go it alone, with you on the outside holding high the banner until the release of these formidable fellows in prison, who are preparing for the struggle with the greatest diligence.

"The great secret of success," Martí said, "is knowing how to wait." We must follow the same tactic we employed in our trial: defend our points of view without antagonizing anyone. There will be plenty of time to crush all the cockroaches.

We must not let anything or anyone discourage us, just as we didn't during even the most difficult moments. A last piece of advice: guard against envy. Whenever anyone has as much glory and prestige as all of you, mediocre people easily come up with reasons or pretexts for probing your weak spots.

Fidel completed the reconstruction of *History Will Absolve Me* in June. On June 27, after he had been in solitary confinement for 134 days, two midshipmen were placed in his cell.

On Friday, July 9, *Bohemia* magazine published an interview with Fidel, illustrated with seven photographs showing him in his cell and in the prison library. The article, by journalist Raúl Martín Sánchez, was entitled "With the Political Prisoners on the Isle of Pines."

On July 26, the first anniversary of the Moncada attack, thou-

---

1. Martínez and Rodríguez were veterans of the Moncada attack. Martínez later became a traitor to the revolution.

sands of leaflets addressed "To the People of Cuba" and signed by the Centennial Youth were distributed in Havana, denouncing once more the crime committed by the dictatorship against the participants in the July 26 actions. The same day a portrait of Raúl Gómez García was unveiled in the Hall of Martyrs of the FEU and a demonstration headed by Melba and Haydée was attacked by the police in the Colón Cemetery.

That same day, Fidel was unexpectedly visited in his cell by Minister of the Interior Ramón O. Hermida, who had come to apologize for having recently offended him. Fidel accepted the apology, "reserving the right to fully explain and resolve this problem when I am at liberty."

Summing up the political events of 1954 several months later, journalist Enrique de la Osa commented in his *Bohemia* magazine column "In Cuba":

There was the extraordinary case of the near crisis in Batista's cabinet over Fidel Castro. It so happened that on July 26, 1954, the first anniversary of the events in Oriente, Ramón Hermida, then minister of the interior, visited Fidel in his prison cell and had a long talk with him, details of which were never released. This enraged Rafael Díaz Balart, the undersecretary of his department, who, in an open letter, bitterly criticized his superior for that visit to "the promoter of that criminal attack." According to Díaz Balart, Hermida had offended the armed forces and the memory of the soldiers killed at the Moncada. Díaz Balart and the minister both resigned, and Batista had to step in to conciliate and overcome the crisis.

Shortly after this, prison conditions were eased for Fidel, as he explained in a letter written in August:

I continue to be isolated from the rest of my comrades. This is undoubtedly designed to hinder the intellectual training of the young men, whom they view as their most implacable adversaries of the future. They have even forbidden them to exchange books with me. Otherwise, I am better. They brought Raúl here. They connected my cell (which you saw in *Bohemia*) with another area four times as large and a big yard, which is open from 7:00 a.m. to 9:30 p.m.. The prison personnel are in charge of cleaning it. We sleep with the lights out; we do not have to appear for line up or formations at any time during the day; and we get up at any hour we choose.

Naturally, I had not requested any of these improvements. We have plenty of water, electric light, food, and clean clothes — all free. We don't even pay rent. Do you think it's better out there? We have visits twice a month. Utter peace reigns. I don't know, though, how much longer we'll be in this "paradise."

In that same letter, he pointed out with the farsighted vision of an exceptional leader:

Our time is approaching. Before, we were a handful; now, we must merge ourselves with the people. Our tactics will be different. Those who view us as a group will be sadly mistaken. We will never be characterized by a group mentality or group tactics. Now, moreover, I can dedicate myself body and soul to my cause. I will put all my time and energy into it. I will begin a new life. I am determined to overcome all obstacles and fight as many battles as may be necessary.

Above all, I see our path and our goal more clearly than ever. I haven't wasted my time in prison, for I have been studying, observing, analyzing, planning, and training the men. I know where the best of Cuba is and how to look for it. When I began I was alone; now we are many.

Throughout 1954, Fidel would have to solve several very complex problems to keep the Moncada action, with its heroic sacrifice, from falling into oblivion, cloaked in silence, and its energizing example for the people lost. At the same time, the vanguard nucleus that had already been created could not be allowed to weaken, for it would be needed to lead the people in the struggle for their liberation.

The ability, tact, and energy with which Fidel handled a whole range of situations related to these two main questions are astonishing — as was the acuteness of his understanding of the true motivations of the various political forces in the country. Totally isolated, he saw much further than those who were directly confronting these problems on the outside.

Even more astounding were the solutions he unhesitatingly proposed for every situation. Their validity and effectiveness, even in those cases that required a long period of time to bring results, showed his exceptional political ability, which, of course, is not enough to explain everything. Revolutionary solutions must be conceived within and adjusted to the concrete social framework from a revolutionary and class standpoint.

The revolutionary base

Today, when looking back at Fidel's ability to interpret the Cuban situation at that time, we have to remember that 27 years have passed and that he was only 27 at the time. Yet he correctly diagnosed the ills of his time and proposed solutions for them. This required developing his talents, and reaffirming the active role Marxism assigns to the individual in history.

There was another factor, one that is not usually taken into account, but without which it is impossible to understand the popular essence of the revolutionary program of the Centennial Youth, which Fidel had drawn up, and the method he devised at the time for putting it into practice. That factor was Fidel's class standpoint.

Without understanding the class position from which Fidel began to outline the solution to what was then called the crisis of Cuba's political institutions there can be no adequate explanation for the scope of his revolutionary program or for his radical method of struggle.

In that sense, although we know with certainty what Fidel's class standpoint was, we do not know the exact chronology of how it developed — when it was that the objective and subjective change in his class allegiance took place.

Fidel Castro was the son of a well-to-do farmer and a boarding student in the exclusive schools of the bourgeoisie and later in the University of Havana, where he received a monthly allowance from his father. We know that his interest in Marxism began during his university days.

Fidel's brief experience in practicing law showed him to be in a process of conscious and objective proletarianization — both ideologically and economically. The social group in which he later based himself and with which he organized the actions of July 26, 1953 — conceived only as the beginning of a *people's* armed insurrection and as a minimum program to be presented in the name of the Centennial Youth — obliges us to ackowledge his outright opposition to the class interests of the large landowners and the bourgeoisie.

When exactly did he change his class allegiance and adopt a non-bourgeois ideology? That is, when did he take up the methodology that provided a consistent approach to the revolutionary transformation of his society?

Fidel himself provided the answer many years later:

> We didn't propose a socialist program on July 26, but we were already socialists then. The leaders were socialists: Abel, Raúl, Montané, and all the rest of the leading nucleus of the Movement were socialists. However, it would have been absolutely incorrect from any point of view to have proposed a socialist program on July 26. Such a program would not have corresponded to that stage of the revolution, which required a program of national liberation, a program that would precede and create all the conditions for socialism.[2]

Clear confirmation of this change was provided during his imprisonment when Fidel's writings present concrete evidence that he had consciously rejected his class origins — "class suicide," as Lenin put it — that prepared him to take an unambiguous stand with the poor and working classes.

It is essential to grasp this all-important defining factor of Fidel's class standpoint in order to understand the genuinely revolutionary attitude of that 27-year-old young man who had

2. Fidel Castro, Speech to the Assembly of Ratification of Mandates, July 26 School City, October 7, 1975.

already been recognized as a potential leader of his people (and from a historical point of view he already was). And it becomes impossible to understand the reasons for his actions and decisions.

The proof that such a change in class allegiance had already taken place, is shown by the definition of the concept "people"[3] that Fidel outlined in *History Will Absolve Me*, a definition in which he completely excluded the exploiting classes.

His perspectives, explanations, instructions, and orders during that period unquestionably showed an utter disregard for the way of life and the interests of the exploiting classes, as well as indicate the absence of all sentimentality typical of petty-bourgeois politics. Fidel had, in fact, totally divorced himself from the fetish of capitalist private property. Following Martí's tactical approach, however, he expressed only as much of this as could be assimilated at the time, given the general level of social and political awareness, taking into account the traditions, idiosyncracies, and language of his people. These early characteristics have been maintained in all Fidel's political writings over the years.

From the specific to the general, from the personal to the most complex aspect of the dialectics of the class struggle, excerpts from several letters Fidel wrote during that period defined his true class standpoint and revolutionary dimension.

On May 2, 1955, shortly before the amnesty was decreed, he wrote his sister Lidia:

---

3. "When we speak of the people, we do not mean those who live in comfort, the conservative elements of the nation, who welcome any oppressive regime, any dictatorship, any despotism, prostrating themselves before the master of the moment until they grind their foreheads into the ground. When we speak of struggle, the *people* means the vast unredeemed masses, to whom everyone makes promises and who are deceived by all; we mean the people who yearn for a better, more dignified, and more just nation; those who are moved by ancestral aspirations of justice, for they have suffered injustice and mockery generation after generation; those who long for great and wise changes in all aspects of their life; people who, to attain those changes, are ready to give even their very last breath — when they believe in something or in someone, especially when they believe in themselves."*History Will Absolve Me*, Fidel Castro's self-defense before the Court in Santiago de Cuba on October 16, 1953.

Why make sacrifices to buy me a fancy shirt, a pair of pants, and other things? I am going to leave here in my old gray wool suit, even if it's the middle of summer. Didn't I send back the other suit that I never asked for and never needed?

Don't think that I am or have become an eccentric. The habit makes the monk, and I am poor. I have nothing; I have never stolen a cent; I have never begged; and I have dedicated my career to a cause. Why should I put on a fancy linen shirt, as if I were rich, a high-ranking official, or an embezzler? I'm not earning anything at present, so anything I have has to have been given me, and I cannot, should not, and refuse to be a burden to anyone.

My greatest struggle since I have been here has been to insist — and I will never tire of doing this — that I don't lack for anything at all: I have needed only books, which I consider to be spiritual goods.

His March 23, 1954, letter, attacking the abstract concept of individual liberty would certainly have outraged any petty bourgeois:

Robespierre was honest and idealistic right to the end. With the revolution endangered, its borders surrounded by enemies, traitors aiming a dagger at its back and the vacillators getting in the way, it was necessary to be hard, inflexible, and severe; to sin by commission but never by omission, for therein lay the road to ruin. A few months of terror were needed to end the terror that had lasted for centuries. Cuba needs many Robespierres.

Two weeks earlier, speaking of the insensitivity of the rich toward the poverty of the people, Fidel had commented ironically on the vanity that the ladies of high society showed in their philanthropic works, which the press covered fully, down to the door-to-door collections they made for this or that hospital. Fidel wrote:

I think the state should resolve this problem by taking the money from the rich. Taxes should be tripled on the mansions in the Country Club and on Fifth Avenue, on the farms used for recreation, on the aristocratic clubs, on the inheritances destined to be squandered, and on the fabulous incomes that are spent on luxury.

Analyzing the class composition of the Orthodox Party, to which he had belonged, he wrote on June 12:

> What business did those who have joined the ranks of the enemy, seeking appointment as senators and representatives, have in a people's party? What were those large landowners, millionaires, and exploiters of peasants and workers doing inside a party whose first duty is to seek social justice? While the masses were fighting in the streets, they were prostituting the Orthodox Party, grabbing positions of power and trying to turn it into just one more traditional party. What a magnificent lesson for the future!

He did not forget this lesson. More than a year later, on October 4, 1955, he wrote Melba Hernández reiterating that the Movement "has a social program with an ambitious content that, first and foremost, defends the interests of the poor and exploited classes," and stated in no uncertain terms:

> You will never see a Fico[4] or a Gerardo Vázquez[5] and Co. in our Movement — only new people, poor people, fighting people, those who have never held any ministerial posts or served as senators or representatives, and who have never taken part in any dirty deals or politicking.

Clearly, anyone who could speak like that and publicly espouse those ideas was not afraid of alienating himself from the support of those classes or of falling out of their good graces. Therefore, he did not belong to them either objectively or subjectively.

---

4. Federico "Fico" Fernández Casas was a large landowner and planter in Oriente Province and owner of the América Sugar Mill.
5. Gerardo Vázquez was the owner of large sugarcane plantations in Camagüey and president of the National Association of Sugar Growers of Cuba.

Fidel spelled this out in a letter whose date is worth remembering: April 15, 1954.

It is curious how similar all the great social reforms have been, from antiquity to the present. Many of the measures taken by the Paris Commune in 1871 were similar to laws decreed by Julius Caesar. The problems of land, housing, debt, and unemployment have arisen in all societies dating back to ancient history.

I am inspired by the grand spectacle of the great revolutions of history, because they have always signified the triumph of aims embodying the welfare and happiness of the vast majority as opposed to a tiny group of vested interests.

Do you know what episode really moves me? The revolution of the black slaves in Haiti. At a time when Napoleon was imitating Caesar and France resembled Rome, the soul of Spartacus was reborn in Toussaint L'Ouverture. How little importance is given to the fact that the African slaves who rebelled set up a free republic, defeating the greatest generals Napoleon had! It's true that Haiti has not progressed very much since then, but have the other Latin American republics done any better?

I keep thinking about these things, because, frankly, how pleased I would be to revolutionize this country from top to bottom! I am sure that all the people could be happy — and for them I would be ready to incur the hatred and ill will of a few thousand individuals, including some of my relatives, half of my acquaintances, two-thirds of my professional colleagues, and four-fifths of my former schoolmates.

Fighting words — and so it turned out to be.

Ideology, discipline, and leadership

At the beginning of August 1954, Fidel received a letter from Luis Conte Agüero, calling on him to help establish "a civic movement, which is becoming a pressing need." It was Conte who most frequently echoed Fidel's denunciations from prison and his widely heard commentaries on the Oriente Radio Network helped shape public opinion and mobilize the people which would soon become a movement for a general political amnesty.

Even so, Conte's opportunist motives were later revealed. His two-faced behavious, seeking honor without sacrifice and glory without risk, was the result of a driving ego that finally led him to betray his country following the triumph of the revolution. Thus it would later become clear how the "civic" attitude of "the most prominent voice in Oriente" (as he conceitedly introduced himself on his program) masked Conte's aspirations to cover himself with the mantle of the July 26 martyrs and the revolutionary honor of its imprisoned vanguard.

Fidel answered him on August 14, once again showing his great ability in handling complex and unforeseen situations, with masterful tact and tactics. He accepted the notion of a civic movement without committing himself to it, presently such solid, logical reasons that obliged Conte to work to free the Moncada prisoners so he could count on them later for the proposed "civic movement."

It is also interesting to note how closely Fidel's views on membership and organization coincide with the Leninist conception of the party, even though, characteristically, the language he uses does not indicate this:

I fully agree with you on the need for it. You cannot imagine how many hours I have spent thinking about it and how many ideas I have, based on my experience over the past few years.

First of all, I think one of the biggest obstacles to establishing such a movement are the excessive personal interests and ambitions of groups and their chiefs; the difficulty of getting every man of worth and prestige to place himself at the service of a cause, a vehicle, an ideology, and a discipline, freeing himself of all vanity or ambition.... That is what I think, and I have repeatedly let you know that I haven't the slightest personal ambition, and neither do my comrades. Our only hope is to serve Cuba so that our comrades will not have died in vain.

Because of its importance, any step taken now would have to be discussed and agreed to by the majority — in the case of our group here, unanimously. It has become very difficult for me to discuss and to exchange opinions with my comrades, but we manage to keep in touch, and I will send them your letter.

Nevertheless, Luis, I have some doubts regarding how useful a contribution we can make now and whether it would not be broader and more meaningful if we were free — which I think is possible if an effective struggle is waged.

First I must organize the July 26 men and bring together firmly united all the combatants in exile, in prison, and throughout the country — more than 80 young men who are all part of this chapter of history and sacrifice. A perfectly disciplined nucleus such as this will be tremendously valuable in terms of training fighting cadres for insurrectional or civic organization. It is evident that a big civic and political movement must have the necessary strength to conquer power, by peaceful or revolutionary means. Otherwise, it will run the risk of having that power snatched away, as happened to the Orthodox Party just two months before the election.

The first task is to unite all our combatants, for it would be a shame to see our ranks depleted because of failure to carry out the initial task of convincing. On the basis of the experience gained prior to July 26, I can assure you that one tested and trustworthy young person is worth as much as a thousand others. Perhaps the hardest and most time-consuming task is to find those youth of quality and train them so that they can be a decisive force from the start.

On the basis of what we now have, we can greatly increase our forces. By that I mean incorporating other forces that are ready to unite in a firm and disciplined manner in order to create the movement necessary to defeat the ruling political system. Those who believe that they alone have the required merits will be contributing to a greater scattering of the nation's moral and human forces, as well as helping to perpetuate petty and sterile habits of struggle — habits that are neither worthy of an intelligent and able people nor capable of crushing the opposition and the solidly united vested interests.

The following characteristics are vital to any genuine civic movement: ideology, discipline, and leadership. All three are essential, but leadership is fundamental. Was it Napoleon who said that one bad opposing general in battle was worth more than 20 good ones? You cannot organize a movement if everyone thinks he has the right to issue public statements without consulting anybody else. Nothing is to be expected from a movement made up of anarchists who at the first disagreement will go off on their own, disrupting and destroying the organization. The propaganda and organization apparatus must be so powerful that it will unmercifully destroy all who try to create tendencies, cliques, and splits, or who rise up against the movement.

The realities of politics must be taken into consideration; that is, we must have our feet solidly on the ground, without ever sacrificing the great reality of principles.

The program must comprehensively, concretely, and courageously take up the serious economic and social issues confronting the country, so that a genuinely new and promising message can be brought to the masses.

The main danger to Fidel's efforts to reorganize the revolutionary movement, was similar to the problem faced prior to the Moncada attack: the divisive and diversionist role played by the supposed insurrectional organizations such as Carlos Prío's Authentic Organization (OA), and the Association of Friends of Aureliano (AAA) led by the former minister of education in the Prío government, Aureliano Sánchez Arango.

The AAA suffered a serious setback in May 1954, when police discovered Aureliano — who had arrived in Cuba clandestinely in February — in a house in the Country Club district. He managed to elude his captors and was given political asylum in the Uruguayan embassy. However, the police found a list of members of his organization when they searched the house and had them arrested and imprisoned. Referring to the incident, Fidel wrote Melba and Haydée on June 18:

I still have no faith whatsoever in the Authentic Party, and I am convinced they have done nothing but waste time and bungle things. The latest events have proved me right. Who would ever think of carrying the full list of members in a briefcase? I really think they are falling apart. They have no ideals or morale; they are corrupt to the core. They cannot help but only harm the cause of the revolution.

The fact is that those organizations, especially Prío's, had financial resources amounting to millions. On a number of occasions, the repressive forces captured complete arsenals they had brought into the country. The fact that they had weapons dazzled many of the regime's opponents who were eager to fight and was instrumental in luring people away from the real revolutionary forces. In the six years of Batista's dictatorship they never carried out a single armed action, although they led many valuable rank-and-file activists to lose their lives, hunted and shot down by the repressive forces.

Having instructed Melba to go to Mexico (in a letter dated April 17, 1954), Fidel sent her this warning in May:

Don't reach any agreements until you arrive in Mexico. I will accept the decision of you and the others, but don't forget that I despise the ambition and presumption of those who have promised so many revolutions but who only aspire to recover the republic's treasury. They will not be sincere friends of ours, because they know that we belong to another generation and that we are true revolutionaries.

Melba's trip confirmed Fidel's caution. She arrived on May 19 and immediately verified that Prío's agents were trying to recruit some of the participants in the July 26 actions who were in exile in Central America. She even managed to obtain a photocopy of a letter in which Carlos Prío gave instructions to penetrate the "*Fidelista* group" to learn of its plans. In that letter, which Melba reported on to Fidel upon her return, Prío described the Moncada group as dangerous elements who would have to be eliminated after he regained power.

Aware of this despicable plan, Fidel wrote on June 18:

What do you all think of the photocopy that M brought from M⁶? Isn't it just what I wrote about to M before her trip? I want you all to preserve it carefully. I know you share my opinion of these people. It would be crazy to make a pact with them, following the road that has led so many Orthodox leaders to ruin.

Now more than ever I am convinced that we must keep the Movement independent, as we did in the most difficult moments, when no one wanted to pay any attention to us. I am aware of the great difficulties you face in your struggle, but do not despair. Always bear in mind what I have told you in each of my letters. Remember that nothing can be attempted until we are out and that it is always necessary to know how to wait for the right moment. Your mission is to prepare the way, keep together the courageous elements — of which there are never many — standing firm, and recruit all those who may be of use. Cuba is full of courageous men, but we must find them.

On June 19, Fidel issued new instructions, insisting firmly on this matter, reminding those outside that the leadership of the Movement was to be found in prison on the Isle of Pines:

As members of the top leadership and as leading representatives of the Movement on the outside, you must strictly follow the decisions made here and do so with the zeal and discipline imposed on you by duty and the responsibilities your positions entail. You know that we have always taken a firm line on these matters, and I mean to do so again today.

Any inclination to form a pact with the Authentic Party constitutes a serious ideological deviation. We did not form a pact with them in the past — when they had millions at their disposal and we were begging for pennies and suffering terrible hardships to purchase weapons because we believed they lacked the capacity, the morality and the ideology to lead

---

6. That Melba Hernández brought from Mexico.

the revolution. So how can we make such a pact today, over the bodies and the blood of those who gave their lives for their noble ideals?

If in the past we weren't misled by their stories, fantasies, and braggadocio, why should we believe them now, when they have shown their true colors, in spite of their stolen millions? If all they did in the past was to hinder us, sabotage us, weaken our ranks, and decimate our cells with their lies and deceits — and then not even have the decency to denounce the regime's crimes — then what principle, idea, or argument could lead us to lower our noble banners before them?

What did Prío do in the United States, where he had every opportunity to widely publicize the barbaric massacre committed in Santiago de Cuba? He kept miserably silent. Moreover, haven't they had more than enough time — just as they have had more than enough money — in the nearly two and a half years since then to fulfill 20 times over, the boast they've made 100 times: to make a revolution?

The revolution cannot mean the return to power of men who have been morally and historically annihilated and who are totally responsible for the situation we now suffer. Always remember that our possibilities for success have been based on the certainty that the people would support the efforts made by honorable men who have upheld their revolutionary principles right from the start. Men who have deceived and betrayed the people can never aspire to that kind of support.

I must warn you of several very important things so you will not let yourselves be impressed. At present, Aureliano has not the slightest chance of leading an insurrection — Aureliano or anyone else — and anyone who claims it is possible is lying shamelessly. We should be the last to be fooled. Therefore, the Movement cannot be compromised by anyone or have anything to do with any insurrectional farce. We must give our consent to any agreement involving such matters. Beware also of those who thrive on intrigue, the petty politicians, and those who play at revolution!

And Fidel later added:

> If we now have men in our ranks who want only to come out shooting and are willing to come to an agreement with the devil himself to get a gun, they must be expelled without any further thought, just as the cowards who back out when the time comes must be shot. The ones who brag the most generally do so out of desperation. We want no gangsters or adventurers, but only men who are aware of their historic destiny, who know how to wait and work patiently for the future of our homeland.
>
> This has been our main concern, and we have guided our steps in this direction, training our leaders through constant study and by building discipline and character. It doesn't matter whether we spend more or less time in prison, as long as we know we will fulfill our mission when the time comes. I assure you that nothing as formidable as this has ever been prepared in Cuba.

Against the electoral farce

The time was not right. They had to wait. At that point in history, various factors came together to confirm Fidel's analysis. The members of the Authentic Party were incapable of organizing any serious attempt at an insurrection, and any support for them would have risked the lives of valuable cadres in efforts that were doomed to failure, and would have only benefitted the dictatorship. The Moncada vanguard was imprisoned, and those who were free would only be dissipating their forces uselessly — which would benefit the hidden enemies of the revolution.

Even though the regime's scheduled election was organized in such a way that the opposition could not possibly win, it reduced the prospects of the people's support for insurrectional actions during those months.

Moreover, any such action under those conditions would lack a leadership with enough authority to mobilize the people. The dishonesty of the regime's call for elections had to be demonstrated, so that people could see with their own eyes the futility of the hope for a solution to the national crisis through electoral means.

Significantly, only 10 days after the trial of the Moncada combatants, Batista had announced there would be a general election on November 1, 1954. Press censorship was lifted and, on October 28, the decree suspending constitutional guarantees that was issued following the July 26 actions expired.

Asked if he would be a presidential candidate, Batista replied, "The grapes are not yet ripe." Obviously, he would be not only a candidate but also the certain "winner." In the last week of July 1954, clearing up a doubt that never really existed, he "accepted" nomination by the Progressive Action, Liberal, Democratic, and Radical Union parties, which then made up Batista's coalition.

In December 1953, the Electoral Court rejected the registration application of a new party, the National United Front, composed of the outlawed Cuban Marxist-Leninists. Thus, the party that represented the interests of the poor and working classes was excluded from the scheduled election.

A few days later, the government's electoral commission announced the rules for the election, that were not subject to appeal: restriction of the right to organize new political parties; maintenance of the Law on Public Order (which curtailed all opposition), and slate balloting (a vote for a representative or senator necessarily implied a vote for the presidential candidate of the same party).

On December 14, former Authentic Party President Ramón Grau San Martín (1944-48) announced that he would run, even without an electoral law. As the only opposition candidate, he obviously counted on capitalizing on the popular hostility toward Batista.

The Montreal globe-trotters (the followers of Authentic Party leaders Prío, Sánchez Arango, and Antonio de Varona and Orthodox Party leader Millo Ochoa) kept on hoping for the miracle that the Yankees might come to the rescue once more. Dreaming of military victories against Batista, they refused to take part in the election.

The position of the Popular Socialist Party and what remained of the Cuban People's (Orthodox) Party was set forth in the December 21 issue of *Carta Semanal*:

Dr. Agramonte refuses to have anything to do with the election unless the government agrees to a "national solution" consisting of reestablishing the guarantees set forth in the 1943 Electoral Code; allowing all sectors of opinion to participate in the election; repealing the Law on Public Order; permitting the exiles to return; freeing the political prisoners; and establishing an impartial administration eight months prior to the election, presided over by a judge from the Supreme Court. He believes that a positive step would be to reestablish direct, free balloting instead of the slate method imposed by the government.

These demands are positive, and, in their most important immediate aspects, they coincide with those voiced by the PSP, except with regard to the impartial administration. What we do not agree with is his approach in presenting these demands. If they are, in part, elements for obtaining a desirable solution for our country, then we do not have to wait for the government to grant them; we must claim them through direct, daily action; we must promote and organize united action by the masses of the people and by all organizations and parties that favor them. The PSP does not limit itself to expressing the wish for a democratic solution; it struggles and fights to obtain it.

The registration period, which was set for February 14-28, wound up rather unexpectedly with the adoption by Batista's Council of Ministers of what came to be called the "last straw decree." Two of the parties that were to participate in the government coalition (Eusebio Mujal's Labor Party and the Democrats) did not obtain the required support of at least 4 percent of the voters, inspite of their going through all the voter registration lists. The same was true of the only two opposition parties, Fico Fernández Casas' splinter group of the Orthodox Party and Grau's Authentic Party. The "last straw decree" stated that all parties that had participated in the reorganization would be accepted, even if they did not meet the voter registration requirement.

That was not all Eusebio Mujal, the gangster heading the

"CTK"[7], got out of that meeting of the Council of Ministers. It also voted to make union dues compulsory for workers. This was clearly a means for strengthening the CTC's tyranny over the labor movement, further enriching Mujal's "Mafia" and providing it with funds for the election campaign.

In March, Fico resigned as president of the pro-election faction of the Orthodox Party and handed it over to the devious Carlos Márquez Sterling.

The electoral code finally adopted by the government guaranteed participation by the two miserable opposition parties by stipulating two seats in the Senate for minority parties, regardless of how few votes they obtained. In order to qualify, however, they would have to run their own presidential candidates in the election. By doing this, Batista guaranteed a split opposition.

This was the overall picture of the pre-electoral scene. On April 2, Fidel wrote the following:

Politics is such a hoax! In my experience, even with the best men and the best parties, it is unbearable. Now, recalling all the meetings tirelessly and fanatically attended by so many idol worshippers who remained seated hour after hour, listening to 20 different speakers engaged in a furious oratorical competition in which all of them said the same thing (and did so not only that day but every day), I have come to the conclusion that our people are infinitely patient and kind. Thinking of it here in this lonely cell, I cannot understand how they applauded instead of hurling their chairs at the charlatans. All these politicians are like actors in a theater — they play their

---

7. The revolutionary vanguard dubbed the Confederation of Cuban Workers (CTC) the "CTK" when it was taken over by corrupt officials, unscrupulous politicians, and gangsters riding the wave of the post-World War II anticommunism and McCarthyism. These gangsters and sell-out leaders had found a gold mine in Clause K of the Ministry of Education's budget — which had originally set up a special fund for contracting teachers who were not on the regular personnel rosters. Established under the government of Ramón Grau San Martín (1944-48) and initially amounting to 200,000 pesos a year, the Clause K fund was gradually increased to tens of millions of pesos and used for all kinds of nonjustifiable budgetary expenditures.

roles, earn the audience's applause, and are damned if they think of anything but election day, about which they're obsessed!

I was one of them. I can only explain it on the basis of inexperience, the environment, and inability to do anything else when your head is full of a million ideas. I was a player in that circus. Like Archimedes, I searched for the pivot on which to move the world. Deep in my heart I was disgusted by it all; I thought I saw hypocrisy and mediocrity everywhere, and time has shown that my instincts did not deceive me.

If I ever manage to do anything, the first thing will be to turn party meetings into a true means for promoting information, education and discipline, generating the energy of the masses. I would end all the clowning and grandiloquence — which is all you see nowadays. No more than four or five speakers should address any meeting. Fewer would be even better. I was a member of a party whose greatest claim to fame was that it was different from the others, yet it turned out to be identical in every respect. The sorriest thing was the utter lack of political content in its slogans, the lack of character in its leaders, and discipline among its members.

Two months later, on June 12, he wrote:

The treacherous coup has pushed decent people and the more politically conscious masses out of the electoral struggle. We are witnessing a battle among thieves: the thieves of yesterday against those of the day before yesterday and those of today — a struggle among traitors. Today's traitors to the constitution are battling yesterday's traitors to the people. It is a struggle between Machado's *porras*[8] and the founders of gang-

---

8. *Porra* was the nickname given to the members of the special police force set up for political repression during the dictatorship of Gerardo Machado, so called because of their frequent use of *porras* (blackjacks) in their brutal torture and frequent murder of opponents of the regime which was eventually overthrown in 1933.

sterism,[9] between tyranny and farce, which will result in tragedy for the people. Any one of them may win, but Cuba will lose, no matter what.

The important thing now is to safeguard our principles; with them, everything will be saved. From the depths of corruption the redeeming ideal will rise purer and cleaner.

A week later, on June 19, he wrote:

It would be interesting to see what would happen if a third political front were established. So many hypocrites would finally take off their masks, seeking seats as senators and representatives and dancing to the government's tune! Then, it would only be necessary for Prío's eager supporters to be nominated in any of those fronts for us to have a perfect starting point for our real struggle. On one side there would be the criminals, thieves, political hacks, apostates, traitors, and other corrupt elements dividing up the republic among themselves. And, on the other side, alongside the people, all those in Cuba who remain unstained, idealistic, and sincerely revolutionary. The sooner these sides are defined, the better.

July 9 saw the publication of Fidel's replies to the reporter who interviewed him for *Bohemia* magazine. Commenting on the rumor that the Orthodox Party would participate in the election, Fidel said:

The members of the Orthodox Party should unite — but unite to fight against the sham elections and continue demanding a

---

9. When the aims of the revolution of the 1930s were frustrated, some of the disillusioned young people who had fought for change and social justice formed organizations that eventually deteriorated into coercive groups based on gangster methods. When the Authentic Party came to power in 1944, some of these individuals obtained sinecures and administrative posts in state agencies and the police force. While not doing any work, they still demanded remuneration. This led to internal battles and struggles that finally reached the point of armed confrontations, assassination attempts, and outright murder — which came to be known in Cuba as "gangsterism."

patriotic, democratic, and honorable solution to the Cuban problem.

Unity achieved for the sole aim of participating in the election would be wretched, opportunistic, and lacking in heroism. The people would be right in thinking that those who did not unite to make the sacrifices demanded by duty would betray the nation if they united only for an easy conquest of elective posts, making a miserable compromise with the de facto regime.

The Popular Socialist Party had been frustrated in its efforts to unite the opposition in a powerful mass movement that would force the regime to accept a true democratic opening in which all of the country's political forces could participate. Being unable to take the road of armed struggle at that time, it took the only realistic position from which, as a party, it could confront the dictatorship. As Fidel explained several years later:

> The political parties that had been ousted from power had millions of embezzled pesos and some weapons. But they lacked morale and the will to struggle. The parties that had been in the opposition lacked the means, the leaders, and a strategy for the struggle. The Marxist-Leninist party, on its own, had neither the means nor the strength, nor were the national and international conditions propitious for carrying out an armed insurrection. In Cuba at that time, it would have been a senseless holocaust.[10]

Unlike the bourgeois opposition, the members of the Popular Socialist Party who voted in the election were not motivated by ambition. No party member could possibly be elected, as their party had been outlawed and they could not even be nominated. In his report to the Eighth National Assembly of the Popular

---

10. Fidel Castro, *Informe Central* (Main Report) to the 1st Party Congress, published by the Department of Revolutionary Orientation of the Central Committee of the Communist Party of Cuba. Havana 1975.

Socialist Party held in August 1960, Blas Roca[11] explained that decision:

> There were only two candidates: Grau and Batista. Neither one could provide a solution to the Cuban crisis. Batista's candidacy showed the real purpose of the election: to "legalize" the regime born of the coup d'état, gain political support through a loyal "opposition" that would be awarded some public positions, and prolong the dictatorship. Grau's candidacy, in opposing the coup, meant a return to the earlier maneuvers and immoral practices.
>
> Under those conditions, taking into account the fact that voting was compulsory and many people would vote for Grau to oppose the March 10 regime, the party decided to guide this action correctly and use the election to stage a broad demonstration of repudiation of the government.
>
> We therefore launched the slogan of the "vote against."
>
> We told the masses that since we have to vote, let's vote against Batista's tyrannical, unpopular government.
>
> We publicly explained that voting for Grau would not solve anything and that we were calling on the people not to vote *for* him but to vote *against* Batista — and the only possible way to vote against Batista in the existing conditions was to put an "X" next to Grau's name. Our "vote against" slogan got a great response among the masses.

An article published in the "In Cuba" section of *Bohemia* magazine evaluated the events as follows:

> By the middle of the year, a surprising phenomenon began to take place.... There was an increase in the comings and goings of visitors and messages at Fifth Avenue,[12] and the "snowball"

---

11. Blas Roca, "Balance de la labor del Partido desde la Ultima Asamblea Nacional y el desarrollo de la Revolución" (Evaluation of the party's work since the last national assembly and the development of the revolution) in *VIII Asamblea Nacional*, (Havana: Ediciones Populares, 1960).
12. The reference is to Ramón Grau San Martín's residence.

R.N. 3859

Fidel Castro Ruz in the National
Men's Prison on the Isle of Pines

Moncada military barracks in Santiago de Cuba, hours after the attack on July 26,
1953, led by Fidel Castro.

R.N. 3839

Raul Castro Ruz

R.N. 3833

Juan Almeida Bosque

R.N. 3817

Pedro Miret Prieto

R.N. 3858

Ramiro Valdés Menéndez

R.N. 3851

Jesús Montané Oropesa

R.N. 3834

Oscar Alcalde Valls

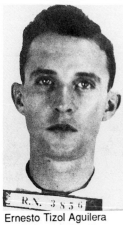

R.N. 3856

Ernesto Tizol Aguilera

R.N. 3857

Israel Tápanes

R.N. 3842

Agustín Díaz Cartaya

R.N. 3836
René Bedia Morales

R.N. 3849
Armando Mestre Martínez

R.N. 3841
Julio Díaz González

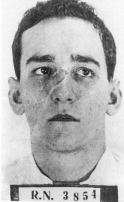

R.N. 3854
Ciro Redondo García

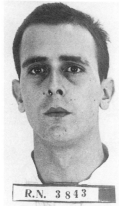

R.N. 3843
Andrés García Díaz

R.N. 3835
Reinaldo Benítez Nápoles

R.N. 4344
Abelardo Crespo Arias

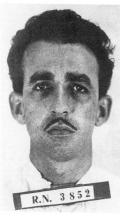

R.N. 3852
José Ponce Díaz

R.N. 3838
Enrique Cámara Pérez

Gabriel Gil Alfonso

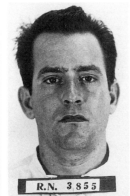
José Suárez Blanco

Rosendo Menéndez

Francisco González

Fidel Labrador García

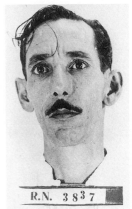
Orlando Cortés Gallardo

Eduardo Rodríguez Alemán

Melba Hernández and Haydée Santamaría behind bars in the National Women's Prison in Guanajay.

The Moncada prisoners in the yard adjacent to their prison ward. First row, left to right: José Ponce, Jesús Montané, Ramiro Valdés, Reinaldo Benítez, José Suárez Blanco, Eduardo Rodríguez Alemán, Julio Díaz; middle row: Enrique Cámara, René Bedia, Agustín Díaz Cartaya, Juan Almeida, Rosendo Menéndez, Orlando Cortés, Mario Chanes, Israel Tápanes, Gabriel Gil; standing in back: Ernesto Tizol, Oscar Alcalde, Francisco González, Armando Mestre, Eduardo Montano, Pedro Miret, Andrés García, Abelardo Crespo, Raúl Castro, Ciro Redondo, Fidel Labrador.

Covers of the first editions of *History Will Absolve Me*.

(above) Fulgencio Batista in Camp Columbia, headquarters of the General Staff of the Armed Forces, on March 10, 1952, the day of the military coup. (below) Batista, Cuban President Andrés Domingo Morales del Castillo, and U.S. Vice-President Richard Nixon during his February 1955 visit showing Washington's approval for Batista's dictatorship.

A section of the National Men's Prison (Model Prison) on the Isle of Pines

General view of the ward that served as a collective cell for the Moncada prisoners.

The Abel Santamaría Ideological Academy: a small blackboard and two wooden tables on which the Moncada prisoners ate under the ledge in the patio. On the day of this photo, the Moncada prisoners were visited by several nuns. Standing at left is Pedro Miret.

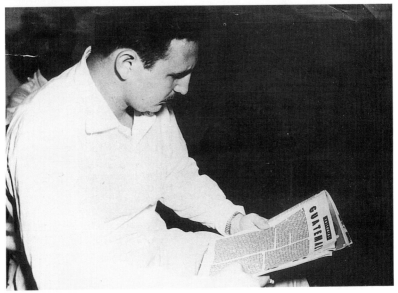

Photo of Fidel Castro in prison taken during *Bohemia's* July 1954 interview.

Some of the most notorious henchmen of the Batista regime. From left to right: Lt. Col. José María Salas Cañizares, who in 1957 would murder Frank País; Gen. Rafael Salas Cañizares, head of the National Police; Col. Orlando Piedra, head of the Bureau of Investigations (in civilian clothes); Captain Larraz; Col. Antonio Blanco Rico, head of the Military Intelligence Service (SIM); and Lt. Col. Lutgardo Martín Pérez.

José Antonio Echeverria, General Secretary of Federation of University Students

(above) Melba Hernández and Haydée Santamaría leaving the National Women's Prison in Guanajay on February 20, 1954, surrounded by supporters. (below) Melba Hernández and Haydée Santamaría laying flowers on the grave of Eduardo Chibás in the Colón Cemetery on the same day.

The fathers of Juan Almeida and Ramiro Valdés.

Sergio Montané, Zenaida Oropesa and
María Estela Aguilara, leaders of the amnesty
committee in Nueva Gerona

María Antonia Figueroa

Margot Machado

Gloria Cuadras

Celia Sánchez

Frank País   Antonio (Ñico) López   José (Pepito) Tey

(Left) Abel Santamaría, the second in command of the Movement, who was brutally tortured and murdered on July 26, 1953. An academy was named after him in the prison on the Isle of Pines by the Moncada prisoners. (Right) Raúl Gómez García, the poet of the young people of the Centennial, who was also murdered on July 26, 1953. The prison library was named after him by the Moncada prisoners.

René Reiné (left), José Valmaña (center) and Gustavo Ameijeiras (right) helped to finance and distribute Fidel Castro's *History Will Absolve Me.*

(left) Fidel Castro embraces Rosario Bosque on the train from Batabanó on the morning of May 16, 1955 and (right) Lidia Castro, Fidel's sister, greets him upon his release.

Raúl Castro, Juan Almeida, and Fidel Castro leaving prison on May 15, 1955.
Behind them is Armando Mestre.

Melba Hernández and Haydée Santamaría greet Fidel on May 15, 1955.

Press conference at the Isle of Pines Hotel on May 15, 1955. Next to Castro is Jesús Montané. Behind them is Mario Rodríguez Alemán, a leading activist in the amnesty committee.

began to gather momentum. The idea of the negative vote as an escape valve took root among the people, and suddenly the November 1 election became meaningful.

By the end of October, there was no room for any more posters on the walls and lampposts. Batista wound up his campaign in Central Park, and the professor of physiology [Grau] did so in Santiago de Cuba. On October 31, however, the electoral framework, which had been built up so laboriously, was undone in a matter of seconds. Olba Benito,[13] addressing the Electoral Court in front of television cameras, denounced in Jacobin terms the wave of persecution and violence that had been unleashed throughout the island and announced Grau's withdrawal.

On the eve of the election, in a last-minute about-face, after having bombarded the people with such slogans as "Bullets or ballots," "With an electoral code or without it," and "To the polls even under gunfire," and so on, Grau took the same abstentionist stand that he had previously ridiculed.

Moreover, his previous stance favored the regime's interests. It was he who made possible the electoral formula put forward by the regime. When he decided to back out, it was already too late. The coalition, free of all opponents, held the election as it wished, staging a scandalous extravaganza of fraud and deception. Just as it imposed the coup of March 10, so it also triumphed on November 1. The Court of Constitutional Guarantees ratified this fast play, and the Electoral Court, when the time came, gave its blessing to the shameful election.

In this expeditious manner, Fulgencio Batista y Zaldívar was "elected" president on November 1, 1954, with 1,262,587 votes — naturally, the largest vote ever given any candidate in the history of the frustrated republic. As in 1940, in a "gentleman's" agreement common to the ethics of bourgeois democracy, the sergeant-

---

13. Grau's representative in the Electoral Court.

turned-general who rose to prominence on September 4 now "legalized" March 10 with November 1.

On October 28, however, three days before the election, an event of singular importance took place in this chapter of Cuban history. In a letter written to his sister Lidia on October 29, Fidel commented:

> Last night I was up until 1:30 a.m., listening to the last political campaign meeting in Oriente, on the Oriente Radio Network. Perhaps you heard it, too, or someone has told you about it. I made a careful study of the psychology of the crowd, whose reaction is an unprecedented development. What a tremendous lesson for the high-and-mighties who were there!

As an expression of the people's consciousness, this "unprecedented development" would recur and hammer on the system's walls over and over again during the next four years. Santiago de Cuba, which had witnessed the dawn of the revolution early on July 26, 1953, also had the privilege of being the site of another breakthrough.

On the evening of October 28, 1954, at the rally that wound up Ramón Grau San Martín's electoral campaign, the people had kept interrupting the speakers, shouting a name that has since been inscribed in history: "Fidel Castro!" — political prisoner 3859, being held in solitary on the Isle of Pines.

CHAPTER 5

It is said that shortly after 1:00 a.m. on January 1, 1959,
Fulgencio Batista y Zaldívar signed his resignation and fled
the country. True and false: he did leave the country, but in
historical terms he had already signed his resignation three
years before, on Friday, May 6, 1955.
It is said that on Friday, May 6, 1955, Batista signed the
Amnesty Law that freed Fidel Castro and 28 other
participants in the Moncada attack from the Isle of Pines
prison, along with several hundred other political prisoners.
True and false: in historical terms what he was signing was
his own departure from the country, while, in fact...

The people signed the amnesty

In the absurd effort to reorganize political parties and the
subsequent electoral campaign, Batista had been forced to approve a minimum number of concessions designed "to create a
climate propitious for holding elections with full guarantees," as
they used to say at the time.

As soon as the election was announced in October 1953,
political amnesty became a key point of discussion. The regime
pardoned its opponents a few at a time and finally decreed what
was later called the "false amnesty" — which specifically excluded
all those who had participated in the July 26 events in Santiago
de Cuba and Bayamo.

After November 1, 1954, the holding of elections was no longer
a pressing demand for the opposition. Consequently, the question
of political prisoners ceased to be a priority to be placed before

the government. Instead of trying to find a viable solution to the problem, the opposition did nothing but complain about the spurious nature of the regime.

No one, not even the occasional writer in search of a profitable subject for a fortnightly column, dared mention the question of the Moncada untouchables for fear of being labeled a subversive. A pamphlet being distributed at the time among the masses had a great deal to do with the fear that reigned among these cautious folk.

The clandestine circulation of *History Will Absolve Me* began in October 1954, coinciding with the discouraging scandal of the rigged election to be held in November. It conferred on solitary prisoner 3859 on the Isle of Pines, extraordinary qualities as an invisible, accusing, organizing presence who was once again preparing war against the dictatorship. In factories, homes, offices, sugar plantations, and schools this figure inspired the heroism of battle. Its author thus became the formidable, untouchable opponent who hit the tyrannical government the hardest. His words, spread through the many groups that read the pamphlet, penetrated everywhere, and fired the people's rebellion against the crimes committed by the regime.

Fidel Castro emerged as conspirator number one, active day and night, appearing in a dozen places at once, eluding the repressive forces that sought to arrest him and halt his activity of raising the consciousness of the masses. Of course, they could not arrest him since he was already in prison. But a legend grew around him while he was there in his solitary confinement cell, physically defenseless.

At the same time, the perseverance of the relatives of the prisoners began to bear fruit. By May 1954 they had drawn up an initial and fairly sizable document. Fidel had already spent 90 days in solitary confinement and was concentrating on reconstructing his defense speech. Two months later, the Moncada group would start their second year in prison. The text of the relatives' message was released on the day before Mother's Day. Although inspired by deep sentiments, it made no concessions on principles, nor was it limited to their personal feelings. It demanded freedom for all the political prisoners. Since there was no money to pay for its publication, it was mimeographed and distributed by hand or sent through the mail. Addressed to "All Cuban mothers," it was entitled "Cuba, Freedom for Your Sons" and read:

We are the suffering mothers of the heroic boys who participated in the St. Ann's Day events,[1] and we ask all happy mothers to extend their maternal tenderness to our desolate hearts and help us bear the burden of our *Via Crucis*.[2] We are approaching the most important date on Cuba's patriotic calendar, commemorating the first time our country affirmed its place in the community of free nations, and joined the great American family. For many Cubans it will be a day of joy in which to relive the history of our nation, the flowering of the ideals of our liberators who made us free and independent citizens.

But this must also be a day of remembrance and civic evaluation. Are the Cuban people really happy? Have we fulfilled the aspirations of the struggle for liberation? These questions could be answered by our sorrowing mothers: Cuba cannot be happy this May 20[3] when its beloved sons cannot enjoy the sun, the breeze, the free and pure air; when the stifling heat of the prisons and penitentiaries deadens their minds and weakens their youthful bodies. With so many Cubans without liberty, we have not fulfilled that freedom for which the founders of our country fought.

On this somber May 20, a day which darkens the lives of all Cuban mothers, we ask for an amnesty that includes Dr.

---

1. This refers to the events of July 26, 1953 (the attack on the Moncada barracks).
2. Christians say that one bears a *Via Crucis* when suffering great problems and painful moments, referring to the march by Jesus of Nazareth bearing the cross with which he was to be crucified.
3. This is a reference to May 20, 1902, when, following the imposition of the Platt Amendment that legalized U.S. intervention in Cuba, the "powers" of the U.S. interventionist government were handed over to a local government that had won an election of dubious impartiality. It was the beginning of the deformed republic and, until the triumph of the revolution, was considered "National Independence Day."

Fidel Castro and his comrades who participated in the Moncada action, soldiers serving time, exiles, all of Cuba's political prisoners. We demand the cells are emptied and the gates opened. We demand liberty for our sons, who were sentenced solely for their ideals.

Honor our flag, victoriously unfurled in 1902 by those strong, noble hands.

Free the Cuban mothers, whose hearts are imprisoned along with their sons.

On behalf of the mothers, the document was signed by María E. Aguilera,[4] Rosario B. de Almeida,[5] Luisa P. de Miret[6] and Zenaida Oropesa de Montané.[7]

This was the historic debut of Cuban Mothers, a humble organization that quickly became the Relatives' Committee for Amnesty for Political Prisoners, registered — according to Juan Almeida's father — in the provincial government's list of associations. Later on, the committee's members would include hundreds of people from all over the country, and it would become the central force behind the powerful amnesty campaign that shook the country during the first half of 1955.

Zenaida Oropesa, Montané's mother, recalled:

The roots of the amnesty campaign were undoubtedly on the Isle of Pines, now the Isle of Youth. There, Juan Almeida and Sergio Montané Soto, the fathers of Juan Almeida Bosque and Jesús Montané, founded a committee for amnesty for the Moncada political prisoners by calling a meeting of the relatives who were visiting the prisoners. These included Rosario Bosque, María Estela Aguilera, Adriana González, Lidia Castro, Mariano Rives, and Magaly and Sergio Montané Oropesa, plus many others.

One of the first tasks was to have some cards engraved

---

4. The mother of Ernesto Tizol.
5. The mother of Juan Almeida.
6. The mother of Pedro Miret.
7. The mother of Jesús Montané.

with a picture of some of the prison's circular buildings and a message. Each relative was sent a quantity and asked to engage in constant propaganda. The cards were also sent to many important individuals, the newspapers, and the radio stations.

The text of the message on those cards is concise, direct, and unambiguous:

We ask for a broad and generous political amnesty! Behind the walls of these circular buildings — imposing steel and cement giants depicted on this card — of the National Men's Prison on the Isle of Pines, the courageous, heroic young men who attacked the Moncada garrison are being held in Building 1.

We ask for a broad and generous amnesty for them and for all others who are in prison or exile because of their love for Cuba and its freedom.

Let there be no more political prisoners and exiles in the land of José Martí and General Antonio Maceo!

Nueva Gerona, Isle of Pines, summer 1954

The main center of this activity shifted back and forth between two humble homes, one in the Poey neighborhood of Havana and the other in Nueva Gerona on the Isle of Pines.

The Almeida Bosques' wood-frame house was on the corner of D Street and Third Avenue in Poey. With Juan imprisoned on the Isle of Pines and his father fired in reprisal from his job as a dairy inspector, the family's 12 children suffered from increasing poverty. Even so, they all worked for the well-being of the prisoners, collecting or buying cigarettes and food so packages could be taken for everyone; checking with the rest of the families before each visit to see if any of them would be unable to go. In that event they would decide that one of the Almeida Bosque daughters would pass as a relative of one of the "boys in jail" and ask to see him. For as Rosario Bosque recalled, "Fidel had said that all of them — or none of them — had to leave the building on visiting day."

The Montané Oropesas' wood-frame house was on what was

then called Benito Ortiz Street, in Nueva Gerona. It had no number. Tizol's mother, María Aguilera, lived there for a while, until she moved to Gerona, where she made a living giving piano lessons. The door was always open at all hours to those coming to the small island from the big one to see their sons, husbands, and brothers — and there were quite a few of them, since most came from working-class backgrounds and had no money to pay for a hotel room. The cost of the trip to Batabanó and then the four pesos to get from Batabanó to Gerona on the steamship *El Pinero* was already quite a drain.

Rosario Bosque later recalled:

We went on the *El Pinero* only once or twice. We usually took a schooner and crowded together at the stern, along with the cargo. All of us — even the little ones — left home at noon on Saturday, and we got there at dawn on Sunday. We sometimes left our packages and bags at a cafeteria where we had some coffee, then paid some visits and waited in the park or in Father Sardiñas'[8] church until it was time for visiting hours at the prison. We had some problems with this, too, because the bus service from Gerona to the prison was suspended, and we had to take taxis that charged two pesos per person. Later, we got them to lower the price to 40 centavos each. In the evening, we had our only meal of the day at the cafeteria, and we embarked on the schooner again at night. We reached Batabanó at dawn on Monday and went straight to Havana: my older daughters, to work in the shop, and my husband, to his business. Meanwhile I went home to Poey with the children and started thinking about our evening meal.

When the beautiful saga of human solidarity and love behind the aid given the Moncada political prisoners is written, it will have to record these stories and include a chapter on Juan Almeida's unemployed father, who walked all over the city looking for

---

8. After the landing of the *Granma*, Guillermo Sardiñas, parish priest in Nueva Gerona, joined the Rebel Army in the Sierra Maestra and rose to the rank of commander.

advertisements for his little paper *La Opinión Libre* (Free Opinion) and devoted the proceeds to helping the prisoners. Following his critical article "Batista, Hunger Does Not Give Good Counsel," however, agents of the Bureau for the Repression of Communist Activities (BRAC) destroyed the printshop on Concordia Street where the paper was published. He walked through the streets of Havana visiting his friends among the writers on the various newspapers, to whom he showed his membership card in the Reporters' Association, and tried to convince them to write articles on amnesty from time to time in order to break the conspiracy of silence.

History should also record the dozens of families in Bayamo and Santiago de Cuba who opened their doors to many participants in the Moncada attack, enabling many of them to escape and either remain underground in Cuba or go into exile. There were also those who frustrated the attempt to bury the Moncada's fallen heroes without identification; after discovering where they were buried in the Santa Efigenia Cemetery, they planted flowers there and maintained the graves. Others put up the Moncada attackers' relatives who went to Santiago for the trial.

Many applauded from the sidewalks whenever a bus went by taking the handcuffed combatants to the Provisional Court. Others protected and cared for wounded survivors in the hospitals or collected food and other things for those in the Boniato prison. Many worked on reprinting the first *Manifesto to the Nation*, which was sold to raise funds to buy the first machine gun — purchased in 1954 with the help of Félix Pena, Frank País, and their Oriente Revolutionary Action group (ARO). In Oriente Province, all these forces would become the center of support and solidarity to the Moncada prisoners on the Isle of Pines.

A group of Santiago de Cuba women headed by Vilma Espín, a young university student, wrote a letter asking for Abelardo Crespo Arias to be transferred to the Calixto García Hospital. María Antonia Figueroa traveled to Havana and to the Colón Cemetery, together with Melba and Haydée, on the first anniversary of the Moncada attack, where they were attacked by the police. In Pilón and Manzanillo money was collected and canned meat and chocolate bars were sent to the Isle of Pines organized by a pro-Martí activist from Oriente named Celia Sánchez.

Then there were also the hundreds of people throughout the country who helped to publish and distribute *History Will Absolve Me* — both the high-quality edition that was printed in New York on October 30 (the same month in which the first Havana edition appeared) and the mimeographed version put out in Margot Machado's academy in Santa Clara.

All these things will have to be recorded when the history of these events is written. Filled with a truly revolutionary and human solidarity, they reaffirm the historic significance of the Moncada period. All those forces later joined the Relatives' Committee and, together with Melba and Haydée, raised the demand for amnesty for their imprisoned heroes.

Many names will undoubtedly be forgotten, but not those of Mercedes Valdés, Alvaro Suárez, Ramón Cantalicio Valdés, Clara García and Evaristo Redondo (Ciro Redondo's parents), María González and Lorenzo Díaz (Julito Díaz's parents), from Artemisa; Amelia Vento Pichardo (Tápanes' mother) and Emilia Guerrero (who helped her), from Matanzas; and Carlota Díaz (Ponce's mother) and Hortensia Nápoles Pastor (Benítez' mother), from Camagüey. They were among the first to sign the amnesty petition circulated by the committee — which, in the end, would have tens of thousands of signatures. They even took the petition from door to door; gave talks in factories, shops, and schools; sent hundreds of telegrams to mobilize the people; and sent delegations to visit radio stations, newspapers, and magazines. They created an amazing organization, which quickly spread from Gerona to Pinar del Río, reaching all parts of the country. Guido García Inclán made daily appeals in his COCO radio commentaries — which, of course, were echoed in Santiago de Cuba by Gloria Cuadras, who was at the heart of the radio and newspaper agitation in Oriente Province.

The efforts of a small group founded in a wood-frame house near Gerona were soon multiplied by the masses. When in the beginning there was nothing more than a determined initiative by a small group of people, Fidel understood its potential for weakening the dictatorship. Under his leadership, this became transformed into a decisive national mobilization pitting the masses against the dictatorship. It was then that the amnesty campaign was unleashed as a powerful, overwhelming movement that could not be contained.

Arouse the nation against Batista

The year 1955 started off very favorably for the regime — so much so that several of its spokesmen, trying to make a benevolent and condescending gesture out of the political defeat that the masses were about to impose on it, favored announcing a generous pardon for its imprisoned opponents. Perhaps unwittingly, they were only puppets whose strings were being pulled from a solitary confinement cell. There, on January 1, 1955, Fidel Castro wrote these instructions to Ñico López, who was planning to return to Cuba from Mexico with Calixto García.[9]

> You should do this publicly and appear before the courts as Moncada combatants. I will explain the reasons for this. Right now, there is very little you can do outside while we are imprisoned. My proposal to you is something worthy of us and would stir public opinion. The trial would have to be reopened, and we would arouse the nation against Batista when he is about to take office on February 24.
>
> This would be a tremendous psychological blow, especially when everyone is calling for amnesty. The trial proceedings would once again become the center of public attention — and an excellent platform for expounding our ideas. This would undoubtedly have repercussions, since all news is being widely publicized at present, thanks to the artificial climate of freedom the regime created to put across the electoral farce in November.
>
> Your arrival in Cuba must be preceded by the public

---

9. Antonio (Ñico) López and Calixto García had participated in the July 26, 1953, attack on the Bayamo garrison, a strategic action carried out to support the Moncada attack. They managed to escape and return to Havana, from where they went into exile: Ñico in Guatemala and Calixto in Costa Rica. At the end of 1954, they were living in Mexico. They both would later participate on the *Granma* expedition, after which Ñico was taken prisoner and murdered.

statements I am enclosing for you to sign and send on to CMQ radio, Miguel Quevedo,[10] Conte Agüero, Pardo Llada,[11] Unión Radio, Manuel Palacio Blanco,[12] *Prensa Libre*, *El Mundo*, and *Diario Nacional*. You should send a letter and a copy of the statement to each of them, regardless of how you may feel about them. Use the same channel I am using now when you send these statements to Cuba; all of them should arrive at the same time. You will receive a cable as soon as they are published.

A few days later, with the same amount of publicity — of course, you must let us know this ahead of time — we will announce the date, place, and exact time of your arrival, so that people (perhaps including journalists) can meet you. We will put people in charge of all these details. You will undoubtedly be arrested immediately and then sent to Santiago de Cuba for trial in the Provisional Court. I am not in favor of asking for any guarantees except the support of public opinion. Under these circumstances, you may be sure that they will not mistreat you in the least. Right now, they are trying to avoid all scandal, because the climate is very favorable to exiles and political prisoners. The return of any exile would get a lot of publicity — especially in your case.

Tell all the other exiled compañeros you think should know about this plan, but make sure it appears as your own idea. I don't want to put any moral pressure on them. I beg you not to forget this elementary discretion. If anybody else decides to return before February 24, the government will go crazy, just when it wants to make a show of political normalcy at all costs. This might become a decisive factor in forcing it to sign the amnesty.

---

10. Miguel Quevedo was owner and editor of *Bohemia* magazine.
11. José Pardo Llada had quietly returned to Cuba from exile. He had a daily radio program with a large audience. At the height of the amnesty campaign, he rivalled journalist Luis Conte Agüero as "opportunist number one."
12. Manuel Palacio Blanco was director of the "Ahora" daily news broadcast on radio station 1060.

Always alert, Fidel foresaw another possibility. Further on in the same letter, he wrote:

> If, by some chance, they do not want to arrest you when you arrive, to avoid exactly what we are aiming at, then present yourselves along with Baudilio Castellanos, who will be your counsel, before the Provisional Court in Santiago. Tell them that you "want to suffer the same fate as your imprisoned comrades," and they will be forced to act.

Fidel saw a positive aspect to the period in prison, which he explained to Ñico López as follows:

> There is no need to tell you that I don't think we are wasting our time in prison. To the contrary, we are preparing the vanguard and the leaders of our Movement ideologically and intellectually. We are young and in no hurry. It would be wonderful to have 80 instead of 29 compañeros here! I have much more faith in those imprisoned here than in those scattered in exile, in terms of what they will be able to do for Cuba.

He defined the political stand of the Moncada combatants within the framework of the general political situation in the country and outlined the overall strategy for the struggle:

> I am absolutely convinced that in present situation we must prepare for a long struggle, that will culminate in the fulfillment of the most cherished dreams of the Cuban people, who truly deserve a better fate. Day by day through our actions we have won their sympathy. Your action would win still greater admiration; and moreover, you would then join us in this workshop where we are forging the leaders of our generation, instilling in them the same thinking and the same doctrines and discipline. Under no circumstances will we have to remain here much longer, thanks to the strength of public pressure calling for our freedom. But even if we should, what does it matter? We have time on our side.

I'm speaking to you frankly, with the bitter but instructive experience of 17 months' harsh imprisonment. For the last 10, I have been isolated from the rest of the compañeros, but the academy continues functioning rigorously and seriously, and the library is becoming more complete. You have no idea how much faith, morale, and spirit of struggle and self-improvement have reigned at all times.

Our enthusiasm and fervor remain as great as ever, as does our readiness for sacrifice and our desire for struggle. While politicians who were never revolutionary — even though they tried to pass themselves off as such — try to use Cuba as a stepping-stone for their base ambitions, we are preparing ourselves for great revolutionary action on the very altar of sacrifice. For us, prison is our academy of struggle, and when the time comes, nothing will be able to stop us.

Meanwhile, I sincerely believe we can expect nothing from the political parties and pseudo-revolutionary groups, whose incapacity has been laid bare to all in the three years that have elapsed since March 10. With our blood, sweat, sacrifice, selflessness, and idealism, we are the only ones who have provided a ray of hope and faith in the disillusioned heart of the nation. Let us be worthy of this, knowing how to wait, knowing how to act, knowing how to grow stronger in adversity.

We have lost a battle, but we have saved the honor of Cuba. We will return to the struggle. Only when not a drop of blood runs in our veins and the last of us dies — only then will they be able to say they have defeated us. We have lacked resources, but we have never been wrong.

Do you remember how our ranks were decimated by the intrigues of the political rogues and false revolutionaries of all stripes, trying to make off with whole cells of our trained members, constantly sowing confusion and lies among them and throughout the country? I don't know if you know how much they slandered our Movement and how cowardly they hushed up the horrible murders of the prisoners within the Moncada garrison. We went to our deaths alone; we have been persecuted and imprisoned alone; and we will go on alone. So let us go forward. It would be a blind, crazy, and treacherous thing to join with those who have neither the authority nor the organization to be the vanguard of the Cuban revolution.

I seek the union of all Cubans — but worthy and noble Cubans, led by men who were never implicated in the shameful past. So what if we don't have any ill-begotten money? Did we, perchance, have any before July 26? That did not stop us — all the more reason for not stopping now, when we can count on the faith of the people, who saw us go empty-handed to our deaths for their freedom.

You are one of the good ones, and I write you all this because I know you will understand me. I send a fraternal embrace to all those who, like you, remain loyal to the principles of those who died; the others, I believe, are not lost. I am firmly convinced that sooner or later they will see I am right and that someday we will all march along the same road to glory that led us to the memorable dawn of July 26.

Ñico and Calixto were then facing absolute poverty. They slept under the stairway of a building and at times went for days without food. The only ones who could give them the money for their return trip were Prío elements with whom they had no relations. Weeks went by in fruitless attempts to get enough money. By March, things changed. Fidel's letter exemplified his talent for keeping the whole situation under control.

In these conditions, with 1955 appearing promising for the regime, the 126 mayors and all the councilmen "elected" on November 1 took office on January 3. The six provincial governors were sworn in on January 15.

On January 23, provisional "President" Andrés Domingo Morales del Castillo — "provisional" because of Batista's electoral leave of absence — signed Legislative Decrees 648, 649, and 650, prohibiting ordinary courts from trying crimes attributed to the military. Since these decrees could not be appealed, they constituted a legal guarantee against such annoyances as the Supreme Court's January 1954 declaration of competence that ruled in favor of a civilian court's jurisdiction in the case surrounding the November 27, 1953, murder of Mario Fortuny.

The November election fraud was consolidated when the recently constituted Consultative Council — created to replace congress by those who carried out the coup — was dissolved on January 27. And in a new insult to the memory of José Martí, the House of Representatives and the Senate were inaugurated in the luxurious rooms of the Capitol on Janaury 28, the anniversary of Martí's birth.

Sixteen Authentic Party representatives, ignoring Grau's election-eve order to boycott the elections and abstain from taking office, took their seats in the 114-member House of Representatives. In the Senate, 18 Authentic Party members — three for each province — accepted the tempting electoral-minority offer to get seats despite the fact that they had received practically no votes. Thirty-six from the ruling coalition also took Senate seats — six for each province. Only two members of the Authentic Party group — Francisco Grau Alsina in the Senate and José Miguel Morales in the House of Representatives — obeyed Grau's order.

While the senators and representatives were taking their seats on January 28, several events showed that there had been no real political changes in the country and that the dictatorship would continue its repression.

Former President Grau was kept from laying a wreath at the foot of the statue of Martí in Havana's Central Park. A large number of police cordoned off his residence on Fifth Avenue in Miramar and several high-ranking officers guarded his front and back doors, preventing him from going out.

The regime had prohibited all public demonstrations on the 102nd anniversary of José Martí's birth. Ignoring the ban, more than 500 young people from the Martí Student Bloc met at Dolores Park in Santiago de Cuba and attempted to march toward the tomb of the Apostle of Cuba's independence in the Santa Efigenia Cemetery. The police cut them off at Aguilera and Calvario streets. Clashes also occurred at the Martí and Crombet parks in Santiago de Cuba, with the police shooting at the students and attacking them with clubs and whips. More than 30 young people were wounded or arrested.

The regime made quite a show of commemorating Martí's anniversary, January 28. It arrested hundreds of people throughout the country on that day, charging them with participating in a supposed conspiracy. Juan Manuel Márquez was among those arrested. All were released a few days later.

Several protests made at the time show that the dictatorship's repressive arm also reached into the cultural sector. Three hundred copies of the October 1954 issue of *Humanismo* magazine, dedicated to the Cry of Yara and published in Mexico, were confiscated by Cuban customs. The same thing happened shortly after with a shipment of Luis Conte Agüero's book *Eduardo Chibás, the Leader*, printed in Mexico by JUS Publishers. The outrages continued as SIM agents broke into the house of the mother of Carlos Rafael Rodríguez and made off with all 3,700 books in the distinguished communist leader's library.

At the end of January, it was the turn of Antonio Núñez Jiménez, a teacher at the Vedado Institute of Secondary Education. All copies of his recently published book *Geography of Cuba* were confiscated by SIM agents in the bookstores that planned to sell them. Even the printing plates were seized from the Lex Publishers shop.

In a state of evident euphoria, Fulgencio Batista gave U.S. Vice-President Richard M. Nixon a warm embrace during the first week of February as he stopped off in Cuba during his tour of Central America. The man responsible for the March 10 "revolution" was thus given the blessing of his mentors.

As a gesture of profuse servility, provisional "President" Andrés Domingo Morales del Castillo convened the last marathon Council of Ministers meeting. The session, held on January 27, the eve of the opening of Congress, had approved Legislative Decree 1875. According to this new legal contrivance, a participant in any activity considered to be communist could be fired from any post in a state body, in the educational system, trade unions, and other bodies. Since it was left to the arbitrary rule of the repressive forces to assess the possible communist content of the activities carried out by its opponents, it became clear just how this measure would be used.

The finishing touch to this scene was the visit to Cuba in April by another big shot in imperialism's continental strategy: Allen Dulles, director of the Central Intelligence Agency. The soul of discretion as befitted his calling, the CIA general manager limited himself to imperiously wagging his index finger, saying the United States was "deeply concerned about the problem of communism in Cuba." That was all he needed to say. A month later, on May 15, 1955, after feverish counseling by U.S. experts in this sphere, Batista decreed the creation of the Bureau for the Repression of Communist Activities (BRAC),[13] which chalked up a sinister list of crimes in the three and a half years of agony that still lay ahead for the enslaved republic.

On February 8, the Executive Committee of the banned Popular Socialist Party met to again denounce the anti-worker character of the "CTK" leadership, openly allied with the dictatorship and imperialism. The PSP called for unity in repudiating compulsory union dues, sanctioned by the outgoing Cabinet on January 27.

The document stated:

The traitors Mujal,[14] José Luis Martínez,[15] Bolaños,[16] and Co., hypocritically claim that compulsory union dues benefit the workers, because some sectors of the bourgeoisie are against it. This is utterly false. Even though it is true that some local employers' groups oppose the measure, it is supported by the worst, most aggressive enemies of the workers: the Yankee imperialists, their companies, and their lackeys, who want to apply the fascist methods of Mussolini, Hitler, and Franco in our country. These dictators used compulsory union dues to

---

13. BRAC was finally created on July 1, 1955, in a morning ceremony presided over by Santiago Rey Pernas, the regime's new minister of the interior. Other participants included General Martín Díaz Tamayo; Colonel Orlando Piedra, chief of the Bureau of Investigations; Lieutenant Colonel Antonio Blanco Rico, chief of SIM; Enrique Fernández Parajón, from the secret police; and other high-ranking officers of the armed forces. Years later Ambassador Arthur Gardner publicly confessed his role in the matter, declaring that he considered himself the "father of BRAC." Captain Castaño, head of BRAC, was shot after the revolution's triumph.
14. Eusebio Mujal was general secretary of the CTC.
15. José Luis Martínez was general secretary of the National Federation of Sugar Workers.
16. Javier Bolaños was general secretary of the National Federation of Railroad Workers.

strengthen fascist, government-sponsored unions with well-paid bureaucrats accustomed to a petty-bourgeois life-style, who are incapable of leading any real working-class, revolutionary, progressive struggle but are always ready to oppose every action by the workers for their demands.

The Yankee imperialists have created that type of parasitic bureaucracy, which feeds off the workers, in the form of the American Federation of Labor and the Congress of Industrial Organizations (AFL-CIO). They now want to set up here the same kind of unions they imposed on Puerto Rico with Iglesias: unions that support Yankee imperialist companies in opposition to national ones and to Cuba's independence. This is why they support and promote compulsory union dues. Meanwhile, as the fascist vice-president of the United States tours our country in an attempt to subject and control it, he grants the hireling Mujal a special audience in which he praises him publicly as the best, most faithful trade union lackey Yankee imperialism has in Cuba.

The PSP document also called on everyone to "join forces in the battle to obtain amnesty for all political and social prisoners, to annul the November electoral farce, to restore democracy, and to call for a new general election — in which all working-class, anti-imperialist, and democratic parties may participate and the people may elect a National Democratic Front government that will bring about a democratic solution to the crisis."[17]

At a joint session on February 18, the House and Senate proclaimed Fulgencio Batista y Zaldívar and Rafael Guas Inclán president and vice-president of the republic, respectively, and — in an ironic observance of the 60th anniversary of the unleashing of Martí's necessary war for independence — on February 24 these illustrious patriarchs were sworn in.

That same day the Constitutional Statutes were annulled,

---

17. National Committee of the Popular Socialist Party, *El Partido Socialista Popular llama a combatir la cuota sindical fascista* (The Popular Socialist Party calls for opposition to the fascist union dues), February 8, 1955. A five-page mimeographed flyer.

replacing the constitution of 1940, adopted 15 years earlier at Guáimaro and proclaimed in the Capitol. It appeared that the constitution was to be enforced once again, at least on paper — though an appendix was tacked on calling for "respect for all mandates emanating from the November election."

Everything seemed to be going smoothly, but the government's true intentions on the constitutional rights of citizens soon became apparent. Following the wave of repression in January, on February 24 Orlando León Lemus, known as "El Colorado," was murdered at 211 Durege Street in Santos Suárez, and the body of José Angel ("Mitico") Fernández was found four kilometers out on the road to the Rancho Boyeros airport, riddled with bullets.

February 24 was also the day that an important document in favor of amnesty appeared. Signed by people representing a wide range of ideological beliefs — with the Communists excluded, of course — it constituted the high point of the right-wing opposition to Batista around the question of freedom for political prisoners (although there were some honorable exceptions).

The text was given broad coverage in the press. Its "repeated repudiation of violence" (in a sense, repudiation of the revolution) expressed the class character of many of the signatories. Published under the title "A Public Appeal," it read as follows:

Aware of our responsibility as citizens and inspired by the same ideals that aroused the enthusiasm and civic faith of the Cuban people in the struggle for emancipation that we now commemorate, we address ourselves to public opinion. We demand freedom for those imprisoned for political reasons and guarantees for the return of all those in exile, with no qualification or exclusions, which might affect the peaceful coexistence we all seek.

Without reservation or hesitation, the signatories of this document and the great majority of the nation has insisted on the need to stabilize the republic. This can be achieved by creating a true climate of civic peace in which democratic institutions can be restored and so citizens who are openly and actively opposed to the present powers that be have the right to voice their political opinions.

Cuba's problem must be discussed in terms of dignity, honor, and civic values. Peace cannot be achieved as long as a group of people tries to manage the interests of the majority and impose its will rather than govern — yet peace is necessary if we are to solve this agonizing national crisis. Freedom for political prisoners is not a result of peace; it is one of its conditions.

Impelled by our repeated repudiation of violence — the very essence of our common ideals — we call on the members of this government to prove that they are really working for peace by applying the constitution of 1940 and respecting law and justice, as they are duty-bound to do. This declaration, along with the people's demands for steps leading to full respect for man's dignity and to national progress, places in your hands the exclusive historic responsibility for providing a solution to this serious conflict, the consequences of which we are trying to avoid with this public appeal. We hope that this solution will be definitive and that it will pave the way for our homeland to achieve harmony and dignity, which have always inspired the best of our national traditions.[18]

Events were clearly following an uneven course of coincidences, encounters, disagreements and — at times — antagonistic contrasts. Amidst much fanfare and reformist rhetoric of an abstract Christian Democratic nature, a new political party briefly emerged in March. The leaders of the so-called Radical National Movement included Amalio Fiallo, Andrés Valdespino, Mario Llerena, and other beatific figures who wanted to go swamp-hopping without

---

18. The document was signed by Cosme de la Torriente, Carlos Márquez Sterling, Manuel Antonio de Varona, Ramón Zaydín, Jorge Mañach, José R. Andreu, Pelayo Cuervo, José Manuel Gutiérrez, Antonio Martínez Fraga, Néstor Carbonell, Manuel Bisbé, Francisco Carone, Félix Lancís, Lincoln Rodón, José Pardo Llada, Héctor Pagés, Luis Casero, Alberto Saumell, Carlos M. Peláez, José Díaz, Rogelio Regalado, José Miguel Morales Gómez, Vicentina Antuña, Roberto Melero Juvier, Antonio G. Cejas, Luis Conte Agüero, Manuel Palacio Blanco, Eduardo Corona, Andrés Valdespino, Rafael Miyar, Luis Felipe Gutiérrez, Max Lesnick, Javier Lezcano, Aramís Taboada, Orlando de la Portilla, and Francisco Ramos Montejo. The text and list of signatories are taken from *Bohemia* magazine, February 27, 1955, p. 62.

getting muddied.

Meanwhile, the Provisional Court of Santiago de Cuba acquitted a young student from the University of Oriente who was accused (rightly, though not enough proof was presented) of engaging in clandestine activities. He was not very well known then, but his name would soon join those of Cuba's national heroes: Frank País.

In a strange legal interpretation, the Provisional Court of Camagüey filed charges against a group of veterans of the war of independence. It was claimed they had engaged in "subversive activities" because they had signed a public document. Against national sovereignty? No, against the imperialist plan of cutting Cuba in two from north to south in Matanzas Province by building a canal — for the benefit of U.S. shipping companies. Simultaneously, what was left of the skeletal Cuban merchant fleet was either sold or leased to other countries.

An imperialist plan

The incongruity of the charges filed in Camagüey was revealed in all its absurdity at a time when the people — with perhaps unprecedented unanimity and organization — dealt the dictatorship and Yankee imperialism a major blow.

The plan for a canal through Cuba had its obscure origins in Decree 1618 (August 14, 1954) declaring the canal a public utility and "setting the regulations governing its construction and financing." As *Bohemia*'s "In Cuba" section succinctly explained: "It came as a surprise to the few Cubans who read the *Gazette*, for the controversial issue had notoriously been kept a dark secret so it could be sprung on the citizens as a fait accompli."

Legislative Decree 1715 of September 30 modified the earlier decree by facilitating financing by contract bidders, who were required to invest only half a million pesos, which could be borrowed from the insurance companies. This reduced their actual investment to practically nothing, especially since the project's estimated overall cost was 500 million pesos.

The full scope of the affair could be seen by December 6, when Legislative Decree 3652 was published. It was clear the government was involved in a plan that would be disastrous for the country's economy, and could only lead to further dependency and loss of political sovereignty. Everybody was quite aware that it was impossible to undertake such a project with Cuban capital.

The concessions that were granted included the creation of a "port authority in charge of all matters relating to public order, strategic aims, and compliance with the terms of the contract." That authority would be assumed by the mysterious concessionary corporation and the navy. Never before had Cuba delegated such constitutional prerogatives to a private entity. The fact that public order, including strategic military aims, would be discussed with the directors of a private company, was the most flagrant violation of national sovereignty.

The concession was to be tax-free for 99 years. The land for the canal was to be seized, and all tenant farmers and squatters living within 300 meters of the 80-kilometer-long canal — which would run from Cárdenas to the Bay of Pigs in the Zapata Swamp — were to be evicted. The enterprise was given the right to register ships, in violation of Cuban law. Workers in the canal zone area would belong to the naval reserve and be subject to military law in the event of a disorder. They would be excluded from trade union activities and denied any legal protection.

The popular repudiation of the project reached explosive proportions. At a press conference held on December 17, Batista cynically declared, "If you were to ask me what was behind the idea of building this canal, I would say it is chiefly our overriding desire to improve the country's economic situation and create jobs. In other words, it falls into the category of projects aimed at fighting unemployment and strengthening our economy." Predictably, he went on to say: "I must tell you frankly that the opposition to the canal through Cuba comes from Communist sources. Since they cannot function legally, they operate through other organizations and elements."

While it was true that the members of the first Cuban Marxist-Leninist party had been among the earliest to oppose the project, nobody could accept the president's view that Roberto Agramonte, Salvador Menéndez Villoch, Amalio Fiallo, Andrés Valdespino, Vicente Rubiera, and Jorge Mañach — who were also among the first to add their voices in opposition — were "elements" through which the Communists operated.

"If General Batista's charges were correct," the "In Cuba" section noted ironically, "we would have to assume that the Communists controlled public opinion, since members of the Orthodox and Authentic parties, Catholics, all kinds of professionals — including doctors, engineers, lawyers, and architects — and workers' organizations have also opposed the project. The opposition is growing every day."

In spite of Mujal's maneuvers, the Maritime Workers Federation issued a manifesto charging, among other things, that the project would close down the other ports, destroy the link between sea and land transportation, displace workers, and reduce them to poverty.

In mid-December, opposition was voiced in two very different events: a meeting of sugarcane workers in Camagüey and a medical conference in Cienfuegos.

When Rear Admiral Rodríguez Calderón stated that the canal through Cuba would "bring life to dead areas," the Federation of University Students (FEU) responded in *Alma Mater* that the navy chief "made that statement without explaining that the living areas will be left to die." In a more extensive manifesto the FEU then issued a call for a forum "in defense of national honor," to be held January 27-28. The call noted, "Having broken the republic's back on March 10, they now seek to break up the national territory. The dismemberment of the nation seems to be their only objective. If national dignity refused to allow the Isle of Pines to be separated from us, how can it now permit a piece of the nation to be cut off?" Later, José Antonio Echeverría declared, "This is not a political campaign political against a de facto regime; it is a struggle to defend the very essence of our nationality, independence, and territorial integrity."

By the end of December, the Latin American Association, led by Salvador Menéndez Villoch and Eduardo Corona, had joined the opposition. In addition, the Orthodox Youth, led by Mario Rivadulla and Max Lesnick, held a national meeting broadcast over radio station COCO with the participation of university professors, student leaders such as Alvaro Barba, and radio commentators such as Armando García Sifredo and Manuel Palacio Blanco. On December 20, CMQ televised an even more effective roundtable discussion in which Joaquín López Montes denounced the unconstitutional aspects of the project, Segundo Ceballos pointed to its economic drawbacks, and Leví Marrero described how useless and even dangerous it was environmentally. "Cuba's position," he said, "does not interfere with the commercial north-south navigation routes. The land to be expropriated is part of the Havana-Matanzas plains, where the sugarcane industry reached its height at the end of the 19th century and whose red clay soil is as fertile as any in the world. Another important factor must also be considered: because of the great number of underground sumps and caves in that area, if the gigantic cut is made, sea water will flood in causing a salt-water invasion that could render large areas permanently unfit for agriculture."

A few days later, university professor Miguel Angel Fleites wrote in the newspaper *Prensa Libre* that, "According to Legislative Decree 1618, the purpose of the canal will be primarily strategic. Let us assume that World War III breaks out, and the United States occupies the canal. What will happen to the Cubans who have to cross what would then be a military zone and foreign territory to get from one part of the island to the other? For all practical purposes, the island would be cut into two territories completely isolated from each other. No one can predict the social, political, and economic consequences of such a state of affairs."

On January 23, a suit was filed in the Court of Constitutional and Social Guarantees, demanding that Legislative Decrees 1617, 1715, and 3652 be declared unconstitutional. The appeal was prepared by Francisco Carone and signed by a group of jurists including Cosme de la Torriente, Pelayo Cuervo Navarro, Carlos Márquez Sterling, Jorge Mañach, and José Manuel Gutiérrez.

The University of Havana was the center of the national protests against the project. This finally halted the government's plan to build the canal and the project slowly sank into oblivion. It was reduced to a simple smuggling operation that continued on a sizable scale for several months, whereby equipment and merchandise entered the country duty-free on the pretext that it would be used for the project that was never begun.

A thousand years of dignity

Meanwhile, on Saturday, March 6, 1955, Fidel sent the following telegram from prison:

> Our deepest thanks to you and your enthusiastic comrades who have spontaneously taken up the cause of our freedom. In this case, what we most appreciate is not the goal itself — for prison is bearable if you hold your head high — but your gesture of civic support. We will stand firm, exhibiting neither impatience nor fear as we endure our fate today. Tomorrow, our first embrace will be for those who remembered us in this difficult hour. Fraternally.

This deferential and courteous message also served to establish a matter of principle: the refusal to give an inch to the dictatorship. A week later, on Sunday, March 14, Fidel wrote his sister Lidia as follows:

> It has been a quiet, calm Sunday, although the week has been filled with all kinds of details and concerns. Even though it is already 11:00 p.m., I was reluctant to put down an interesting book in order to write you these lines, as I had promised myself I would do. My best hours are those when I am oblivious to everything and can concentrate on learning something new and useful, or on just trying to gain a better understanding of humanity.
>
> Even though I am always eager to have long talks with you, I prefer to wait until visiting day. Today I especially wanted to tell you that on Saturday, March 6, I sent a telegram to some of the fellows who organized a meeting in support of our freedom broadcast over Hispano-Cubano radio. Since these communications are apt to be changed along the way, I am enclosing the full text of that telegram for the record. It just so happens that on the day of the broadcast there was a blackout in this ward all morning and I was unable to listen to it.

After copying down the complete text of the telegram, Fidel continued:

> As you see — with all the necessary delicacy, so it would not seem to be a rebuff — I expressed my gratitude not for the proposal for amnesty but for their gesture towards us, since at times we have been quite forgotten here. I know that some of them deserve a good talking to, but I also have things I wish to express. In this case, I can't help but be grateful to those fellows whom I scarcely know but who, week after week, have been talking about us. It doesn't matter to me which group or tendency they belong to! I'm tired of those petty intrigues! Besides, I am not begging for amnesty and never will. I have enough dignity to spend 20 years here or die of rage first. So let me at least be courteous. The rest of the world be damned, and let the devil take those petty critics who are always looking for some way to try our patience.

March 1955, however, would be remembered for an event of singular importance at a time when, following the halting of the canal through Cuba, the amnesty campaign was the central issue.

On February 24, 1955, in reply to questions posed by journalist Marta Rojas, Batista made the following comment about the possibility of amnesty:

> I applaud the laws governing pardon. The government promulgated one such law recently, but it seems to me the Amnesty Law should be as broad as the people want it to be. I would not be averse to approving an act of pardon passed by the Congress if it would bring the nation long-term peace.
>
> Thus, the law must be consistent with a generally accepted desire of preserving peace between the government and the opposition, so that its results are precisely what the people are striving for. An amnesty that encourages disorder and unrest would be meaningless. If a law of pardon were to grant exceptional benefits to those who have broken the laws of the republic so that these groups could then go on disturbing family life, the economy, our institutions, and the nation itself,

it would not be beneficial.[19]

Pressured by the people, however, the new "elected" regime decided to display the same magnanimity that the monarchs of the past had shown during great festivities, by allowing the draft of an amnesty bill to be presented and discussed in the Senate and House of Representatives on March 10, the third anniversary of the coup.

Great care was taken with the proposal — that seemingly came from the "opposition" — to provide the formulations that would most likely satisfy the dictator's pride. Arturo Hernández Tellaheche presented the proposal in the Senate, and Juan Amador Rodríguez in the House. Both documents were read in their respective legislative bodies on the same day, which led to a dilemma over how they should be handled. To solve the problem, a bicameral commission was formed to determine the chronological order of the debates, since both of these brand new congressional bodies claimed the privilege of discussing the bill first. This excessive legalism was nothing but a delaying tactic by Batista to gain time and pressure the "opposition" to accept a shameful compromise formula.

"The House," according to its president, Gastón Godoy, "claims priority in introducing and discussing the Amnesty Bill, which we all want to see put into effect, because it believes that this conforms to a correct interpretation of the Law of Relations. The bill will be discussed as soon as this interpretation has been accepted by the Commission on Justice and Law."

It was significant that Andrés Rivero Agüero, one of the main figures in Batista's ruling team, publicly backed the amnesty in the midst of this controversy. Everyone was well aware of the fact that Rivero was really speaking for Batista himself. "It is quite possible," said Rivero, the former minister of education, future prime minister, and presidential candidate in the 1958 election, "that the Amnesty Law will become a reality, not only because it

19. Marta Rojas, "Carlos Prío puede y debe regresar a Cuba, dice el general Batista" (Carlos Prío can and should return to Cuba, General Batista says), *Bohemia*, February 27, 1955, p. 59.

is supported by all citizens, but because the president of the republic and his cabinet fully share the people's feeling." Then he added something that no member of the regime had dared to say until then: "It is quite possible that this law will include those imprisoned for the events at the Moncada garrison."

The dictatorship was clearly beginning to negotiate on this matter once again, hoping to further paralyze the passive opposition with high-sounding phrases. Because of the opposition's many shadings and its slight importance, it is not necessary to analyze why it was willing to go along with the conditions the government intended to set for "granting" amnesty. What is much more important is the reaction of those who were always disregarded in such discussions: the "Moncada boys." It is important to recognize that the government spokesmen seemed to lack both the skill and the determination of their opponents. The tyrant finally lost the battle of attempted bribery. The document containing Fidel's reply is a stroke of genius. Two paragraphs from the letter that accompanied it read:

This is a time of doubt, vacillation, compromise, letters to Nixon,[20] ambitions, etc., so we must be firmer than ever. Two or three days ago, Agustín Tamargo's column "Time in Cuba" carried a report that Guas[21] had made efforts to see me and

---

20. Fidel was referring to the letter Carlos Prío had sent to U.S. Vice-President Richard Nixon that month, when he learned of the latter's plans to visit Cuba. The idea for the letter came from Guillermo Alonso Pujol, vice-president of the republic deposed by the March 10 coup. Drawn up by Carlos Hevia (Authentic Party candidate for president in the aborted 1952 election), Pedro Martínez Fraga, and René Fiallo, it was delivered to Nixon at the White House by Teodoro Tejeda Setién, Luis Gustavo Fernández, and Fabio Ruiz, national police chief under Prío. The letter was yet another demonstration of the class dependency on Yankee imperialism of the right-wing opposition to Batista and had no effect whatsoever in deterring Eisenhower's representative from visiting the Caribbean. It was essentially an invitation to the United States to intervene in Cuba's internal affairs. The intervention already existed, but in favor of Batista. Prío sought to turn it around to benefit himself, but that was a useless effort. The White House and the State Department expressed their approval and satisfaction with "the efforts of President Batista's government," just as they approved of Trujillo in the Dominican Republic, Pérez Jiménez in Venezuela, and Somoza in Nicaragua.
21. Rafael (Felo) Guas Inclán.

that Guido[22] said I had assured him that, if I were freed, I would devote myself to legal political activities.

I don't know what the intention was — it might even have been mentioned in order to help the campaign. I cannot, however, allow such statements to go unchallenged. I don't think Guido would have said such a thing anyway, because we have never discussed the matter. You know that right now many people are getting ready for politicking, and they hope we will at least show some sign of weakness. There is not the slightest doubt that after nearly two years in prison, solitary confinement, etc., etc., I would be prepared to go through another, similar period — and as many more as may be necessary — rather than give the slightest ground to those who would like to undermine our moral stature. I will give this to the compañeros to read and sign as well, to indicate that I am expressing their views, but it should appear over my signature alone. This time the responsibility is mine — just as the question of the two-month sentence reduction was theirs.

He passed the document on to the other Moncada prisoners, and they all approved it. It was dated March 19, 1955, and was published in the March 27 issue of *Bohemia*:

To be imprisoned is to be condemned to silence; to listen to what is said and to read what is written without being able to comment; to be attacked by cowards who take advantage of the circumstances to fight those who cannot defend themselves and who make statements that would deserve an immediate reply from us if we were not physically prevented from doing so.

We know that all this must be borne with stoicism, calmness, and courage, as part of the sacrifice and bitter price that every ideal demands. Nevertheless, there are times when it is necessary to overcome all obstacles because it is impossible to keep quiet without having your dignity wounded. I am not

---

22. Guido García Inclán.

writing this to seek the applause that so often exceeds the apparent merits of a theatrical gesture but is denied to those who do their duty simply and naturally. I write this from an upright conscience, out of the consideration, respect, and loyalty I owe the people.

As in his other writings, Fidel displayed a consciousness of history and a concern for the people:

The interest in our freedom shown by so many citizens springs from the masses' innate sense of justice and the deep human feelings of a people that is not and cannot be indifferent. This now irrepressible feeling has been submerged in an orgy of demagogy, hypocrisy, opportunism, and bad faith.

Probably thousands of citizens and perhaps more than a few officials of the regime have wondered what the political prisoners think of all this. Interest has grown over whether the amnesty will be applied to the Moncada group — those excluded from all amnesties, the target of all the worst cruelty, and the key to the whole problem. I do not know whether we are more hated or feared! Some have said, "Even the Moncada group will be included." They cannot mention us without inserting "even," "included," or "excluded." They raise doubts and vacillate, knowing for a fact that if a survey were made, 99 percent of the people would demand amnesty for us, because it is not so easy to fool the people or hide the truth from them.

They are not sure, however, what the 1 percent of those in uniform think. And they fear — with good reason — that they might offend them, because they have been poisoning the military against us — falsifying the facts, imposing prior censorship for 90 days, and decreeing the Law of Public Order. All this was done in order to cover up what happened at the Moncada, which side behaved in a humane way in that battle, and which side committed the actions that history will someday record with horror.

How strange have been the regime's actions toward us! In public they call us murderers and in private, gentlemen. In public they fight us with bitterness, yet in private they come to make our acquaintance. One day it's an army colonel with his staff who presents me with a cigar and offers me a book, all very courteously.[23] Another day three ministers appear, all smiles, friendly and respectful. One of them says, "Don't worry, all this will pass. I myself planted lots of bombs and was getting ready to kill Machado at the Country Club; I was also a political prisoner."[24]

The usurper held a press conference in Santiago de Cuba in which he stated that public opinion did not support us. A few days later, a most unusual event took place: at a mass meeting held by a party to which I do not belong — the largest mobilization of the campaign, according to the commentators — the people of Oriente constantly shouted our names and demanded our freedom. What a tremendous response by brave and loyal people who know full well what took place at the Moncada!

It is now up to us to respond, also in a civic spirit. The regime has issued us a moral challenge, declaring that there will be amnesty if the prisoners and exiles retreat from their stance, if there is a tacit or expressed commitment to respect the government.

The Pharisees once asked Christ whether or not they should pay tribute to Caesar. Any reply he made would be bound to offend either Caesar or the people. The Pharisees of all times have used that trick. Today they are trying either to discredit us in the eyes of the people or find a pretext for keeping us in prison.

I am not at all interested in convincing the regime to grant the amnesty. That does not matter to me in the least. What I am interested in, is to show how false its statements are, how hypocritical its words, and what a vile, cowardly maneuver it is using against the men who are in prison for having fought against it.

---

23. Fidel is referring to Colonel Dámaso Sogo's visit to his cell.
24. Fidel is referring to the visit of Gastón Godoy, Marino López Blanco, and Ramón O. Hermida on July 26, 1954.

The government officials have said they can afford to be generous because they are strong — while really they are vengeful because they are weak. They have said they bear us no hatred, yet they have treated us in a way no other group of Cubans has ever been treated.

"There will be amnesty when there is peace." What moral right do men who have spent three years publicly stating that they made their coup d'état to bring peace to the republic have for saying that? There is no peace; the coup d'état did not bring any peace. So now, after three years of dictatorship, the regime has admitted it lied by finally confessing that there has been no peace in Cuba since the day it seized power.

For many months they said, "The best proof that there is no dictatorship is the fact that there are no political prisoners." Now, with so many in prison and in exile, they cannot say any longer that this is a constitutional, democratic regime. They are damned by their own words.

"The regime's opponents will have to retreat from their stance before there can be amnesty." In other words, the regime commits a crime against our people and then holds us as hostages — just as the Nazis did in the countries they occupied. Today we are therefore more than political prisoners; we are hostages of the dictatorship.

"There must be a commitment to respect the regime before there can be amnesty." The miserable creatures who suggested this assume that those of us who have spent 20 months in exile, imprisoned on this island, have lost our sense of purpose because of the excessive hardships imposed on us. Those officials, in the comfortable, well-paid posts they would like to keep forever, have the gall to use such terms to men a thousand times more honorable than they, who are kept behind bars.

This writer has spent 16 months in solitary confinement but feels he has enough energy to respond with dignity. Our imprisonment is unjust. I do not see how those who stormed the garrisons to overthrow the legitimate constitution, which the people had approved, robbing them of their sovereignty and freedom, can possibly have any justice on their side or the right to rule the republic against the will of the people. Meanwhile those who sought to have the constitution respected, who fought to give sovereignty and freedom back to the people, and who remained loyal to their principles rot in prison.

Look at the records of those in power, and you will see that they are full of crooked deals, corruption, and ill-gotten wealth. Compare them with the lives of those who died in Santiago de Cuba and those of us in prison here, which are without blemish or dishonor. Our personal freedom is an inalienable right as citizens born in a nation that recognizes no master of any kind. We can be deprived of these and all other rights by force, but no one can ever make us agree to regain them by unworthy compromise. We will not give up one iota of our honor in return for our freedom.

The ones who must commit themselves to accepting and respecting the laws of the republic are those who ignominiously violated them on March 10. Those who must respect sovereignty and the will of the nation are those who scandalously made a mockery of them on November 1. Those who must foster a climate of tranquility and peaceful coexistence in the country are those who for three years have kept the country in turmoil and on the brink of disaster. It is they who bear the responsibility. Without the March 10 coup the battle of July 26 would not have been necessary, and no Cuban would now be suffering political imprisonment.

We are not disturbers of the peace or blind proponents of violence; we would not resort to violence if the better homeland for which we long could be attained with the weapons of reason and intelligence. No people would follow a group of adventurers who tried to submerge the country in civil conflict if injustice did not predominate and peaceful and legal means had not been denied to all citizens in the civic battle of ideas.

We believe, as did Martí, that "he who promotes a war in a country where it can be avoided is a criminal, just as he who fails to promote a war that is inevitable is also a criminal." We would never encourage the Cuban nation to fight a civil war that could be avoided. I insist, however, that whenever circumstances in Cuba reach a point of such ignominy as those that followed the sinister coup of March 10, it would be a crime not to promote the inevitable rebellion.

If we considered that a change in circumstances and a positive climate of constitutional guarantees demanded a change of tactics in the struggle, we would make that change. But we would do so solely out of respect for the interests and aspirations of the nation — never because of a compromise with the government. That would be cowardly and shameful. If that is what is demanded of us in exchange for our freedom, our reply is a resounding "No."

No, we are not tired. After 20 months, we feel as firm and upright as on the first day. We do not want amnesty at the expense of honor. We will not suffer the great humiliation of submitting to ignoble oppressors. A thousand years in prison before we submit to humiliation! A thousand years in prison before we sacrifice our dignity! We proclaim this quite calmly, without fear or hatred.

If what is needed at this moment are Cubans who will sacrifice themselves in order to save our people's civic pride, we offer ourselves gladly. We are young and have no petty ambitions. The political hacks have nothing to fear from us as they move — in more or less cunning ways — toward the carnival of personal aspirations, forgetting the great injustices injuring our homeland.

We will not ask them for amnesty, nor even to improve the conditions of our imprisonment, through which the regime has demonstrated all its hatred and brutality. As Antonio Maceo once said, "The only thing we would accept with pleasure from our enemies would be a bloody gallows — which other, more fortunate compañeros have known how to face with heads high and the calm knowledge that they were dying for the just and sacred cause of freedom."

Today, some 77 years after the heroic protest by the Bronze Titan, we, as his spiritual heirs, also reject all such

shameful compromises.[25]
Fidel Castro
Isle of Pines, March 19, 1955

Infamy once again
The die was now cast. The massive mobilization of the people was leading towards a revolutionary situation. To keep Fidel and the rest of the Moncada prisoners in jail and run the risk of a popular explosion; or give in to the noble rebel who would not submit: these were the alternatives faced by the dictatorship. But the people's immediate action soon gave the rogues in power no choice.

May 15 was preceded by ever-deepening convulsions. There would be more actions such as the street demonstrations of the most militant youth, starting in Havana and spreading from town to town. The Orthodox Youth, led by Martínez Tinguao, went on a "civic tour" and got into a fight when police attacked Andrés Luján,[26] Israel Escalona,[27] Efigenio Ameijeiras,[28] Santiago Terry, and many others in San José de las Lajas. The young men were staunchly supported by the Martí Women's Civic Front, under the leadership of Aida Pelayo.

Ever broader sectors of the population joined the popular clamor, protesting the regime's disgraceful response. The following news article reflects the growing unrest:

All Cuba calls for the Amnesty Law. The whole country fervently demands legislation that will send back to their troubled homes all these good and patriotic Cubans. The pressure of the people is such that government officials admit that even

---

25. One of the leaders of the Cuban independence war, General Antonio Maceo, was known as the Bronze Titan. In 1878 he issued the Baraguá Protest, repudiating the treaty with Spain that ended the Ten Years War.
26. Andrés Luján (Chibás) came on the *Granma* expedition and was killed shortly after the landing.
27. Israel Escalona was killed two years later in the underground urban struggle.
28. Efigenio Ameijeiras went into exile, returned on the *Granma*, and fought in the mountains under the direct command of Fidel and Raúl throughout the duration of the war. He became a commander in the Rebel Army.

their own followers favor total political amnesty.

The regime is determined not to approve it for the moment, because no one has come forth to pay the exorbitant and humiliating price so "generously" demanded by these merchants. Instead, the usurpers of power have now taken the offensive, filling newspapers with statements supporting the law but at the same time heaping the basest insults on those who would benefit from it.

This tactic, this strategic shift toward angry opposition to the call for amnesty, is a very serious error. No matter how many opposition newspapers and radio stations they close down they will be unable to alter or stem what is now a deep national conviction, a collective aspiration.[29]

Once again dignity was countered with infamy. Fidel was brought before the prison Administrative Council and again sentenced to total isolation. An attempt was made at the prison court to prove complicity in smuggling out of prison the document repudiating any amnesty contingent on the sacrifice of principles. And, as at the Santiago de Cuba trial, the conclusive evidence for exonerating the other defendants — in this case, some of the prison guards and the censor — came, strangely enough, from the accused himself, as shown by the following document:

The following members of the Administrative Council of the National Prison of the Isle of Pines met at 3:00 p.m. on March 26, 1955: Professor Artemio Silva Camejo, spokesman for education; Jacobo Costa Izquierdo, spokesman for work; First Lieutenant Luis Montesinos, delegate for the supervisor; Dr. Antolín Santurtún, medical director and chairman of the council; and Dr. César Cuní y Téllez, acting secretary.

The plenary meeting of the council was called to study and forward the document drawn up by the head of Internal Order and the attached copy of *Bohemia* magazine, dated

---

29. *Diario Nacional*, April 5. 1955.

March 25,[30] containing on pages 63 and 94 the article "Letter on Amnesty" signed by Fidel Castro Ruz, prisoner no. 3859, convicted in Case 37 of 1953 by the Provisional Court of Santiago de Cuba for violating the stability of the republic.

First Lieutenant Pedro Rodríguez Coto, in charge of Internal Order, here declares that neither he nor his personnel gave orders permitting the said article to leave prison.

Mr. José Miguel Rives, director of archives and official censor, here declares that he did not clear any correspondence that might have included the said article.

Fidel Castro Ruz, prisoner no. 3859, here declares: "I assume full responsibility for the article, in which my ideas are correctly expressed. I give my word of honor, however, that no official of this prison is guilty of any negligence or lack of vigilance regarding this matter. I have nothing else to declare." The document is signed by those present.[31]

That same day the secretary of the Administrative Council sent the chairman of the Supreme Council for Social Defense a notice certifying the decision "to sentence the prisoner to 30 days solitary confinement."

Three days later, the Administrative Council met again to study another document sent by the prison's head of Internal Order concerning Fidel's article in *Bohemia* magazine. According to the document: "His accomplice is his brother Raúl Castro Ruz, who shares Fidel's cell and who is also here serving his sentence for Case 37 of 1953 of the Provisional Court of Santiago de Cuba, in which he was convicted for having violated the stability of the republic." This time, the council did not even bother to call in the new defendant but decided "to apply to prisoner Raúl Castro Ruz the same sentence it has given Fidel Castro Ruz."

On March 27 *Bohemia* published a statement by FEU President José Antonio Echeverría, who, with his characteristic militancy,

---

30. The issue of *Bohemia* referred to was actually dated March 27, 1955.
31. The document is signed by Fidel Castro Ruz, First Lieutenant Pedro R. Coto, José Miguel Pérez Pantoja, First Lieutenant Luis Montesinos, Dr. Antolín Santurtún Zabala, Artemio Silva Camejo, and Dr. César Cuní y Téllez.

attacked the regime and the opportunist politicians and defended the political prisoners:

> The call for general amnesty is the demand of all citizens, to which the students have given our full support. We cannot remain indifferent when so many comrades are held as political prisoners for defending the honor of our nation, besmirched by the March 10 coup. We denounce, however, the contemptible spectacle of all those politicians who, after taking every possible advantage of the shameful November 1 election to get a few crumbs from the regime, now parade as defenders of our imprisoned comrades, whose ideals they have betrayed.
>
> The cry of the people is stronger than ever: Free every one of these worthy enemies of the dictatorship! Any attempt to exclude the Moncada fighters from the amnesty will be repudiated by public opinion. We must not expect any spontaneous generosity from this regime, which will only consent to a general political amnesty when the pressure of public opinion becomes irresistible. We must therefore unite all our forces to free our brothers from the belly of the monster. We therefore repeat:
>
> Free all the fighters against the dictatorship!

In its April 5 edition, the *Diario Nacional* protested the fact that Fidel's sisters had not been allowed to see him on the first Friday of that month, because of his firm stand against the government. This is how his new sentence to solitary confinement was made public:

> In every home, neighborhood, town, and province of Cuba, people are talking about amnesty, and of course about Fidel Castro. But although he is the center of this national discussion, he cannot speak out on the matter. The rulers consider a political prisoner to be an object, with no right to express his opinions.

"Is it fair to lock a person up in solitary confinement just because he has said he does not want amnesty if it means sacrificing his honor?" the writer Luis Conte Agüero asked, adding:

> Fidel's situation in the Model Prison cannot continue. Every-
> thing points to the need to transfer him and the rest of the
> Moncada prisoners to the La Cabaña prison at once. Tragedy is
> stalking his cell, and it would be wise to avoid it. Besides,
> their transfer to La Cabaña would be in compliance with the
> sentence of the Provisional Court of Santiago de Cuba, which
> ordered them to be confined in that military prison.

The April 10 edition of *Bohemia* magazine included an item in the
"In Cuba" section protesting the fact that Fidel had once again
been sentenced to solitary confinement:

> While the conscience of the nation categorically demands
> political amnesty and the legislative bodies are discussing the
> terms of what is not a handout but a public duty, the
> authorities respond by throwing Fidel Castro into solitary
> confinement and leaving him there, according to his relatives,
> with no radio,[32] letters, newspapers, magazines, or even sun-
> light.

In this article, Enrique de la Osa described Fidel's document
(which the magazine had already published) as a "monument of
integrity and personal self-sacrifice," and wrote of the regime:

> The government has acted in a petty way. Defeated, impris-
> oned, sentenced by the courts, this staunch Moncada combat-
> ant is a man whose enemies may or may not agree with him,
> but have to respect him. To isolate him completely is to con-
> centrate the attack on this upright figure of the opposition.
> Moreover, this is being done by a regime whose representa-
> tives are supposedly far from harboring grudges, rancor, or
> revenge. Paradoxically their own actions are making a symbol

---

32. Since July 1954, Fidel had had a small radio in his cell — a Silvertone 3004,
serial number 757130, bought at the Sears Roebuck store at the corner of Amistad
and Reina streets, in Havana.

out of the solitary prisoner on the Isle of Pines.

Events gather momentum

April was a month of an incredible show of servility. The regime gave Electric Bond and Share 10 million pesos "for its industrial expansion," according to the report detailing the money that an underdeveloped country was giving the company that exploited it and, besides, charged it the highest electricity rates in all Latin America. William S. Stafford, representative of this multi-million-dollar consortium, happily received the check from Jorge "Yoyo" García-Montes, recently appointed prime minister of the Batista regime, who represented the Cuban National Finance Agency, a state body supposedly created to develop the country.

Events gathered momentum, however, and public pressure for amnesty reached a point that was very dangerous for the regime.

This already extremely heated atmosphere was exacerbated by the reappearance of Luis Orlando Rodríguez' newspaper *La Calle* whose circulation at times reached an unprecedented 50,000 copies. This paper had been closed down on August 16, 1952, the first anniversary of the death of Eduardo Chibás, when its very first issue was seized by the police. Luis Orlando was not able to resume publication until Thursday, April 1, 1955, when he became the main spokesman for the amnesty campaign.

Other events in April, when Fidel's new sentence to solitary confinement was made public, brought into view the strategic polarization of forces that was developing in the country.

On April 14, police seized another arsenal belonging to one of Prío's groups. A dozen M-1 rifles, several Garands, 1,500 grenades, and 20,000 bullets were captured at 327 Rabí Street, in the Víbora section of Havana.

Rumors that an election would be held at the end of the following year brought forward a new proto-party whose stand was in shameful contrast to the amnesty campaign. Called the Movement of the Nation, it included the ever-present Jorge Mañach, former member of the ABC and the Orthodox Party; José Pardo Llada, the accommodating former member of the Orthodox Party and Montreal group; economists Justo Carrillo and Rufo López Fresquet, former leaders of Action for Liberty; Vicente

Rubiera, sell-out union leader of the telephone workers; Jorge Quintana, the obese president of the Reporters' Association; and other, lesser personalities. The "shifters," as it was soon called because of its founders' ambiguous and shifting political positions, broke up into many factions and disappeared into thin air within a few months. Emerging in a moment of recklessness, however, it entered the political arena with a rash of promises to the people.

Meanwhile, FEU President José Antonio Echeverría denounced the poor timing of these political maneuvers. Echeverría, who had won respect in street clashes with the police, by his militant opposition to the 1954 election, as head of the protest against the "break up Cuba" canal, and for going to Central America and to join the Costa Rican people's armed battle against Somoza's aggression,[33] denounced these untimely political maneuvers. In an article published in *Bohemia* on April 17, Echeverría wrote:

> We have said, and we repeat, that the prevailing national situation permits only two positions, two parties: with Cuba and against Batista, or with Batista and against Cuba.
>
> The March 10 regime has consistently shown its determination to hold on to power indefinitely, using force against the sovereign will of our people. The recent November 1 "election," by which Batista kept himself in power in flagrant violation of the nation's will, makes it quite clear that there is no place for an opposition movement that naively believes it can wrest away that power at the polls. Only by militant national action that reaffirms the principles of the Cuban revolution, which is already underway in our homeland, will this dark period in the history of our republic be erased.

As the nation's forces became increasingly polarized, this road to

---

33. On January 11, 1955, Nicaraguan dictator Anastasio Somoza organized a mercenary force to invade Costa Rica aimed at ousting the government of President José Figueres. Echeverría and a number of other Cuban student leaders volunteered to fight against the invasion of Costa Rica, thereby receiving military training which would prove useful in the revolutionary struggle in Cuba.

reaffirming the principles of the Cuban revolution to which José Antonio referred ran through a cell in the prison hospital on the Isle of Pines.

And along this road the wave of popular pressure was already becoming an irresistible force — leaving the government with but one alternative.

On Tuesday, May 2, the House of Representatives approved the Amnesty Law, after the Presidential Palace had hastily given it the green light. The Senate adopted it on Wednesday, May 3, and sent it on to the "president."

One hundred and twelve amnesty laws had been approved during the republic's 53 years of frustrations. This was number 113 — a symbolic number, since it happened to be the prison number that Spanish colonialism had given a 16-year-old political prisoner in 1870: José Martí. With that same number Fidel Castro was released under this Amnesty Law.

On Friday, May 6, Prime Minister García Montes sent this official statement to the press: "The president of the republic has just signed the law on amnesty for political crimes passed by the Congress. In honor of Mother's Day, the president has immediately endorsed the constitutional measure,[34] making this generous initiative the law of the land."

The people had broken the locks, and the prison doors opened on Sunday, May 15.

Tactical and strategic vision

First and foremost, from a general tactical point of view, the amnesty campaign had succeeded in freeing Fidel and his comrades. But another objective had already been achieved before this victory. It had consolidated a series of conditions that would be of decisive importance for the future development of the revolution:

1. It attacked and weakened the dictatorship within the limits of the legal framework.

2. In appealing to positive sentiments of justice, it stimulated

---

34. Signed by Fulgencio Batista, Prime Minister Jorge García-Montes, and Minister of Justice César E. Camacho, Law 2 was published the following day in the *Official Gazette*. (See appendix for the complete text.)

political activity against the regime among broad sectors that had thus far demonstrated only an inactive opposition.

3. It gained widespread publicity that attracted and revived the public interest in the prisoners and the actions of July 26, 1953; and about their conduct, ideals, program, and point of view, which differed from those of the rest of the opposition on how to confront the dictatorship.

4. It became a vehicle for the legal creation of discussion groups, many of whose members from that initial contact later joined the revolutionary movement.

5. A number of other activities besides the amnesty campaign were carried out, including assisting the combatants who had not been arrested; providing support for the families of the dead; collecting and sending supplies to the prisoners; and, very importantly, printing, distributing, and publicizing *History Will Absolve Me*. This helped reestablish contact with many other scattered members of the organization — both those who had and had not participated in the July 26 actions — and incorporated many others. These activities also forged ties with various revolutionary groups that later would become part of the July 26 Revolutionary Movement, which was soon to be established.

From a broader, strategic perspective, it can be compared with the Battle of El Jigüe in July 1958, three years later. In military terms, that battle constituted the turning point of the war in favor of the Rebel Army and accelerated the triumph of the revolution. In a similar way, the battle waged by the Moncada group during their imprisonment and the battle the people waged to set them free represented, in historical terms, the turning point in the country's political situation in favor of the revolutionary vanguard that emerged at the Moncada. This in turn meant the liquidation of the dictatorship and with it the oppressive system of social injustice and exploitation.

The leaders of the March coup, who were forced to approve the amnesty, failed to foresee these results. The defeat imposed on them by the unanimous action of the people was counteracted, in their eyes, by the indecisiveness, division, weakness, and lack of prestige of the splintered traditional parties that made up the legal opposition.

The regime's arrogance kept it from understanding what had happened that day in May.

When the doors of the National Men's Prison on the Isle of Pines swung open, the members of the vanguard who had been inside were reunited both with one another and with those who had remained outside, as they took up the banner of their fallen comrades.

It was May 15. The revolution — whose bright dawn had been first announced by the bells at the La Demajagua Sugar Mill[35] which had fallen and then risen again at Baraguá;[36] its colors were raised at Baire;[37] to fall again and be revived three times during the shameful Republic — this same revolution, set back but still undefeated was now released beyond the prison bars.

It was May 15, 1955, just four days before the 60th anniversary of José Martí's death at Dos Rios.[38] Four days later, the dialogue between the disciples and their teacher continued in freedom — the freedom of a revolution that could not be imprisoned. With a pledge signed in blood, this same revolution would carry with it the eternal destiny of a people.

---

35. On October 10, 1868, Carlos Manuel de Céspedes, whom Cubans consider the father of his country, freed the slaves who worked in his La Demajagua Sugar Mill; proclaimed a war of independence against Spain; and, with a group of his followers, began that war.

36. Baraguá, on the eastern coast of what used to be Oriente Province, was where Gen. Antonio Maceo repudiated the Zanjón Pact that put an end to the Ten Years' War, begun under the leadership of Céspedes on October 10, 1868. Maceo's action is recorded in Cuban history as the Baraguá Protest.

37. Baire, in the eastern part of the country, symbolizes the reinitiation of the war of independence on February 24, 1895, under the leadership of José Martí.

38. Dos Ríos was the place in Oriente Province where José Martí was killed in combat against the Spanish army on May 19, 1895.

Glossary

AAA — Also known as the Triple A, an underground organization led by Aureliano Sánchez, former minister in the government of Carlos Prío overthrown by Fulgencio Batista on March 10, 1952. It grouped together former student leaders in the struggle against the Machado dictatorship (1927-33) and politicians from the Authentic Party governments. Its strategy was based on convincing leaders of the armed forces to carry out a coup d'état against Batista. The AAA had virtually disappeared by the time of the overthrow of the Batista dictatorship on January 1, 1959.

Agramonte Loynaz, Ignacio (1841-1873) — Lawyer; came from a rich family in Camagüey. Together with other patriots in the region he joined the 1868 uprising against Spanish rule led by de Céspedes, establishing a reputation as a brilliant military leader. A signatory to the constitution of Guáimaro (1869), he was killed in the battle of Jimaguayú on May 11, 1873 at the age of 32. His body was burnt by Spanish troops. He is known in Cuban history as the Major.

Alcalde Valls, Oscar (1926-) — Former accountant; member of the Civil Committee of the revolutionary movement led by Fidel Castro. A participant in the attack on the Moncada military barracks on July 26, 1953, he was sentenced to 13 years' imprisonment and released May 15, 1955. He is currently president of the People's Savings Bank in Cuba.

Almeida Bosque, Juan (1927-) — Former bricklayer. A participant in the Moncada attack, he was sentenced to 10 years' imprisonment and released May 15, 1955. A member of the *Granma* expedition of 1956, he became a Rebel Army commander in February 1958 and in March 1958 was named head of the "Mario Muñoz Monroy" Third Front of Oriente. In 1959, after the victory of the revolution, he was commander of the air force and head of the Rebel Army. In later years he held a number of posts including head of the army in central Cuba, vice-minister of the Revolutionary Armed Forces, chief of operations of the army general staff, and head of the construction industry. Currently he is a member of the Political Bureau of the Central Committee of the Communist Party of Cuba, president of its National Control and Revision Commission, vice-president of the Council of State, and chairman of the Commission to Perpetuate the Memory of Commander Ernesto Che Guevara.

Authentic Party (Partido Revolucionario Cubano (Auténtico) — Cuban Revolutionary (Authentic) Party) — Taking its name from the party founded by José Martí, it was organized in June 1934 by Ramón Grau San Martín and other anti-Machado fighters. Its first participation in elections was the contest for delegates to the 1940 Constituent Assembly and that year's general elections. In 1944 its candidate Grau San Martín was elected president, and in 1948 Carlos Prío was elected on its ticket. Frustrating the hopes of the mass of people, these administrations were characterized by a notable increase in corruption and graft. At the same time, the country's political system degenerated into virtual anarchy, and widespread attacks were launched against the workers' movement. The party became commonly known as the Authentic Party.

Authentic Youth (Juventud Auténtica) — Youth group of the Cuban Revolutionary (Authentic) Party.

Batista y Zaldívar, Rubén Fulgencio (1901-1973) — Former army sergeant. Together with other noncomissioned officers he led a rebellion on September 4, 1933, that overthrew the army's high command and helped install a government composed of representatives of the anti-Machado forces. He was then named colonel and head of the army. On January 15, 1934, with the complicity of the U.S. ambassador, Jefferson Caffery, he overthrew the provisional government of Ramón Grau San Martín (within which the anti-imperialist fighter Antonio Guiteras had played an outstanding role). As dictator and head of the general staff, Batista appointed and removed presidential figureheads. Popular struggles forced him to permit the convening of a Constituent Assembly, which in 1940 approved a new constitution. He was elected president that year in elections widely viewed as having been rigged. He left Cuba to live in the United States after finishing his term in 1944, with a stolen fortune estimated at 16 million pesos. Returning to Cuba in 1948, he headed the March 10, 1952, coup that overthrew President Carlos Prío. With support from the U.S. government he established another dictatorship, the most repressive in the country's history. He fled Cuba with an estimated fortune of over $200 million on January 1, 1959 following the victory of the revolutionary forces led by Fidel Castro. He died in exile in 1973.

Bedía Morales, René (1923-1956) — Former house painter. A participant in the Moncada attack, he was sentenced to 10 years' imprisonment and released May 15, 1955. A *Granma* expeditionary, he was killed by government troops on December 8, 1956, in the foothills of the Sierra Maestra. He was 33 years old.

Benítez Nápoles, Reinaldo (1927-) — Former store employee. Wounded in the Moncada attack, he was sentenced to 10 years' imprisonment and released May 15, 1955. A participant in the *Granma* expedition, he was captured and sentenced to six years' in prison, but was freed on January 1, 1959. He is currently retired.

Bohemia — Weekly magazine founded in 1908. The largest-circulation weekly in Cuba, it had a circulation of 255,000 in early 1955. In the 1950s it was one of the main forums open to the forces opposed to the Batista dictatorship.

Bravo Pardo, Flavio (1921-1988) — A member of Cuba's first Communist Party since 1937. Founder of the Socialist Youth in 1944, he served as its chairman until 1956. In 1945 he became a member of the Central Committee of the Popular Socialist Party. While functioning underground, he served on the party's Political Bureau and was secretary of education and propaganda responsible for its underground press. After the revolution's victory he held a number of posts, among them as an organizer of the National Revolutionary Militias and as chief of operations of the Oriente army and the general staff. He was a combatant at the Bay of Pigs (Playa Girón). In 1965 he became a member of the Central Committee of the new Communist Party. In 1970 he was in charge of the consumer goods' industry and of domestic trade. He became vice-prime minister in 1972 and was a member of the Council of State and vice-president of the Council of Ministers. At the time of his death in 1988 he was president of the National

Assembly of People's Power.

Bronze Titan — Name given by Cuban history to General Antonio Maceo, one of the most brilliant and outstanding leaders of the independence forces of the 19th century.

Cámara Pérez, Gregorio Enrique (1929-) — Former shoemaker. A participant in the Moncada attack, he was sentenced to 10 years' imprisonment and released May 15, 1955. A *Granma* expeditionary, he was captured and sentenced to six years in prison, but was freed on January 1, 1959. He is currently retired.

Carta Semanal — Weekly underground newspaper published after the March 10, 1952 coup, reflecting the views of the Popular Socialist Party.

Castellanos García, Baudilio (1928-) — Lawyer; former leader of the Federation of University Students and fellow student of Fidel Castro at the University of Havana. He was the principal defense attorney for the imprisoned Moncada fighters in the trial of 1953. A member of the provincial leadership of the July 26 Movement at its founding in 1955. He also served as principal defense attorney for the members of the *Granma* expedition who were captured in 1956. Currently he is legal adviser for the Ministry of the Electrical Industry.

Castro Ruz, Fidel (1926-) — Law graduate from the University of Havana where he was first involved in politics. Joined Revolutionary Insurrectional Union (UIR), a student action group, in 1946. Founding member of the Cuban People's Party (Orthodox) in 1947, becoming a leader of its left wing. That same year he was part of an aborted armed expedition that had planned to go to the Dominican Republic to help overthrow the dictatorship of Rafael Trujillo. Attending a student conference in Bogotá, Colombia, in 1948, he participated in the *Bogotazo*, a massive rebellion that erupted while he was there. After graduating from law school, he ran for a position in the House of Representatives on the Orthodox ticket in the 1952 elections; the elections never took place because of the Batista coup of March 10, 1952. In response to the coup he began plans for an insurrection that were to culminate with the attack on the Moncada military barracks in Santiago de Cuba on July 26, 1953. The attack was crushed and he was subsequently arrested, surviving an attempt to summarily

execute him. He was tried and sentenced to 15 years imprisonment. His defense speech, *History Will Absolve Me*, later became
the program of the July 26 Movement. After being released from
prison on the Isle of Pines in 1955 as a result of a mass public
campaign, he went to Mexico where he began to organize the
forces that were to become the Rebel Army. Sailing on the yacht
Granma with 81 other guerrillas including his brother Raúl, Che
Guevara, Camilo Cienfuegos, and Juan Almeida, he landed in the
province of Oriente on December 2, 1956. It was from the nearby
Sierra Maestra mountains that he led the revolutionary war to
victory. With the flight of Batista on January 1, 1959, the war
came to an end, and Fidel Castro arrived triumphantly in Havana
on January 8. He served as prime minister of the revolutionary
government from February 1959 until December 1976, when he
became president of the Council of State and the Council of
Ministers. He has been the first secretary of the Communist Party
of Cuba since its founding in 1965.

Castro Ruz, Raúl Modesto (1931-) — Former student of social
sciences at the University of Havana, where he quickly allied
himself to the Marxist left. A leader of the José Martí Congress for
the Rights of Youth in 1953, he was a delegate to the international
youth congress in Vienna that same year. From there he traveled
to Romania. He participated in the Moncada attack and was
sentenced to 13 years' imprisonment. Released May 15, 1955, he
was forced shortly thereafter to take asylum in the Mexican
Embassy and go into exile. He was a member of the *Granma*
expedition and headed the Rebel Army's rearguard platoon. In
February 1958 he became a Rebel Army commander in charge of
a column in northeast Oriente Province, and headed the "Frank
País" Second Front of Oriente until the end of the war. In 1959 he
became minister of the Revolutionary Armed Forces, a post he
continues to hold. He is currently second secretary of the
Communist Party of Cuba and a member of its Central Committee and Political Bureau. Since 1959 he has been vice-president of
the Council of Ministers. He has served as first vice-president of
the Council of State since 1976.

Centennial Youth — Young people who engaged in intensive
political and revolutionary activity in 1953 in response to the

institutional crisis following the March 10, 1952, military coup. The term was derived from the fact that 1953 was the centennial of José Martí's birth (January 28, 1853). Since the most important event of 1953 in Cuba was the attack on the Moncada military garrison led by Fidel Castro, the veterans of that attack became identified in contemporary Cuban history as the Centennial Youth or the Centennial Generation.

Céspedes Castillo, Carlos Manuel de (1819-1874) — Lawyer, poet, narrator, dramatist; wealthy landowner in southwest of the old province of Oriente. At his La Demajagua sugar mill on October 10, 1868, he freed his slaves, proclaimed the Republic of Cuba, and launched Cuba's first war against Spanish colonialism in what became known as the Cry of Yara. He was supreme commander of the Cuban independence army until April 12, 1869, when the first Cuban constitution was drafted in Guáimaro and he was proclaimed president of the Republic in Arms, holding this post until October 27, 1873. Killed in battle against the Spanish army in San Lorenzo, Sierra Maestra, on February 27, 1874. He is regarded in Cuban history as the Father of the Nation.

Chibás y Rivas, Eduardo René (1907-1951) — Member of the 1927 University Student Directorate. Together with Antonio Guiteras and others he helped lead the struggle against Machado's unconstitutional extension of his presidential term in 1927. In the 1930s he fought both the Machado and Caffery-Batista-Mendieta dictatorships. A member of the Authentic Party, he was a delegate to the 1940 Constituent Assembly and was later a representative and senator of the Cuban Revolutionary (Authentic) Party. In 1947 he founded the Cuban People's (Orthodox) Party and became its central leader. In 1951 he publicly committed suicide to protest the rampant vice and corruption in Cuban political life.

Conte Agüero, Luis (1924-) — Journalist; graduate in philosophy and letters, and a former leader of the Federation of University Students at the University of Havana. In 1947 he was a founding member of the Cuban People's (Orthodox) Party. A leader of the Orthodox Youth, he served as head of the party's Secretariat. During the years of the Batista dictatorship he opposed the perspective of armed struggle. After the revolution's victory in 1959 he fled to the United States, where he has written various works against the Cuban revolution.

Cuban People's Party — See Orthodox Party

Cuban Revolutionary (Authentic) Party — See Authentic Party

Díaz González, Julio (1929-1957) — Former store employee and student. A participant in the Moncada attack, he was sentenced to 10 years' imprisonment and was released on May 15, 1955. A *Granma* expeditionary, he became a captain in the Rebel Army. He was killed at the Battle of El Uvero in the Sierra Maestra on May 28, 1957, at the age of 27.

Echeverría Bianchi, José Antonio (1932-1957) — Architectural student at the University of Havana and a leader of the revolutionary radicalization of university students in the struggle against the Batista dictatorship. In 1954 he was elected president of the Federation of University Students, a position he held until his death. He was an organizer of many student street demonstrations in the years 1952-56 and was injured and jailed a number of times. After having belonged to various insurrectional organizations, in 1955 he founded the Revolutionary Directorate, and became its central leader. In September 1956 he met with Fidel Castro and they issued a unity pact known as the Mexico Letter. He carried out intensive underground and semi-underground activity, including urban armed struggle. This culminated in the heroic assault on the Presidential Palace on March 13, 1957, which resulted in his death. Together with Julio Antonio Mella he is viewed as a symbol of Cuba's revolutionary students. He was 24 years of age when killed.

El Jigüe, Battle of — Took place July 10-20, 1958, in the southern part of the Sierra Maestra, between Rebel Army forces led by Fidel Castro and government troops, planes, and ships. Government forces suffered close to 100 casualties, 260 prisoners, and the loss of 300 weapons. It was the most important in a series of battles that routed Batista's army in the Sierra Maestra and enabled the Rebel Army to launch a counteroffensive, which continued up to the revolution's victory on January 1, 1959.

Espín Guillois, Vilma (1930-) — Former chemical engineer; participant in student struggles in Oriente Province. A member of Frank País' group, she belonged to the Revolutionary National Movement, Oriente Revolutionary Action, Revolutionary National

Action, and the July 26 Movement. A participant in the November 30, 1956, Santiago de Cuba uprising, she went underground in April 1957 and was named the July 26 Movement's coordinator in Oriente Province. In July 1958 she joined the Rebel Army and served in the "Frank País" Second Front of Oriente until the triumph of the revolution. She has been president of the Federation of Cuban Women since its founding in 1960. She has also served as chair of the Commission for Social Prevention (1967-71), director of industrial development for the food industry (1969-73), president of the Infancy Institute (1971-present), and vice president of the World Federation of Democratic Women (1973-present). She has been a member of the Communist Party's Central Committee since 1965, and has served on the Council of State since 1976.

Federation of University Students (Federación Estudiantil Universitaria — FEU) — Founded by Julio Antonio Mella in 1923 as an organization of students at the University of Havana. It has played an important role in Cuban political life, particularly in the struggle against the Machado dictatorship (1927-33), the first Batista dictatorship (1934-44), and the second Batista dictatorship (1952-58). Currently it incorporates all Cuban university students in the 14 provinces of the country.

Federation of University Students of Oriente (Federación Estudiantil Universitaria de Oriente — FEU-O) — Organization of students at the University of Oriente in Santiago de Cuba. During the struggle against Batista it played an active role under the leadership of Pepito Tey.

Fortuny Rodríguez, Mario (1911-1953) — Student of batchelor degree; he was incorporated at an early age into revolutionary life through involvement in the Anti-Imperialist League of Cuba. From 1927 he took part in the struggle against the Machado dictatorship. Member of the Alliance of the Student Left. Participating in many street actions and acts of sabotage, he was detained several times and in 1930, at the age of 19, was sent to prison on the Isle of Pines. After the fall of the Machado government he commenced work at the Emergency Hospital in Havana from where he continued political activity, now in the fight against the first Batista dictatorship. He was one of the organizers of the March 1935 general strike. Following the failure of the strike and being forced from his job, he commenced work as a retailer. After the coup of March 10, 1952 he founded, with others from the generation of fighters from the 1930s, the AAA or Triple A, an underground organization led by Aureliano Sánchez. Among his tasks was to capture military officials. He was eventually captured himself by the police on November 26, 1953 and shot the next day. Despite suffering savage torture he did not reveal to the Batista forces any of his extensive knowledge of the whereabouts of the AAA's secret arms caches nor the location of its leading members.

García-Montes Hernández, Jorge (Yoyo) (b. 1897-) — Lawyer. Began his political life in 1922 as a member of the rightist Conservative Party when he was elected to the House of Representatives for the province of Las Villas. Re-elected in 1926, he supported the unconstitutional extension of the term of the government that initiated the dictatorship of Gerardo Machado. Again elected to parliament in 1932, although the term was cut short with the downfall of the dictatorship in August 1933. In 1946 he was once again elected to the House of Representatives, this time for the rightist Democrat Party. As the head of this party in Las Villas, he supported the candidature of Fulgencio Batista when he nominated for the Senate in 1946. The following year he founded along with Batista the Unitary Action Party (PAU). Re-elected to parliament in 1950 he went on to become the parliamentary leader for the PAU in the lower chamber. He supported the coup of March 10, 1952 and was designated vice-president of the Consultative Council, an unconstitutional legislative body that substituted itself for the Congress (both the House of Representatives and the Senate). Becoming senator in the electoral farce of November 1, 1954, he was designated prime minister from February 24, 1955. Once again elected a senator in the false election of November 1, 1958 he was to seek refuge in the United States following the triumph of the revolution.

Gil Alfonso, Gabriel (1924-) — Former restaurant worker. A participant in the Moncada attack, he was sentenced to 10 years' imprisonment and released May 15, 1955. A participant in the *Granma* expedition, he was captured again and sentenced to six years in prison, but was freed on January 1, 1959. He is currently retired.

Gómez Báez, Máximo (1836-1905) — Born in Bani, in the Dominican Republic, he went to Cuba in 1865. After joining the 1868 pro-independence uprising led by de Céspedes, he soon became head of the Army of the Republic in Arms in Oriente Province. By the end of the war in 1878 he had become supreme commander of the Liberation Army. He later spent many years in exile, where he took on numerous political and organizational tasks in collaboration with José Martí. After the relaunching of the independence war in 1895, he returned to Cuba as supreme commander of the Cuban Mambí independence army. Renowned for his military talents, his brilliant and victorious campaigns against the Spanish army are still the subject of study today. He led, together with Antonio Maceo, the famous westward invasion from Oriente to the other end of the country in 1895-96. He died in Havana in 1905, seven years after the end of the final war of independence.

Gómez García, Raúl (1928-1953) — Poet, school teacher, and student of pedagogy at the University of Havana. Following Batista's coup he edited an underground newspaper, *Son los mismos*. After joining the revolutionary movement led by Fidel Castro with the group of Abel Santamaría, he drafted what became known as the Moncada Manifesto, explaining the political aims and immediate objectives of the popular armed insurrection to be sparked by the Moncada assault. He was captured and murdered by government troops during the Moncada attack. He was 25 years of age.

González Hernández, Francisco (1926-) — Former store employee. A participant in the Moncada attack, he was sentenced to 10 years' imprisonment and released May 15, 1955. He was a member of the *Granma* expedition and was captured and sentenced to six years in prison, but was freed on January 1, 1959. He is currently retired.

Granma — Small sporting yacht used to transport Fidel Castro and 81 other revolutionaries from Mexico to Cuba, November 25 - December 2, 1956, to begin the war against the Batista dictatorship from the mountains of the Sierra Maestra in the province of

Oriente.

Grau San Martín, Ramón (1887-1969) — Doctor; professor of physiology at the University of Havana. One month after the fall of the Machado dictatorship in August 1933, he became a member of a new government collegium. He served as Cuba's provisional president from September 10, 1933 until January 15, 1934, when he was overthrown by Fulgencio Batista with the support of the U.S. ambassador, Jefferson Caffery. In 1934 he founded the Cuban Revolutionary (Authentic) Party. He was president of the Constituent Assembly that met in 1940; that same year he was defeated by Batista in presidential elections widely viewed as fraudulent. From 1944 to 1948 he was Cuba's president in an administration marked by graft and corruption, which he had earned a reputation for opposing in the 1930s. At the same time he helped lead an anticommunist witch-hunt against leaders of the trade union movement as part of the "cold war" initiated by the United States. In 1954 he was a presidential candidate — as the only opposition figure — in Batista's electoral maneuver, but later withdrew his candidacy.

Guas Inclán, Rafael (Felo) (1896-1975) — Lawyer. His political life began by being elected to the House of Representatives on the ticket of the rightist Liberal Party. Re-elected in 1930. As president of the lower house of Congress he was decisive in allowing the illegal extension of the term of the government; a move that initiated the Machado dictatorship. As a delegate to the Consitituent Assembly he proposed in 1940 the candidature of Fulgencio Batista to the position of president. This same year he was elected governor of the province of Havana; re-elected in 1944. In 1948 he took a seat in the Senate. As part of an electoral pact he supported the presidential candidate of the Authentic Party in the 1952 elections, which were aborted because of the March 10, 1952 coup. As national leader of the Liberal Party he gave his support to the Batista regime. In return he was rewarded with the position of minister of communications (1953-54), and later the post of vice-president, taking office on February 24, 1955. Following the triumph of the revolution he went to the United States.

Guevara de la Serna, Ernesto (Che) (1928-1967) — Born in Rosario, Argentina. After graduating as a doctor in 1953, he headed north to Guatemala, then in the midst of a revolutionary process. With the U.S.-instigated overthrow of President Jacobo Arbenz in June 1954 he went to Mexico, where in 1955 he met Fidel Castro and joined the July 26 Movement. In November-December 1956 he traveled to Cuba aboard the *Granma* as medical officer. In July 1957, after participating in the Rebel Army's early battles, he became the first combatant to obtain the rank of commander and was assigned to lead a second guerrilla column. As head of the "Ciro Redondo" Column No. 8, in August 1958 he began the march to Las Villas Province in the center of the country, together with the "Antonio Maceo" Column No. 2 led by Camilo Cienfuegos. Once there he led an effective military campaign that routed the dictatorship's troops in this region, culminating in the capture of Santa Clara on January 1, 1959. On January 2, he arrived in Havana and occupied the La Cabaña fortress. As a leading and early proponent of the revolution's measures, he became one of its most popular leaders. He carried out numerous responsibilities in the new government, including head of the Deparment of Industrialization of the National Institute of Agrarian Reform (INRA), president of the National Bank, and minister of industry. He also represented the Cuban revolution abroad on numerous occasions, including to a meeting of the Organization of American States in Punta del Este in 1961, to the General Assembly of the United Nations in 1964, and to Algeria in 1965 for a conference of Asia-Africa solidarity. In 1965 he left Cuba to support the revolutionary movement in Africa, and in 1966 he went to Bolivia to lead a guerrilla movement there. He was captured by Bolivian government troops on October 8, 1967, and murdered the following day.

Guitart Rosell, Renato (1931-1953) — A member of the Military Committeee of the revolutionary movement led by Fidel Castro, he was the only person from Oriente Province who knew in advance of the plans to attack the Moncada garrison. He led the vanguard squad that opened up the entrance to the garrison and was the first revolutionary killed in the actions of July 26, 1953. He was 21 years old at the time of his death.

Guiteras Holmes, Antonio (Tony) (1906-1935) — Doctor of pharmacy. As a student at the University of Havana he joined

Mella in the Movement for University Reform. In 1927 he became part of the University Student Directorate to fight Machado's illegal extension of his presidential term. While advocating armed struggle and unity in the fight against the dictatorship, he participated in various conspiratorial actions. In 1930 he prepared an unsuccessful uprising in Santiago de Cuba and was imprisoned until the following year. He then founded the Revolutionary Union, with the stated objective of socialism. He later attempted to organize an uprising throughout Oriente Province that included the seizure of the Moncada garrison; although unsuccessful, his forces were able to capture the town of San Luis. After Machado's downfall, Guiteras became a member of Grau's cabinet, serving as secretary of the interior, war, and naval affairs. As a defender of Cuban sovereignty and an opponent of U.S. intervention, he decreed the seizure of various U.S. corporations, including the U.S.-owned Cuban Electricity Company. Following the overthrow of the Grau government in 1934 by Batista, Guiteras went underground and formed first the TNT and later Young Cuba, an organization with a socialist, nationalist, and anti-imperialist program. Attracting followers throughout the country the new organization propagated armed struggle to gain power. On May 8, 1935, he was killed in an armed clash while attempting to leave Cuba for Mexico in order to organize an armed expedition. He was 28 years old when killed.

Hernández Rodríguez del Rey, Melba (1922-) — Lawyer. As a member of Abel Santamaría's group she joined the revolutionary movement led by Fidel Castro and was one of two women to participate in the Moncada attack on July 26, 1953. Sentenced to seven months' imprisonment, she was released February 20, 1954. When the July 26 Movement was founded in June 1955, she became a member of its National Directorate. Returning to Cuba from Mexico after the *Granma* landing, she carried out intensive underground activity and later joined the Rebel Army in the "Mario Muñoz Monroy" Third Front of Oriente. Since 1959 she has held a number of leadership and diplomatic positions. She was founder and president of the Committee in Solidarity with Vietnam and the Peoples of Indochina. Currently she is vice-president of the Anti-Imperialist Tribunal of Our America, a member of the Central Committee of the Communist Party, and director of its Center for Studies of Asia and Oceania.

July 26 Revolutionary Movement (Movimiento Revolucionario 26 de Julio — MR-26-7) — Underground revolutionary organization led by Fidel Castro. Prior to the attack on the Moncada garrison it was known simply as the Movement. Following the political amnesty of May 15, 1955, it was restructured and in June 1955 adopted the name July 26 Revolutionary Movement, in honor of those killed that day in 1953. Also known as the July 26 Movement, it became the largest, best structured, and most active underground organization fighting the second Batista dictatorship of 1952-58. It was active both within and outside of Cuba, having a presence throughout Latin America and in the United States. After the *Granma* landing on December 2, 1956, it continued to function as the principal logistical support for the Rebel Army, as well as the organization leading the urban struggle. During this period Fidel Castro was its general secretary in addition to his responsibility as commander in chief of the Rebel Army.

López Fernández, Antonio (Ñico) (1932-1956) — Former stevedore, he came from a poor background and barely finished primary school. A member of the Orthodox Youth, he was known for militancy in social and political struggles. He later became leader of a cell of the revolutionary movement led by Fidel Castro, who regarded him highly. A participant in the attack on the Bayamo military barracks on July 26, 1953, he was able to escape and go into exile. While in Guatemala, he met Ernesto Che Guevara and they became close friends. He later went to Mexico before returning to Cuba May 29, 1955, following the general amnesty. When the July 26 Movement was founded in June 1955, he became a member of its National Directorate and headed its Youth Brigades, helping to organize the movement throughout the country. In mid-1956 he joined Fidel Castro in Mexico and participated in the *Granma* expedition as part of its general staff. On December 8, 1956, several days after the landing, he was captured by government forces in Boca del Toro in the Sierra Maestra and murdered. He was 24 years old.

Luis Santa Coloma, Reinaldo Boris (1928-1953) — Outstanding trade union and student leader. A leader of the revolutionary movement led by Fidel Castro, he belonged to its Civil Committee. A participant in the Moncada attack, he was taken prisoner, horribly mutilated, and murdered. He was 24 years old at the time of his death.

Maceo Grajales, Antonio (1845-1896) — Former administrator of crop sales for a family farm. Two days after the October 10, 1868, independence uprising led by de Céspedes, he joined the war as a simple soldier. As a result of his heroism and military abilities, he was repeatedly promoted until by the end of the Ten Years War, he had reached the rank of general in the Liberation Army. He opposed the Zanjón Pact that ended the war because it did not result in Cuba's independence, and on March 15, 1878, he issued the Baraguá Protest, regarded in Cuban history as a symbol of firmness, honor, and revolutionary intransigence, and he continued the struggle alone. When the Spanish army avoided combat, in 1878 he was forced into exile in Jamaica and later the United States, attempting unsuccessfully to relaunch the war. Living in Honduras in 1881, he was named a division general in that country's army. After various unsuccessful attempts to restart the Cuban independence war, he joined with Martí and landed in Oriente on April 12, 1895, with the rank of lieutenant general of the Liberation Army. Together with supreme commander Máximo Gómez, he carried out the military feat of the westward invasion from Oriente to Mantua, the last township in the west of Cuba (October 22, 1895, to January 22, 1896). Surrounded by Spanish troops in Pinar del Río Province, he waged another successful military campaign, breaking out of the encirclement and entering Havana Province, where on December 7, 1896, he was killed in the battle of San Pedro, Punta Brava, 20 kilometers from the capital. He had been wounded 24 times in the hundreds of battles in which he had taken part. He was firm in his opposition to an alliance with the United States and rejected the possible military participation of the United States in the Cuban independence struggle. Known in Cuban history as the "Bronze Titan," the date of his death is commemorated as the Day of Martyrs for the Independence of the Homeland.

Machado Morales, Gerardo (1871-1939) — A participant in the final war of independence against Spanish colonialism of 1895-98, where he obtained the rank of general. Secretary of the interior (1908), he later held various public and elective posts. Elected president in 1925, he forced through a constitutional modification in 1927 that extended his presidential term for six more years beginning from 1928. This move caused a wave of protest throughout the country that was met with fierce repression. Under the Machado dictatorship a series of repressive measures against the left-wing movement were initiated, including the banning of the Communist Party. In response large mass movements of students and workers arose. With an economic policy subservient to U.S. imperialism, he received Washington's support. However, in the midst of a massive revolutionary upheaval, U.S. Ambassador Sumner Welles made attempts to replace Machado with another right-wing government in order to contain the revolutionary upsurge. In the midst of a prolonged general strike that completely paralysed the country, the army — under pressure from Welles — withdrew its support for Machado, forcing him to resign and abandon the country on August 12, 1933. His replacement, Carlos M. de Céspedes Quesada, was ousted by a civilian-military movement on September 4 of that year. Despite the record of his brutal dictatorship, Machado obtained asylum in the United States. He died in Miami in 1939.

Mañach Lobato, Jorge (1898-1961) — Graduate from Harvard in 1920 and professor of romance languages there; doctor of law (1924) and philosophy and letters (1925) at the University of Havana. Narrator, journalist, critic, editor of various magazines and newspapers. During the 1920s he participated in various social and political protests. In the 1930s he was a founding member of the ABC, an underground organization of petty-bourgeois intellectuals with fascist-like traits that confronted the Machado dictatorship. Secretary of public instruction in the right-wing government of Carlos Mendieta (1934-35), he lived in exile in the United States, 1935-39. A delegate to the 1940 Constituent Assembly, he became a senator and a professor of the history of philosophy at the University of Havana that same year. In 1944 he became minister of state in Batista's government. In 1947 he joined the Orthodox Party. He was director of the radio program "University on the Air" and was founder of the TV program

"Meet the Press," 1952-57. In 1957 he went into exile in Spain. Returning to Cuba in 1959 after the victory of the revolution, he left shortly thereafter and died in Puerto Rico in 1961.

Marinello Vidarreta, Juan (1898-1977) — Lawyer and doctor of philosophy and letters; poet, essayist, critic. One of the most outstanding Latin American contemporary prose writers, he founded numerous progressive cultural publications over the course of several decades. Together with Rubén Martínez Villena, he was a member of the Minority Group, the Anti-Imperialist League, and the first Communist Party of Cuba. As a result of his opposition to Machado, he was imprisoned. In 1937 he went into exile in Mexico and became professor at the Autonomous University of Mexico. He edited the Communist Party's newspaper *La Palabra*. In 1937 he participated in the Congress of Writers for the Defense of Culture held in Madrid. Elected delegate to the Constituent Assembly in 1940, the House of Representatives in 1942, and the Senate in 1944. From that year is president of the Popular Socialist Party. During the second Batista dictatorship of the 1950s he was jailed several times. Following the victory of the revolution, he held various responsibilities, including as Cuban ambassador to UNESCO, rector of the University of Havana, and chairman of the Movement for Peace and Sovereignty of the Peoples. A member of the Central Committee of the Communist Party, at the time of his death in 1977, he was president of the National Assembly of People's Power.

Márquez-Sterling Guiral, Carlos (1898-) — Lawyer. Two years after the fall of the Machado dictatorship he was elected to the House of Representatives in 1936 on the ticket of the Liberal Party. With the support of the rightist and counterrevolutionary parties, the only parties that participated in these elections, he was elected president of the lower house of Congress. He was a delegate to the Constituent Assembly of 1940; re-elected to the House of Representatives. Minister of labor (1941) and minister of education (1943) of Batista's government (1940-44). Following his failure to become a Senate candidate for the Liberal Party in 1944 and also a failed attempt to create a Labor Party, he joined the Orthodox Party. After the death of Chibás he was in the center of the many factional divisions that engulfed the party. Prior to the

March 10, 1952 coup he adopted legalist and opportunist positions, always with the objective of advancing the possibilities of his re-entering electoral politics. In 1955 he finally withdrew from the Orthodox Party and was later part of the Free People's Party. In an electoral maneuver he was presidential candidate in the fraudulent elections of November 1, 1958, just two months prior to the fall of the Batista dictatorship. With the victory of the revolution on January 1, 1959, he fled to the United States.

Márquez, Juan Manuel (1915-1956) — While a youth he was imprisoned in the 1930s for his opposition to Machado. Subsequently he became an active opponent of Batista's first dictatorship. A former member of the Authentic Party, he became a founding leader of the Orthodox Party in 1947. Joining the July 26 Movement in 1955, he participated in the *Granma* expedition as its second-in-command. He was captured and murdered by government troops on December 16, 1956, two weeks after the landing.

Martí Pérez, José Julián (1853-1895) — Known as the "Teacher" and the "Apostle"; Cuba's national hero. Lawyer, poet, novelist, dramatist, critic, journalist; founder, editor, and correspondent for numerous magazines and newspapers. His literary and political output, which currently fill 28 thick volumes, make him one of the outstanding figures of Latin American letters. In 1869, at the age of 16, he was imprisoned, put to forced labor, and exiled. His fervent participation in every Cuban independence struggle and conspiracy from 1868 on led him to a life of permanent harassment, with the majority of his years spent in exile. Between 1878 and 1895 he worked constantly to achieve the unity of Cuba's patriotic forces. In 1892 he founded the Cuban Revolutionary Party (PRC) in order to fight for the independence of Cuba and Puerto Rico. The PRC was an organization completely different from any other up to that time, with a centralized leadership, democratic in its public methods of work, and mass based. The PRC was anticolonialist in its origin, pro-independence in its immediate goals, and internationalist in its strategic aims. It was the first antiimperialist party organization in history, and the first party of that nature aimed at winning national liberation through armed popular insurrection. Champion of equality, the PRC defended the unity of "Our America" in opposition to U.S. imperialism. The ideas of Martí have constituted an entire code of ethics and norms of political conduct for the Cuban people. The day before his death he wrote: "Every day I am in danger of giving my life for my country and duty, a duty I understand and wish to fulfill: to prevent the United States, before it is too late, from spreading throughout the Antilles once Cuba is independent and falling with added weight on the lands of the Americas. Everything I have done until now and will do in the future is toward this end. I have had to do this silently and indirectly, since there are some things that must be kept hidden in order to be achieved. To proclaim things as they are would create difficulties too vast to be able to achieve the goals." Landing in Oriente immediately following the start of the war he had organized (February 24, 1895, the Cry of Baire), he was proclaimed president of the Republic in Arms by the Liberation Army. On May 19, 1895, he was killed in battle at Dos Ríos. At the time of his death he was 42 years of age.

Mella, Julio Antonio (1903-1929) — Real name was Nicanor McPartland. Former law student at the University of Havana and initiator of the Movement for University Reform in Cuba. In 1923 he founded the Federation of University Students. Member of the Cuban section of the Anti-Imperialist League that linked student and worker struggles. In 1925 he became a founding member of the first Communist Party of Cuba. The following year, persecution by the Machado dictatorship forced him into exile. While living in Mexico he was a member of the executive committees of the Anti-Imperialist League of the Americas, the Mexican Communist Party, the United Trade Union Federation, and the Association of Proletarian Students. He later helped lead the campaign to save the lives of Sacco and Vanzetti, who were executed in the United States. He actively supported Augusto César Sandino in his struggle against U.S. military intervention in Nicaragua. He also founded the anti-Machado Association of Recent Cuban Emigres, and organized the Continental Committee for the Congress Against Colonial Oppression and Imperialism, held 1927 in Brussels. That same year he participated in the Fourth Congress of the Red International of Labor Unions and the conference of the International Red Aid in Moscow. While preparing an armed expedition to return to Cuba, he was assassinated in Mexico on January 10, 1929, at the age of 25.

Mestre Martínez, Armando (1927-1956) — Former bricklayer and student. A participant in the Moncada attack, he was sentenced to 10 years' imprisonment and released on May 15, 1955. He helped organize the July 26 Movement in Havana before going into exile in Mexico. A *Granma* expeditionary, he was captured and murdered in Nicquero on the coast of Oriente on December 8, 1956, several days after the landing. He was 29 years old.

Miret Prieto, Pedro (1927-) — Former public employee and student of agricultural engineering. A member of the Military Committee of the revolutionary movement led by Fidel Castro, he was the principal trainer of its combatants. Wounded in the Moncada attack, he was sentenced to 13 years' imprisonment and was released May 15, 1955. When the July 26 Movement was founded in June 1955, he was military head for its National Directorate. Jailed in Mexico at the time of the *Granma* expedition, he returned to Cuba in 1958 with an air shipment of arms and joined the ranks of the "José Martí" Column No. 1 of Fidel Castro in the Sierra Maestra, obtaining the rank of Rebel Army commander. Since 1959 he has held a number of posts, including undersecretary of defense (1959), minister of agriculture (1959), minister of minerals (1969), and vice-prime minister for the industrial sector since 1972. Currently he serves on the Council of State and is a member of the Communist Party of Cuba's Central Committee.

Moncada garrison — Military fortress in Santiago de Cuba, the country's second largest city located 800 kilometers from Havana on the southern coast of the former Oriente Province, which contained Cuba's principal mountain ranges. The Moncada garrison was the base for the army's "Antonio Maceo" Regiment No. 1. It was attacked by Fidel Castro and his revolutionary movement on July 26, 1953. From that day the revolutionaries who took part in the assault were known as "Moncadistas."

Monroe Doctrine — Hegemonistic program proclaimed by U.S. President James Monroe in a message to Congress December 2, 1823, declaring that the "two Americas" would be closed to new colonization by European governments. This policy would later be summed up in the well-known phrase, "America for the Americans." While preventing extracontinental powers from intervening in the Americas, it permitted the United States to intervene in both North and South America, as has been shown in the history of the last century and a half of expansionism and interventionism.

Montané Oropesa, Jesús Sergio (1923-) — Former accountant. Together with Abel Santamaría's group he joined the revolutionary movement led by Fidel Castro, becoming a member of its National Directorate and Civil Committee. A participant in the Moncada attack, he was sentenced to 10 years' imprisonment and was released May 15, 1955. When the July 26 Movement was founded in June 1955, he became a member of its National Directorate. A *Granma* expeditionary, he was captured and sentenced to six years in prison, but was freed on January 1, 1959. Since 1959 he has held a number of posts: governor of the Isle of Pines, national director of prisons (1959), subdirector of the National Institute of the Tourist Industry (1959-61), military adjudant of the general staff (1962-63), minister of communications (1963-72). In 1973-74 he served as organization secretary of the Central Committee of the Communist Party of Cuba, and since 1974 has been assistant to the first secretary of the party's Central Committee. He is currently a deputy to the National Assembly of People's Power and a member of the Communist Party's Central Committee.

Movement — See July 26 Revolutionary Movement

Mujal Barniol, Eusebio (El catalán) (1915-1985) — Of working class origin, a member of the first Communist Party of Cuba in the 1930s. He later joined the Authentic Party. A delegate to the Constituent Assembly of 1940, he was elected to the House of Representatives and re-elected in 1944. He was member of the Senate, 1948-52. From the 1930s he held leading posts in the trade union movement in Oriente Province. He founded the National Workers Commission of the Authentic Party. In an illegitimate act of 1947 this body was decreed by President Grau to be the leadership of the Confederation of Cuban Workers (CTC) and Mujal became the CTC's general secretary under the wave of the

McCarthyist repression by the government in which working-class, communist, and independent leaders were removed from trade union positions. With the backing of the government Mujal assumed control of the CTC, using police and gangster support to murder left-wing workers' leaders. When Batista's 1952 coup took place Mujal renounced the Authentic Party and aligned the CTC with the Batista dictatorship. In Cuban history Mujal symbolizes yellow unionism, betrayers of the working class. A millionaire, he fled Cuba on January 1, 1959 for the United States, where he died in 1985.

Ochoa Ochoa, Emilio L. (Millo) (1907-) — Dentist. Member of the University Student Directorate of 1930, he fought against the Batista dictatorship. A founder of the Authentic Party, he was leader of this organization in the province of Oriente. Delegate to the Constituent Assembly in 1940; elected to the Senate in this year and reelected in 1944. In 1947 he left the Authentic Party and joined with Chibás to form the Orthodox Party. In 1948 he led a group of legislators that opposed the line of political independence of Chibás. His attempt to become governor of Oriente on a ticket of the Liberal and Democrat parties ends in defeat. Following the split of the majority of the parliamentary faction — with the exception of Ochoa and Pelayo Cuervo — Chibás was able to regain control of the party. In 1950 Ochoa was elected to the House of Representatives. With the suicide of Chibás in 1951 he became president of the Orthodox Party. He ran for the position of vice-president in the 1952 elections. After the 1952 coup the divisions in the Orthodox Party deepen and Ochoa led a faction that signed the Montreal Pact with the Authentic Party faction of Prío. This subsequently created a split in the leadership of the Orthodox Party. He went into exile and then returned. In early 1955 he repudiated the Montreal Pact. Going into exile again he joined with former soldiers in a tiny organization known as "XYZ" which was inactive up until the victory of the revolution in 1959, at which time he returned to Cuba. He later left the country going to Venezuela and then to the United States.

Orthodox Party (Partido del Pueblo Cubano — Cuban People's Party) — Founded May 15, 1947, by Senator Eduardo Chibás and other political leaders who split from the Authentic Party as a result of the widespread corruption during the administration of President Ramón Grau San Martín. Political figures of other tendencies also joined the party's ranks. Commonly known as the Orthodox Party, it had a wide base of popular support, primarily youth discontented with the rampant political corruption in the country. Its slogan "Honor Against Money" and its symbol, a broom "to sweep away bad government leaders," received a broad popular response. Its members became known as *Orthodoxos*. With Chibás's death in 1951 it split into various currents. Its most radical wing, led by Fidel Castro, formally split from the party in June 1955 at the time when the July 26 Movement was formed.

Orthodox Youth (Juventud Ortodoxo) — Youth group of the Cuban People's (Orthodox) Party. It was from its membership that recruits were won to the revolutionary movement led by Fidel Castro.

Osa Perdomo, Enrique de la (1907-) — Poet, journalist, historian; editor of numerous publications beginning with his student days, including *Atuei* and *Alma Mater*. A fighter against the Machado dictatorship, he carried out underground work, was imprisoned, and went into exile in the United States, where he joined the Association of Recent Cuban Emigrants founded by Mella in Mexico. An opponent of Batista's first dictatorship, in 1943 he founded the "In Cuba" section of the magazine *Bohemia*. Before Batista's 1952 coup he joined Action for Liberty. Later he joined the ranks of the July 26 Movement. After the victory of the revolution he was editor of *Bohemia* and the newspaper *Revolución*. He is the author of numerous books.

País García, Frank (1934-1957) — Former student, teacher, poet, and musician. President of the Association of Students of the Teachers Training School in Santiago de Cuba and vice-president of the Federation of University Students of Oriente. An active opponent of the March 1952 coup of Batista, he founded the Revolutionary Student Directorate that same year and in 1953 helped organize the José Martí Student Bloc. In 1952-53, he belonged to Action for Liberty, and in 1953-54 to the Revolutionary National Movement. In 1954 he founded Oriente Revolutionary Action, an underground organization that adopted the perspective of armed struggle. In 1955 this group changed its name to Revolutionary National Action, and carried out numerous urban activities including sabotage, attacks on army garrisons, and weapons seizures. After the Moncada attack, he planned an operation to rescue the prisoners while they were in the Boniato jail but it could not be carried out. He sought to link the student movement of Oriente with struggles of workers and peasants. He was actively involved in solidarity with the people of Guatemala following the CIA-backed overthrow of the Arbenz government in 1954. His group collaborated with the student movement in the rest of the country, including José Antonio Echeverría, with whom he developed efforts to rid the University of Havana of the problem of "gangsterism." In 1955 his group joined the July 26 Movement and he became its action head for Oriente Province, where the organization achieved its highest level in terms of militancy, economic resources, supply of weapons, and military training. Traveling to Mexico in June and October 1956, he met Fidel Castro and elaborated plans for an insurrectionary action to support Fidel's arrival in Cuba. In this work Celia Sánchez would play an important role. On November 30, 1956, he led a well-executed uprising in Santiago de Cuba and other parts of Oriente, initially intended to coincide with the arrival of the *Granma*. These were outstanding examples of underground urban armed struggle. He was named national action head of the July 26 Movement after the *Granma* landing and helped restructure it under the instructions of Fidel Castro. In March 1957 he sent 50 armed men to the Sierra Maestra as the first reinforcement of the guerrilla forces. He led all the urban armed actions with an exceptional capacity and established an efficient base of logistical support for the Rebel Army. In June 1957 he unsuccessfully attempted to open a second front in northern Oriente Province. On July 30, 1957, he was captured and murdered by government forces in Santiago de Cuba, at the age of 23. He is viewed as a symbol of the underground combatant and the day of his death is commemorated yearly as the Day of the Martyrs of the Revolution.

Pardo Llada, José (1923-) — Journalist, radio commentator; for 15 years his radio news program was the most popular on national radio. As a member of the Orthodox Party he was elected to the House of Representatives in 1950 with the highest vote ever recorded in the neocolonial republic. Until the death of Eduardo Chibás he directed the radio program of the Orthodox Party, broadcast every Sunday evening. Following the March 10, 1952 coup he assumed a legalist response along with the majority of Orthodox Party leaders. Having been detained several times and also having had his radio program frequently censured, he went into exile in 1953. Together with Emilio Ochoa he became part of a group of Orthodox figures who signed the Montreal Pact with ex-president Prío, commiting themselves not to carry out armed actions against the dictatorship. Returning to Cuba in March 1954 he subsequently renounced the Montreal compromise. In this same year he abandoned the Orthodox movement. In April 1955 he founded with Jorge Mañach and others the Nation Movement, a party with electoral aims that was to later disintegrate. At the end of 1958 he traveled to the Sierra Maestra as a journalist. In 1959-60 he continued to practice journalism and in this capacity accompanied Fidel and other leaders of the revolutionary government on various overseas tours. Just days prior to the U.S.-backed mercenary invasion at the Bay of Pigs (Playa Girón) he left the country. From that time on he has lived in Colombia.

Pena Díaz, Félix Lutgerio (1930-1959) — Former leader of the student movement and commerce student. Active in the student struggles during the Authentic Party administrations, as a member of the Orthodox Youth he participated in protest demonstrations in Santiago de Cuba after the March 1952 coup. Together with Frank País, Pepito Tey, and others, he helped found the Revolutionary Student Directorate (1952) and the José Martí Student Bloc (1953). He was a member of Action for Liberty (1953-54) and later of Oriente Revolutionary Action and Revolutionary National Action (1954-55). Head of the July 26 Movement's Youth Brigades in Oriente, he participated in the Santiago de Cuba uprising of November 30, 1956. In March 1957 he joined the first contingent of reinforcements sent to the Sierra Maestra by Frank País and participated in the battles of Column No. 1. In March 1958 he was promoted to captain and joined Column No. 6 under the command of Raúl Castro, which invaded northern Oriente Province and set up the "Frank País" Second Front of Oriente. Named commander of Column No. 18 in September

1958, his unit entered Guantánamo on January 1, 1959 with columns no. 6 and 20 of commanders Efigenio Ameijeiras and Demetrio Montseny. After the triumph of the revolution he presided on the Revolutionary Tribunal which mistakenly judged air pilots of the Batista dictatorship who were guilty of war crimes. He commited suicide on April 11, 1959 at the age of 28.

Ponce Díaz, José (1926-) — Former printer. A participant in the Moncada attack, he was sentenced to 10 years' imprisonment and released May 15, 1955. A member of the *Granma* expedition, he was captured shortly after the landing and sentenced to six years in prison, but was freed on January 1, 1959. He is currently retired.

Prío Socarrás, Carlos (1903-1977) — Lawyer. A noted student leader in the struggle against the Machado dictatorship, he joined the University Student Directorate in 1930. Was imprisoned on the Isle of Pines. He was part of a civilian group that gave support and a political orientation to the insurrectionary movement of soldiers of September 4, 1933. In 1934 he helped found the Cuban Revolutionary (Authentic) Party and the Authentic Organization, which fruitlessly attempted to organize an armed popular uprising against the first Batista dictatorship. In 1940 he was elected a delegate to the Constituent Assembly. In the Grau administration of 1944-48 he was a senator and minister of labor, in which he helped carry out the anticommunist witch-hunt of the labor movement. In 1946-48 he served as prime minister. As president (1948-52) he took some positive steps such as the establishment of the National Bank, the Agricultural and Industrial Loans Bank, the Accounts Tribunal, and the Constitutional Guarantees Tribunal, but during his administration the theft of public funds and political corruption grew, as did repression of the democratic workers' movement and the violent activities of the gangsters. He was overthrown seven months before his term was due to end by the March 10, 1952, coup. In March 1952 he went into exile in the United States. He financed the purchase of large stocks of arms in order to launch an armed uprising against Batista, which never succeeded. Supporting the AAA, a new form of the Authentic Party, he signed the Montreal Pact (June 1953) with a faction of the Orthodox Party. Arriving in Cuba in August 1955, he was expelled by Batista in May 1956 and returned to the United States. At a crucial time he gave financial assistance to the *Granma* expedition. Prío was always negotiating for the United States to intervene against Batista and maneuvering for his overthrow which was finally achieved by the triumph of the revolution. After January 1, 1959, he returned to Cuba but left again for the United States where 18 years later he committed suicide.

Rebel Army — Name of the revolutionary armed forces commanded by Fidel Castro after the landing of the *Granma* expeditionaries on December 2, 1956.

Redondo García, Ciro (1931-1957) — Former store employee. A participant in the Moncada attack, he was sentenced to 10 years' imprisonment and released May 15, 1955. On December 2, 1956, he landed in Cuba aboard the *Granma*. With the rank of captain in the Rebel Army, he was killed November 29, 1957, in the Battle of Mar Verde in the Sierra Maestra. He was 26 years old.

Rivero Agüero, Andrés (1905-) — Lawyer. He became active in political life after the fall of Gerardo Machado. He was political secretary of Fulgencio Batista during the first Batista dictatorship, and later minister of agriculture (1941-42). As prominent spokesperson for the party founded by Batista, the Unitary Action Party (PAU), he supported the coup of March 10, 1952 and was designated minister of education until August 1954. As chief in the province of Pinar del Río of the new Batista party, Progressive Action (PAP), he obtained a seat in the Senate in the electoral farce of November 1, 1954. In the final years of the dictatorship he occupied the post of prime minister. Designated by Batista as his successor, he was the candidate for president in the fraudulent elections of November 1, 1958, just two months before the fall of the despotic regime. On the first of January 1959 he fled the country and sought refuge in the United States.

Roa García, Raúl (1907-1982) — Lawyer, essayist, journalist, sociologist, and historian. Author of hundreds of articles and numerous books. Teacher at the "José Martí" Popular University in 1927. Member of the Anti-Imperialist League of Cuba. A prominent student leader in the struggle against the Machado dictatorship, he carried out underground activity and suffered imprisonment. In 1930 he was a founder of the University Student

Directorate. In 1931 he became a member of the Central Committee of the Student Left Wing and in 1933 belonged to the Commission for University Reform. As a fighter against the first Batista dictatorship after 1934, he was forced into exile in the United States, where with Pablo de la Torriente Brau and others he helped found the Anti-Imperialist Cuban Revolutionary Organization. In 1940 he became assistant dean of the faculty of Social Sciences of the University of Havana; he was to later serve as dean until 1963. He held the post of cultural director for the Ministry of Education in 1948 and belonged to numerous Cuban and international cultural and scientific institutions. A member of the underground AAA following Batista's March 1952 coup, he went into exile and later joined the July 26 Movement. Following the 1959 revolution he was Cuba's ambassador to the Organization of American States (1959) and for over a decade was minister of foreign relations. He became known as the "Chancellor of Dignity." At the time of his death in 1982 he was a member of the Central Committee of the Communist Party of Cuba and vice-president of the National Assembly of People's Power.

Roca, Blas (1908-1987) — Real name, Francisco Wilfredo Calderío; former shoemaker. As general secretary of the Manzanillo shoemakers' union in 1930 he was elected general secretary of the Manzanillo Workers Federation. In 1929 he joined the first Communist Party of Cuba and in 1934 became its general secretary, a post he held until the party's dissolution in 1961, when it joined in the fusion to create the Integrated Revolutionary Organizations. During that time the party was also known as the Communist Revolutionary Union (1940-44) and Popular Socialist Party (1944-61). He was jailed several times. He headed the Cuban delegation to the Seventh World Congress of the Communist International in 1935 and was elected to its Executive Committee. In 1940 he was elected delegate to the Constituent Assembly and was a member of the House of Representatives from 1940 to 1952. Editor of the newspaper *Hoy*, 1962-65, he was author of numerous political essays and wrote the book *The Fundamentals of Socialism in Cuba*. A member of the Central Committee of the current Communist Party of Cuba at its founding in 1965, he headed the Constitutional Study Commission and the Judicial Study

Commission. He was a member of the party's Political Bureau from 1975 until his death on April 25, 1987.

Rodríguez Pérez, Léster (1931-) — Former engineering student. Together with Fidel Castro in 1950, he joined the September 30 Committee aimed at fighting gangsterism at the University of Havana. After the March 1952 coup, he participated in student protests at the university. He was also part of the January 10 Committee that erected a bust of Julio Antonio Mella. In 1953 he was elected president of the José Martí Congress for the Democratic Rights of Youth. A participant in the Moncada attack, he was able to escape and go into exile in Mexico. He returned to Cuba secretly in April 1955, shortly before the amnesty. With the founding of the July 26 Movement in June 1955, he was designated its coordinator for Oriente Province. With Frank País he helped organize the Santiago de Cuba uprising of November 30, 1956. Subsequently jailed, he was acquitted and went into exile, where he served as the July 26 Movement's representative in the United States. In 1958 he returned to Cuba with an arms shipment and joined the "Frank País" Second Front of Oriente, where he achieved the rank of captain of the Rebel Army. Since the victory of the revolution in 1959, he has held a number of leading posts in state administration. He is now retired.

Rodríguez Rodríguez, Carlos Rafael (1913-) — Lawyer, economist, journalist, essayist. A prominent student leader in the struggle against the Machado dictatorship, he was a member of the Student Left Wing in the early 1930s. During the revolutionary period following the overthrow of Machado, he served as mayor of Cienfuegos. In 1936 he joined the first Communist Party of Cuba (later to become the Popular Socialist Party or PSP), becoming a member of its Central Committee in 1939 and editing several of its theoretical journals. Minister without portfolio during the constitutional government of Batista in the 1940s. Active in the struggle of the PSP against the March 10, 1952 coup and the new Batista dictatorship. In June 1958 he was sent to the Sierra Maestra as a representative of the PSP to work with Fidel Castro and the Rebel Army. Following the victory of the revolution he has held various posts and responsibilities: president of the National Institute of Agrarian Reform (1962-65); minister-president of the National Commission of Economic, Scientific, and Technical Collaboration (1965-76); Cuba's permanent representative to the Council of Mutual Economic Assistance; and vice-prime minister for the foreign agencies sector (1972-76). He is currently a member of the Political Bureau and Central Committee of the Communist Party of Cuba and is vice-president of the Council of State and the Council of Ministers.

Rodríguez Rodríguez, Luis Orlando (1917-1989) — Lawyer, journalist. A member of the Revolutionary Student Directorate in Havana in 1930, he founded the anti-Machado underground newspaper *El Estudiante*. He participated in an unsuccessful attempt to assassinate Machado's police chief, Arsenio Ortíz. In 1934 he joined the Authentic Party and fought against the first Batista dictatorship. In 1940 he founded the Confederation of Students and the Authentic Youth, of which he was national secretary. During 1944-46, he was director of sports in the Grau administration, but resigned in protest of the Authentic Party's corruption. In 1947 he became a founding member with Chibás of the Orthodox Party. Elected a member of the House of Representatives in 1950, he was deposed following the 1952 coup and immediately became active in the struggle against Batista. He founded the newspaper *La Calle*, which was closed by the dictatorship in 1955. In 1956 he became a member of the July 26 Movement. Joining the Rebel Army in 1957, he became the first editor of its newspaper *El Cubano Libre* (The Free Cuban) and director of Radio Rebelde. He finished the war with the rank of captain. Following the 1959 victory he served as minister of government and spent over 20 years in diplomatic service.

Sánchez Arango, Aureliano (1907-1976) — Lawyer. Began his political involvement with Julio Antonio Mella in the struggle for university reform in 1923. In 1927 he was a member of the University Student Directorate that opposed the Machado dictatorship. He was a member of the Anti-Imperialist League, and in 1928 joined the Communist Party. Expelled from Cuba, he returned secretly in 1930, but was imprisoned. He was a central leader of the left wing of the University of Havana students' organization, and one of the most brilliant left-wing student leaders of the Generation of the 1930s. Later, he opposed the

Grau-Guiteras government, participating in the general strike of March 1935. Abandoning Marxism, he joined the Cuban Youth. In 1937 the attempt to form the Democratic Revolutionary Party failed and he retired from active political life. He became a professor of labor legislation in the department of law at the University of Havana for many years. He was minister of education (1948-51) and minister of state (1951-2) until the Batista coup of March 1952. Exiled, he returned secretly in May 1952 to assist the AAA, which was financed by Prío. He left Cuba in 1953 and returned at the beginning of 1954, becoming one of the most wanted persons by the repressive forces. He made a spectacular escape in May 1954, seeking asylum in an embassy and traveling to Mexico. Many of his followers were assassinated, imprisoned or exiled. In October 1954, the police raided his main arms warehouse in Havana. All this, along with the suspension of economic support from Prío, a number of failed attempts to ship arms to Cuba, and his deteriorating morale led to the disillusionment of most of his followers and the end of his insurrectional projects. He gained the support of the Dominican dictator, Rafael Leónidas Trujillo. Following the triumph of the revolution in January 1959 he arrived with a shipment of arms. Shortly afterwards he left to live in the United States.

Sánchez Manduley, Celia (1920-1980) — Dentist. Following Batista's March 1952 coup, she joined the struggle against the dictatorship and supported the revolutionary assault on the Moncada barracks, collecting aid for those imprisoned on the Isle of Pines and actively participating in the campaign to win their release. In 1955 she joined the July 26 Movement in Oriente, and became Frank País's principal organizational cadre in the southwestern coast of this province, the area of the *Granma* landing. The network of activists and material resources she had organized played a decisive role in enabling the Rebel Army forces led by Fidel Castro to become established in the Sierra Maestra. She served as conduit between the Rebel Army and the July 26 Movement in the cities, organizing the reinforcement of combatants and weapons to the Sierra Maestra. She was the first woman to join the guerrilla forces, serving for the remainder of the war as aide to Fidel Castro, a position she continued to hold after the revolution's victory in 1959. From its founding until her death in 1980 she was a member of the Central Committee of the Communist Party of Cuba and secretary of the Council of State and the Council of Ministers.

Santamaría Cuadrado, Abel Benigno (1927-1953) — Former office worker and student. After the March 1952 coup he organized a group of young radical members of the Orthodox Party attempting to pressure the party's leadership to adopt a more energetic opposition to the dictatorship. He founded the underground newspapers *Son Los Mismos*, and later *El Acusador*. In May 1952 he joined forces with Fidel Castro and became second-in-command of the revolutionary movement Fidel organized, undertaking broad responsibilities in propaganda, agitation, organization, and military training. As a leader of the attack on the Moncada barracks in 1953, he was captured, tortured (his eyes were gouged out), and murdered that same day. Characterized by Fidel as the "soul of the movement," he is viewed as a symbol of the revolutionary martyrs of July 26, 1953. He was 26 years old at the time of his death.

Santamaría Cuadrado, Haydée (1925-1980) — Former office worker. Together with her brother Abel, she joined the revolutionary movement led by Fidel Castro in 1952. With Melba Hernández she was one of two women participating in the Moncada attack. Sentenced to seven months imprisonment, she was released February 20, 1954. She was a member of the National Directorate of the July 26 Movement from its founding in June 1955. A participant in the November 30, 1956, uprising in Santiago de Cuba, she undertook intensive underground and international activity during the course of the war. After the victory of the revolution, she served as director of Casa de las Américas and was a member of the Central Committee of the Communist Party of Cuba, posts she held at the time of her death in 1980.

Sardiñas Menéndez, Guillermo Isaías (1917-1964) — Catholic priest; doctor in cannon law, parish priest in Nueva Gerona on the Isle of Pines (1954-57). He was a founding member of the July 26 Movement on the Isle of Pines. Seven months after the landing in Cuba of the *Granma* he joined the Rebel Army in the Sierra Maestra in June 1957 and finished the war with the rank of commander. He died in Havana on December 21, 1964.

SIM (Servicio de Inteligencia Militar — Military Intelligence Service). The army's investigative unit, transformed by the Batista dictatorship into a body devoted to torturing and murdering the opponents of the regime.

Suárez Blanco, José A. (1927-) — Member of the National Directorate of the Orthodox Youth and its leader in Pinar del Río. He helped recruit the largest number of combatants to the revolutionary movement led by Fidel Castro before July 26, 1953. A participant in the Moncada attack, he was sentenced to 10 years' imprisonment and released on May 15, 1955. A member of the National Directorate of the July 26 Movement, he was its leader in the provinces of Pinar del Río and Havana up to the time of the *Granma* landing. He subsequently went into exile and returned following the victory of the revolution. He is currently retired.

Tey Saint-Blancard, José (Pepito) (1934-1956) — Student leader and former railroad worker. Vice-president of the Association of Students at the Teacher Training School of Santiago de Cuba, and president of the Federation of University Students of Oriente. Chief assistant of Frank País, with whom he closely collaborated until his death. Together with País he participated in the street demonstrations protesting Batista's March 1952 coup. He became a member of the Revolutionary Student Directorate (1952), the José Martí Student Bloc (1953), Action for Liberty (1952-53), the Revolutionary National Movement (1953-54), Oriente Revolutionary Action (1954), Revolutionary National Action (1955), and the July 26 Movement (1955-56). Working with José Antonio Echeverría, as the president of the Federation of University Students in Oriente, he helped plan the first unsuccessful attempt at organizing an assault on the Presidential Palace in April 1955. Among the exceptional group of young revolutionaries of Oriente, he is noted for his left-wing views. He was considered one of their most daring underground fighters. He was killed during the November 30, 1956, uprising in Santiago de Cuba in an attack on the police station, one of the most heroic actions of this day. He was 22 years old at the time of his death.

Torriente Brau, Pablo de la (1901-1936) — Journalist, essayist, narrator, author. As a young fighter against the Machado dictatorship (1927-33), he interrupted his study of diplomatic law at the University of Havana. He was wounded in a student demonstration, jailed, forced to go underground, and later went into exile in the United States. During the first Batista dictatorship, he went into exile again and in New York founded the Anti-Imperialist Cuban Revolutionary Organization and its newspaper *Frente Unico*. He took part in antifascist demonstrations that were organized during this period in the United States. In 1936 he went to Belgium to participate in the Congress for Peace, and then on to Spain as a combatant in its civil war and as a correspondent for the *New Masses* (New York) and *El Machete*, newspaper of the Mexican Communist Party. Obtaining the post of political commissar in the republican forces, he was killed in battle in Majadahonda, Madrid, on December 19, 1936. He was 35 years old.

Valdés Menéndez, Ramiro (1932-) — Former industrial worker. A participant in the Moncada attack, he was sentenced to 10 years' imprisonment and released May 15, 1955. A *Granma* expeditionary, he served as second-in-command of the "Ciro Redondo" invasion column led by Che Guevara, finishing the war with the rank of commander of the Rebel Army. Following the 1959 victory he served as minister of the interior (1961-68 and 1979-87) and was a member of the Political Bureau of the Communist Party's Central Committee (1975-87). He is currently a member of the party's Central Committee and is vice-president of the Council of State and the Council of Ministers.

Appendix 1

Moncada combatants killed on or immediately after July 26, 1953

Abad Alemán Rodríguez
Gerardo Antonio Alvarez Alvarez
Tomás Alvarez Breto
Juan Manuel Ameijeiras Delgado
Gilberto Barón Martínez
Antonio Betancourt Flores
Flores Betancourt Rodríguez
Hugo Camejo Valdés
Gregorio Careaga Medina
Pablo Cartas Rodríguez
Fernando Chenard Piña
Alfredo Corcho Cinta
Rigoberto Corcho López
Giraldo Córdova Cardín
José Francisco Costa Velázquez
Juan Domínguez Díaz
Víctor Escalona Benítez
Gildo Miguel Fleitas López
Rafael Freyre Torres
Jacinto García Espinosa
Raúl Gómez García
Manuel Gómez Reyes
Virgilio Gómez Reyes
Luciano González Camejo
Guillermo Granados Lara
Angelo de la Guardia Guerra Díaz
René Renato Miguel Guitart Rosell
Lázaro Hernández Arroyo
Emilio Hernández Cruz
Manuel Enrique Isla Pérez
José Antonio Labrador Díaz
Reinaldo Boris Luis Santa Coloma
José de Jesús Maderas Fernández
Pedro Marrero Aizpurúa

Marcos Martí Rodríguez
Mario Martínez Araras
Wilfredo Matheu Orihuela
Horacio Matheu Orihuela
Roberto Mederos Rodríguez
Ramón Ricardo Méndez Cabezón
Mario Muñoz Monroy
Carmelo Noa Gil
Miguel Angel Oramas Alfonso
Oscar Alberto Ortega
Julio Máximo Reyes Cairo
Ismael Ricondo Fernández
Félix Rivero Vasallo
Asunción Manuel María Rojo Pérez
Manuel Saíz Sánchez
Rolando San Román y de las Llanas
Abel Benigno Santamaría Cuadrado
Osvaldo Socarrás Martínez
Elpidio Casimiro Sosa González
José Luis Tasende de las Muñecas
José Testa Zaragoza
Julio Trigo López
Andrés Valdés Fuentes
Armando Valle López
Pedro Véliz Hernández

Appendix 2

Text of sentence passed October 6, 1953

Continuation of Minutes, Provisional Court

Minutes, pages 2944-2951

In the city of Santiago de Cuba, on October 6, 1953, the day set to continue the trial of Provisional Court Case 37 of 1953 the Chamber of Justice of this Court was presided over by Chief Justice Adolfo Nieto Piñeiro Osorio and Associate Justices Ricardo Díaz Olivera, Juan F. Mejías Valdivieso, and myself.

Mr. Francisco Mendieta Hechavarría appeared as state prosecutor. Recaredo García Fernández served as defense counsel for José M. Villa Romero, Silverio Emilio Brito Oquendo, José A. Batista Lotti, Ramón Campa Delgado, Heriberto Sánchez Tamayo, José Fernando Pila Teleña, Raúl del Mazo Serra, and Pedro Celestino Aguilera González. Domingo Estrada Beatón served as defense counsel for Oscar Gras Escalona, Mario Burman Corman, and Lázara Pérez Cuesta. Baudilio Castellanos García served as defense counsel for Ulises Sarmientos Vargas, Isidro Peñalver O'Relly, Humberto Valdés Casañas, Manuel Vázquez Tio, Jesús Blanco Alba, Carlos Merilles Acosta, Raúl Castro Ruz, Jesús Montané Oropesa, Israel Tápanes Vento Aguilera, Reinaldo Benítez Nápoles, Ernesto Tizol Aguilera, Eduardo Montano Benítez, Oscar Alcalde Valls, Juan Almeida Bosque, Armando Mestre Martínez, Antonio San Román Llanes, Generoso Llanes Machado, Moto Mendel Weiss, Mauro Suárez Suárez, Enrique Cámara Pérez, Angel Valdés Rodríguez, Rafael Núñez Leyva, and Angel L. Díaz Francisco. Andrés Silva Adán served as defense counsel for Guillermo Elizalde Sotolongo, Genaro Hernández Martínez, Rolando Guerrero Bello, René Betancourt Castillo, and Ignacio Fiterre Rivera. Luis A. Gómez Domínguez served as defense counsel for Orlando Cortés Gallardo and Eduardo Rodríguez Alemán. Juan José García Benítez served as defense counsel for Emilio Ochoa Ochoa. Jorge Nariño Brauet served as defense counsel for José Vázquez Rojas. Raúl de Villalvilla Carbonell served as defense counsel for Leonel A. de los Santos Gómez Pérez, Ramón Serrano Alfonso, and Juan Manuel Martínez. Elizardo Díaz Lorenzo served as defense counsel for Fidel Labrador, Julio Díaz González, and Ramón Pez Ferro. Miguel A. Pérez Lamy served as defense counsel for Antonio Pérez Mujica, José Antonio Cabrera, Armando Díaz Cantelar, and Rolando Hevia Ruiz. Rafael Cisneros Ponteau served as defense counsel for Juan M. Lloza Perera and Bernardo Hernández y Hernández. Gerardo Hernández Vera served as defense counsel for Aníbal Quesada Granados and Abelardo del Pozo García. José Valls Tamayo served as counsel for defendants Luis Casero Guillén and Arturo Hernández Tellaheche. Lucas Moran Arce served as defense counsel for José Luis González Ruiz. Eduardo Eljaiek Eldidy served as defense counsel for Angel Eros Sánchez and Fernando Fernández Catá. José María Badell Romero served as defense counsel for Manuel Lorenzo Acosta. Roberto Rosillo Rodríguez served as defense counsel for Vicente Chávez, Sergio González Machado, and Fernando Limia Rodríguez. Rubén Alonso Alvarez served as defense counsel for Humberto Lamothe Coronado, Aracelio Azcuy Cruz, Oscar Alvarado González, Rafael Valdés Calvo, Sergio Mejías Pérez, and Dr. José Manuel Gutiérrez Planas. Baudilio Castellanos García served as defense counsel for Haydée Santamaría, Gabriel Gil Alfonso, Gerardo Sosa Rodríguez, Rosendo Menéndez, Ramiro Valdés Menéndez, José Ponce Díaz, Ciro Redondo García, José Suárez Blanco, Francisco González Hernández, Tomás Rodríguez, Pedro Miret Prieto, Ramón Callao Díaz, Mario Chanes de Armas, Luis Pérez Cabrejas, René Bedia Morales, Florentino Hernández Enríquez, Gustavo E. Ameijeiras Romo, Porfirio Loynaz Hechavarría Cordovés, Cecilio Timoteo Benítez León, Marino Collazo Cordero, Andrés García Díaz, and Agustín Díaz Cartaya. Luis Pérez Rey served as defense counsel for Joaquín Ordoqui Mesa and Lázaro Peña González. Jorge Pagliery Cardero served as defense counsel for Melba Hernández y Rodríguez del Rey. Héctor Canciano Labory served as defense counsel for Luis Arrastría Navarrete. Conrado Castelis Cordero served as defense counsel for Aida Pelayo. Attorneys Roberto García Ibáñez and Ramiro Arango Alsina, both defendants, exercised their right to act as their own counsels.

The Chief Justice declared the Court in session. At this point I reported on a written message from Recaredo García Fernández, defense counsel for José M. Villa Romero, Silverio Emilio Brito Oquendo, José A. Batista Lotti, Ramón Campa Delgado, Heriberto Sánchez Tamayo, José Fernández Pila Teleña, Raúl del Mazo Serra, and Pedro Celestino Aguilera González, requesting this Court to excuse him from this trial in order to attend the hearing on case 376 of 1952, being tried at the Northern Trial Court and to appoint an ex-officio counsel to defend his clients. The Court granted these requests and appointed Dr. Roberto Rosillo Rodríguez as ex-officio counsel to represent the above-mentioned defendants, who expressed their consent. At this point, defense attorney Andrés Silva Adán told the Court that, although an order had been issued for the release of defendants Ignacio Fiterre Rivera and René Betancourt Castillo, they had been rearrested within the prison itself by members of the Military Intelligence Service as soon as they were released from this trial and that no reasons for this new arrest had been given. Defense attorney Raúl de Villalvilla Carbonell reported similar occurrences in the cases of defendants Ramón Serrano Alfonso and Humberto Lamothe Coronado. Since all these defendants had informed their lawyers that they had no further cases pending against them, the lawyers requested that the Court inquire of the chief of the military district as to the reasons for the arrest of these defendants, to which the Court agreed.

Attorney Andrés Silva Adán, defense counsel for Guillermo Elizalde Sotolongo, Genaro Hernández Martínez, Rolando Guerrero Bello, Ignacio Fiterre Rivera, and René Betancourt Castillo, then reported that he would leave the courtroom to act as ex-officio counsel in the Fourth Chamber of this Court. The Court agreed and appointed Roberto Rosillo Rodríguez as ex-officio counsel, regarding attorney Andrés Silva Adán as having ceased to represent the above-mentioned defendants, who expressed their consent.

The Chief Justice then gave the floor to Jorge Pagliery Cardero, defense counsel for Melba Hernández y Rodríguez del Rey, who spoke on behalf of his clients. The Court agreed to a brief recess, following which the Chief Justice gave the floor to attorney Baudilio Castellanos García, who spoke on behalf of his clients since the Court had extended its session until the end of the trial. The Court adjourned for deliberations.

In continuing the trial, the Court, having examined the evidence and the documents presented and having heard the statements made by the parties, decided TO SENTENCE defendants Ernesto Tizol Aguilera, Oscar Alcalde Valls, Pedro Miret Prieto, and Raúl Castro Ruz for directing a crime against state powers, as defined and proscribed in Article 147, but not in 148, of the Social Defense Code, in connection with Article 150 of the said Code, to THIRTEEN YEARS' IMPRISONMENT, to be served in the La Cabaña fortress, since this is a political crime, according to Article 161 of the Social Defense Code, whose Article 70-A provides that such sentences may be served only in a military fortress. The commanding officer there must be instructed that the said prisoners are to be kept isolated from the others. They are to be credited for all time served under provisional imprisonment in connection with this case. Additional provisions of the sentence include denying them the right to active and passive suffrage, to hold public office, to practice liberal professions, and to act on behalf of minors or disabled persons in civil proceedings while serving the main sentence. Moreover, the means or equipment used to commit the crime are to be confiscated for a period of time equal to that of the sentence. There will be a probationary period, equal to the time of the sentence, during which the probationers must appear before their local chief of police every 30 days and are forbidden to change their place of residence without prior written authorization from the said officers.

Also, on the same grounds, the Court decided TO SENTENCE defendants Andrés García Díaz, Enrique Cámara Pérez, Agustín Díaz Cartaya, René Bedia Morales, Eduardo Montano Benítez, José Suárez Blanco, Mario Chanes de Armas, Juan Almeida Bosque, Armando Mestre Martínez, Francisco González Hernández, Ciro Redondo García, José Ponce Díaz, Ramiro Valdés Menéndez, Julio Díaz González, Israel Tápanes Vento Aguilera, Jesús Montané Oropesa, Reinaldo Benítez Nápoles, Fidel Labrador García, and Gabriel Gil Alfonso as participants in a crime against state powers, as defined and proscribed in Article 147, in connection with Article 150, both of the Social Defense Code, to TEN YEARS' IMPRISONMENT, to be served in the La Cabaña fortress, since this is a political crime, according to Article 161 of the Social Defense Code, whose Article 70-A stipulates that such sentences may be served only in a military fortress. The commanding officer there must be instructed that the said prisoners are to be kept isolated from the others. They are to be credited for all time served in provisional imprisonment in connection with this case. Additional provisions of the sentence include denying them the right to active and passive suffrage, to hold public office, to practice liberal professions, and to act on behalf of minors or disabled persons in civil proceedings while serving the main sentence. Moreover, the means or equipment used to commit the crime are to be confiscated for a period of time equal to that of the sentence. There will be a probationary period, equal to the time of the sentence, during which the probationers must appear before their local chief of police every 30 days and are forbidden to change their place of residence without prior written authorization from the said officers.

Also, on the same grounds, the Court decided TO SENTENCE defendants Orlando Cortés Gallardo, Eduardo Rodríguez Alemán, and Manuel Lorenzo Acosta as participants in a crime against state powers, as defined and proscribed in Article 147, in connection with paragraph 2 of Article 157 of the Social Defense Code, to THREE YEARS' IMPRISONMENT, to be served in the La Cabaña fortress, since this a political crime, according to Article 161 of the Social Defense Code, whose Article 70 — correction, Article 70-A — provides that such sentences may be served only in a military fortress. The commanding officer there must be instructed that the said prisoners are to be kept isolated from the others. They are to be credited for all time served in provisional imprisonment in connection with this case. Additional provisions of the sentence include denying them the right to active and passive suffrage, to hold public office, to practice liberal professions, and to act on behalf of minors or disabled persons in civil proceedings while serving the main sentence. Moreover, the means or equipment used to commit the crime are to be confiscated for a period of time equal to that of the sentence. There will be a probationary period, equal to the time of the sentence, during which the probationers must appear before their local chief of police every 30 days and are forbidden to change their place of residence without prior written authorization from the said officers.

Also, and on the same grounds, the Court decided TO SENTENCE defendants Haydée Santamaría Cuadrado and Melba Hernández y Rodríguez del Rey as participants — since they aided the armed body — in a crime against the state powers, as defined and proscribed in Article 160, in connection with 147, both of the Social Defense Code, to SEVEN MONTHS' IMPRISONMENT. This sentence is to be served in the National Women's Prison, where they are to be kept isolated from common prisoners, since this is a political crime, as the person in charge of the said establishment will be notified. They are to be credited for all time served in provisional imprisonment in connection with this case. Additional provisions of this sentence include denying them the right to active and passive suffrage for a period of time equal to that of the main sentence, while the means or equipment used to commit the crime are to be confiscated.

We also impose on all defendants — with the exception of Orlando Cortés Gallardo, Eduardo Rodríguez Alemán, Manuel Lorenzo Acosta, Haydée Santamaría Cuadrado, and Melba Hernández y Rodríguez del Rey — the civil obligation of indemnifying the heirs of Second Lieutenants Pedro Feraud Mejías and Andrés Morales Alvarez with the sum of 5000 pesos in official currency; the heirs of Sergeants Ramón Silverio Enríquez and Luis Oliva with the sum of 4000 pesos; the heirs of Corporals Isidro C. Izquierdo Rodríguez and Nemesio Traba Montero with the sum of 3000 pesos; the heirs of soldiers Manuel Alvarez Morgado, Urbano Sánchez Avila, José Sánchez Pruna, Eusebio Baró Melodio, Felino Miró Ruiz, José Vázquez, Ibraín Galano Liranza, Pedro Guilarte, and Ramiro Saturnino Santiesteban with the sum of 2000 pesos; the heirs of Band Corporal Manuel Miras Nieves with the sum of 3000 pesos; the heirs of National Police Sergeant Jerónimo Suárez Camejo with the sum of 4000 pesos; the heirs of National Policeman Pedro H. Pompa

Castañeda with the sum of 2000 pesos; the heirs of National Policeman Roberto Ferrándiz with the sum of 2000 pesos; Lieutenant Juan E. Piña Martínez with the sum of 30 pesos; Corporal Gerardo Hechavarría Granados with 30 pesos; Corporal José Llanes León with 50 pesos; Corporal Norberto Batista Seguí with 50 pesos; Corporal Eugenio Alcolea with 50 pesos; Corporal Mauricio Feraud Mejías with 100 pesos; Corporal Héctor Reyes Muñoz with 50 pesos; soldier Clemente Godó Estenoz with 30 pesos; soldier Argeo Sarmiento Moreno with 20 pesos; soldier Lázaro Tejadilla with 30 pesos; soldier José Fonseca with 10 pesos; soldier Pedro Guilarte with 50 pesos; soldier Diocles Martínez with 20 pesos; soldier Pedro Chacón with 20 pesos; soldier Luis Frómeta Naranjo with 30 pesos; soldier Marino Ruiz with 30 pesos; soldier Cosme Aguila Cuevas with 30 pesos; soldier Daniel Lavastida Martínez with 30 pesos; soldier Luis H. Hodelin with 100 pesos; soldier Angel Duvalón Gilbert with 50 pesos; National Policeman Patricio Moreno with 100 pesos; National Policeman Evelio Xenis López with 50 pesos; military man Antonio Blanco Rodríguez with 30 pesos; soldier Pedro Porto with 20 pesos; soldier Emilio Reyes Rodríguez with 20 pesos; soldier Alberto Hernández with 50 pesos; soldier Luis Enríquez Naranjo with 50 pesos; and soldier Emilio Reyes with 50 pesos in addition to indemnifying the Cuban state with 2471 and 20 centavos, the cost of the damage to the installations of the Moncada garrison, the Military Hospital, the Military District, the Civilian Hospital, and the Palace of Justice. All these sums are to be paid collectively in the manner established by Article 121 and those that follow in the Social Defense Code. The individuals who default in their payments are subject to one day in jail for every three pesos not paid, up to a period not exceeding six months, subject to the limitations contained in Article 117 of the Social Defense Code.

We also impose on all defendants, without exception, the civil obligation of paying the expenses incurred by experts and witnesses for their court appearances during this trial, which we set at three hundred pesos in official currency; the defense attorneys' fees, which we set at two hundred pesos each, in official currency, to be paid in the manner established in Article 122 and those that follow in the Social Defense Code. The individuals who default in their payments are subject to one day in jail for every three pesos not paid, up to a period not exceeding six months, subject to the limitations contained in Article 117 of the said Code.

Also, having examined the evidence and the documents presented at this trial and having heard the statements made by the parties — which have failed to prove participation in the previously mentioned crime against state powers — the Court has decided TO FREELY ACQUIT defendants José M. Villa Romero, Silverio Emilio Brito Oquendo, José A. Batista Lotti, Ramón Campa Delgado, Eriberto Sánchez Tamayo, José Fernando Pila Teleña, Raúl del Mazo Serra, Pedro Celestino Aguilera González, Mario Burman Corman, Lázara Pérez Cuesta, Oscar Gras Escalona, Ulises Sarmiento Vargas, Isidro Peñalver O'Relly, Humberto Valdés Casañas, Manuel Vázquez Tió, Jesús Blanco Alba, Carlos Merilles Acosta, Antonio San Ramón Llanes, Generoso Reinaldo Llanes Machado, Moto Mendel Weiss, Mauro Suárez Suárez, Angel Valdés Rodríguez, Angel L. Díaz Francisco, Gerardo Sosa Rodríguez, Tomás Rodríguez Rodríguez, Ramón Callao Díaz, Luis Pérez Cabrejas, Gustavo Ameijeiras Romo, Pordorio Loynaz Hechavarría Cordovés, Cecilio Timoteo Benítez León, Marino Collazo Cordero, Rafael Núñez Leyva, Guillermo Elizalde Sotolongo, Genaro Hernández Martínez, Rolando Guerrero Bello, Ignacio Fiterre Rivera, René Betancourt Castillo, Emilio Ochoa Ochoa, José Vázquez Rojas, Leonel Antonio de los Santos Gómez Pérez, Ramón Serrano Alfonso, Juan Manuel Martínez, Ramón Pez Ferro, Antonio Pérez Mujica, and José Antonio Cabrera, Armando Díaz Cantelar, Rolando Hevia Ruiz, Juan M. Lloza Perera, Bernardo Hernández Hernández, Lázaro Peña González, Joaquín Ordoqui Mesa, Aníbal Quesada Granados, Abelardo del Pozo García, Luis Casero Guillén, Arturo Hernández Tellaheche, José Luis González Ruiz, Angel Eros Sánchez, Fernando Fernández Catá, Vicente Chávez Fernández, Sergio González Machado, Fernando Limia Rodríguez, Humberto Valdés Casañas — correction, Humberto Lamothe Coronado — Aracelio Azcuy Cruz, Oscar Alvarado González, Rafael Valdés Calvo, Sergio Mejías Pérez, José M. Gutiérrez Planas, Luis Arrastría Navarrete, Aida Pelayo Pelayo, Roberto García Ibáñez, Ramiro Arango Alsina, and Florentino Hernández Enríquez.

The Court orders the immediate release of this last defendant, who is imprisoned; and will today issue instructions effecting his release in connection with this trial only, noting that no decision was made regarding the material evidence, which is still necessary in the Court, since there are other defendants who have not yet been tried.

The session having been adjourned, the present record was drawn up as certification thereof and signed before me by the Justices, which I certify: Adolfo Nieto, Ricardo Díaz, Dr. J.F. Mejías, Dr. Raúl Mascaró.

Note: On October 6, instructions were issued to the chief of the Maceo Regiment, and a release order was issued to the prison, which I certify — Dr. Mascaró.

Appendix 3

Text of sentence passed October 16, 1953

Minutes, pages 3099-105

FIRST HEARING, PROVISIONAL COURT: In the city of Santiago de Cuba, on October 16, 1953, the day set to begin the trial of Provisional Court Case 37 of 1953, the First Chamber of this District Court was convened in the city's Civilian Hospital, composed of Chief Justice Adolfo Nieto Piñeiro Osorio and Associate Justices Ricardo Díaz Olivera, Juan F. Mejías Valdivieso, and myself. Mr. Francisco Mendieta Hechevarría appeared as State Prosecutor. Marcial Rodríguez Gutiérrez served as counsel for defendant GERARDO POLL CABRERA, and the ex-officio court-appointed attorney served as counsel for defendants FIDEL CASTRO RUZ and ABELARDO CRESPO ARIAS.

The Chief Justice declared the Court in session and advised attorney Fidel Castro Ruz, a defendant, of the charges. Asked if he wished to testify, the defendant replied in the affirmative and spoke on his own behalf, stating that Raúl de Aguiar, Armando Valle, and a third comrade of his had been arrested at Alto Cedro on July 26 and killed on the spot by Corporal Maceo, acting chief of the Rural Guard post at Alto Cedro, and Sergeant Montes de Oca, chief of the Miranda post. He said that one of those responsible for the torture and homicide at the Moncada garrison was Sergeant Eulalio González, the "Tiger," who, while riding on a public bus, had encountered the mother of one of the young men he had killed and had bragged to her that he had gouged out her son's eyes and would do it again. He said that Lieutenant Camps, who arrested his brother, had treated him in a gentlemanly fashion, and so had the military officer who arrested him; and that it was General Martín Díaz Martín — correction, Martín Díaz Tamayo — who had ordered the prisoners murdered at the Moncada garrison.

The Court decided that the defendant's statements would be included in the record. After he had finished presenting evidence in his deposition, the defendant expressed his wish to act as his own counsel, since he is a lawyer, and the Court agreed. The defendant then took his seat in the area reserved for counsels. Defendant Abelardo Crespo Arias was then advised of the charges against him. Asked if he wished to testify, the defendant replied in the affirmative and spoke on his own behalf. Next, defendant Gerardo Poll Caballero [sic] was advised of the charges against him. Asked if he wished to testify, he replied in the affirmative and spoke on his own behalf.

The Court then began interrogating witnesses. The following appeared and testified under oath, having been advised of the penalties for perjury: Lieutenant Colonel Angel González Alfonso, Major Rafael Morales Alvarez, medical Captain Eduardo Pérez Sainz de la Peña, and Major Andrés Pérez Chaumont. At this point, the Court decided to interrupt the interrogation of witnesses in order to appraise the medical experts' evidence, and it summoned Dr. Alipio Rodríguez López and Dr. José Ramón Cabrales Arjona, who appeared and affirmed that they would properly and faithfully fulfill the duties incumbent on them.

The following military men who had been wounded were then called to testify: Evelio Xenis López, Luis Frómeta Naranjo, Angel Duvalón, Víctor Manuel Hernández, Clemente Godó Estenoz, Argeo Sarmiento Moreno, José Llanes León, Pedro Porto, Mauricio Faraud Mejías, Eugenio Alcolea, Miguel Mariano Ruiz, Juan P. Navarro Molina, Norberto Batista Seguí, Antonio D. Blanco Rodríguez, Diocles Martínez, Gerardo Hechavarría Granados, Juan N. Piña Martínez, Alberto Hernández Rodríguez, Néstor Reyes, Emilio Reyes Rodríguez, and Luis Enrique Naranjo. As secretary, I then read the medical experts the opinions they had expressed in previous hearings of this trial, and they swore that they were true.

The following witnesses then appeared and testified under oath as the Court again began the interrogation: Colonel Alberto del Río Chaviano, Juan E. Piña Martínez, Gerardo Hechavarría Granados, Norberto Batista Seguí, Eugenio Alcolea, Héctor Reyes Muñoz, Argeo Moreno Sarmiento, Lázaro Tejadilla, Diocles Martínez, Miguel Mariano Ruiz (who is the same witness as Marino Ruiz), Cosme Aguila Cuevas, Evelio Xenis, Antonio Blanco Rodríguez, Pedro Porto, Emilio Reyes Aguilera, Luis Enrique Naranjo, medical Lieutenant Erik Juan Pita, and provincial secret police investigator Vicente Rigual.

Expert appraisers José Oñate Areas and Lieutenant Rodolfo Hernández Pérez were then summoned, but only the latter appeared. The Court, with the parties' consent, therefore replaced the former with Lieutenant Vicente Camps, who appeared. The two took the oath, affirmed they would properly and faithfully comply with their duties and stated that Lieutenant Rodolfo Hernández Pérez ratified the opinions recorded on pages 354 and 356 and that Lieutenant Vicente Camps concurred.

Ballistics experts Eusebio Berrio and Heriberto Amador Cruz were summoned, but only the former appeared. The Court replaced the latter with Captain Pedro A. Rodríguez Medrano, who appeared. The two took their oaths, affirming they would properly and faithfully comply with their duties, seeking only the truth, and stated that Lieutenant Berrio completely concurred with the opinion already recorded and that Captain Pedro A. Rodríguez Medrano concurred.

Interrogation of witnesses then continued, and the following were summoned, appeared, took the oath, and testified: medical Captain Mario Porro Varela and National Police Major Rafael Izquierdo — correction, José Izquierdo Rodríguez. At the request of Dr. Marcial Rodríguez Gutiérrez, the following witnesses for the defense were summoned, appeared, took the oath, and testified: Rafael Casacó (who stated that he was a brother-in-law of defendant Gerardo Poll Cabrera and was advised of his legal rights before he testified), Oscar Bolívar, Celedonio Marsillí, Manuel Serrano, Emilio Urrutia Portuondo, and Reynaldo Traba Montero. At this point, the Court called for expert medical evidence, and medical experts Drs. Arturo de Feria Mora and Fernando Blanc Corbín were summoned, appeared, affirmed they would properly and faithfully fulfill the duties incumbent on them, and expressed their opinion.

The Court waived interrogation of the remaining witnesses, considering their testimony unnecessary, and called on the prosecutor to sum up his case. The prosecutor requested acquittal of defendant Gerardo Poll Cabrera and asked that defendants Fidel Castro Ruz and Abelardo Crespo Arias be sentenced under Article 148-B of the Social Defense Code, for the reasons explained. The Chief Justice gave the floor to Gerardo Poll Cabrera's defense counsel, who supported the request made by the prosecutor on behalf of his defendant. The Court then gave the floor to Baudilio Castellanos García, counsel for the defense of Abelardo Crespo Arias, who spoke on behalf of his defendant. The Chief Justice then gave the floor to attorney Fidel Castro Ruz, who spoke in his own defense, the Court having prolonged the session until the end of the trial. Following the defendant's address, in which he acted as his own counsel, the Court adjourned to deliberate.

On continuing the trial, after having examined the evidence presented, having taken into consideration the documents and heard the statements made by the parties, the Court decided TO SENTENCE defendant FIDEL CASTRO RUZ, as chiefly responsible for a crime committed against state powers, as defined and proscribed in Article 147 (but not 148) of the Social Defense Code, in connection with Article 150 of the said Code, to FIFTEEN YEARS' IMPRISONMENT, to be served in the La Cabaña fortress, since it is a political crime as defined in Article

161 of the Social Defense Code, whose Article 70-A provides that such sentences may be served only in a military fortress. The commanding officer there must be instructed that the prisoner is to be kept isolated from the common prisoners. The prisoner is to be credited for all time served in provisional imprisonment in connection with this trial. Additional provisions of the sentence include denying him the right to active and passive suffrage, to hold public office, to practice liberal professions, and to act on behalf of minors or disabled persons in civil proceedings while serving the main sentence. Moreover, the means or equipment used to commit the crime are to be confiscated for a period of time equal to the sentence. There will be a probationary period equal to the time of the sentence, during which the probationer must appear before his local chief of police every 30 days and is forbidden to change his place of residence without prior written authorization from the said officer.

Also, on the same grounds, the Court decided TO SENTENCE defendant ABELARDO CRESPO ARIAS as a participant in a crime against state powers, as defined and proscribed in Article 147, in connection with Article 150, both of the Social Defense Code, to TEN YEARS' IMPRISONMENT, to be served in the La Cabaña fortress, since it is a political crime, as defined in Article 161 of the Social Defense Code, whose Article 70-A provides that such sentences may be served only in a military fortress. The commanding officer there must be instructed that the said prisoner is to be kept isolated from the others. The prisoner is to be credited for all time served in provisional imprisonment in connection with this case. Additional provisions of the sentence include denying him the right to active and passive suffrage, to hold public office, to practice liberal professions, and to act on behalf of minors or disabled persons in civil proceedings while serving the main sentence. Moreover, the means or equipment used to commit the crime are to be confiscated for a period of time equal to that of the sentence. There will be a probationary period, equal to the time of the sentence, during which the probationer must appear before his local chief of police every 30 days and is forbidden to change his place of residence without prior written authorization from the said officers.

At this point, Dr. Baudilio Castellanos García, the defendant's counsel, requested that, before his client is transferred to the La Cabaña fortress, he be hospitalized in the Students' Clinic of Calixto García Hospital, to which he has access, since he is seriously wounded -- as recorded in the proceedings -- and there are better scientific resources there for his treatment and recovery. The Court decided that, before the said defendant is transferred to the La Cabaña fortress, he should be transferred, under proper custody and guard, to the Students' Clinic of Calixto García Hospital, where he will receive proper treatment and will remain under adequate custody until his condition permits him to be transferred to the La Cabaña fortress without endangering his life.

We also impose on defendants Fidel Castro Ruz and Abelardo Crespo Arias the civil obligation of indemnifying the heirs of Second Lieutenants Pedro Faraud Mejías and Andrés Morales Alvarez with the sum of 5000 pesos in official currency; the heirs of Sergeants Ramón Silverio Enríquez and Luis Oliva with the sum of 4000 pesos; the heirs of Corporals Isidro C. Izquierdo Rodríguez and Nemesio Traba Montero with the sum of 3000 pesos; the heirs of soldiers Manuel Alvarez Morgado, Urbano Sánchez Avila, Jesús Sánchez Pruna, Eusebio Baró Melodio, Felino Miró Ruiz, José Vázquez, Ibrahím Galano Liranza, Pedro Guilarte, and Ramiro Saturnino Santiesteban with the sum of 2000 pesos; the heirs of Band Corporal Manuel Mirás Nieves with the sum of 3000 pesos; the heirs of National Police Sergeant Jerónimo Suárez Camejo with the sum of thousand pesos; the heirs of National Policeman Pedro M. Pompa Castañeda with the sum of 2000 pesos; the heirs of National Policeman Roberto Ferrandiz with the sum of 1000 pesos; and to indemnify Lieutenant Juan E. Piña Martínez with the sum of 30 pesos; Corporal Gerardo Hechavarría Granados with 30 pesos; Corporal José Llanes León with 50 pesos; Corporal Norberto Batista Seguí with 50 pesos; Corporal Eugenio Alcolea with 50 pesos; Corporal Mauricio Feraud Mejías with 100 pesos; Corporal Héctor Reyes Muñoz with 50 pesos; soldier Clemente Godó Estenoz with 30 pesos; soldier Argeo Sarmiento Moreno with 20 pesos; soldier Lázaro Tejadilla with 30 pesos; soldier José Fonseca with 10 pesos; soldier Pedro Guilarte with 100 pesos; soldier Diocles Martínez with 20 pesos; soldier Pedro Chacón with 20 pesos; soldier Luis Frómeta Naranjo with 30 pesos; soldier Marino Ruiz with 30 pesos; soldier Cosme Aguila Cuevas with 30 pesos; soldier Daniel Lavastida Martínez with 30 pesos; soldier Luis H. Hodelín with 100 pesos; soldier Angel Duvalón Gilbert with 50 pesos; National Policeman Patricio Moreno with 100 pesos; Policeman Evelio Xenis López with 50 pesos; military man Antonio Blanco Rodríguez with thirty pesos; soldier Pedro Porto with 20 pesos; military man Emilio Reyes Rodríguez with 20 pesos; military man Alberto Hernández with 50 pesos; soldier Luis Enrique Naranjo with 50 pesos; and soldier Emilio Reyes with 100 pesos, in addition to indemnifying the Cuban state with 2471 pesos and 22 centavos, the cost of the damage to the installations of the Moncada garrison, the Military Hospital, the Military District, the Civilian Hospital, and the Palace of

Justice.

All these sums are to be paid collectively in the manner established by Article 121 and those that follow in the Social Defense Code. The individuals who default in their payments are subject to one day in jail for every three pesos not paid, not to exceed a period of six months, subject to the limitations contained in Article 117 of the Social Defense Code.

We also impose on both defendants the civil obligation of paying the expenses incurred by experts and witnesses for their Court appearances during this trial, which we set at 300 pesos in official currency; the defense attorneys' fees, which we set at 200 pesos each, in official currency, to be paid in the manner established in Article 122 and those that follow in the Social Defense Code. The individuals who default in their payments are subject to one day in jail for every three pesos not paid, not to exceed a period of six months, subject to the limitations contained in Article 117 of the said Code.

Also, having examined the evidence and the documents presented at this trial and having heard the statements made by the parties, the Court has decided TO FREELY ACQUIT defendant Gerardo Poll Cabrera, as his participation in the above-mentioned crime against state powers has not been proven. The Court orders that the necessary instructions be issued today for the immediate release of the said defendant in connection with this trial only, while making it known that no decision was made regarding the material evidence, which is still necessary in the courtroom, since there are other defendants who have not yet been tried.

The session having been adjourned, the present minutes were drawn up as certification thereof and signed before me by the Justices, which I certify: Adolfo Nieto, R. Díaz Olivera, Dr. Juan F. Mejías, Dr. Raúl Mascaró.

Appendix 4

Excerpts from José Martí's works underlined by Fidel Castro in prison

In 1948, Lex Publishers in Havana published José Martí's *Obras Completas* (Collected works) in two thick volumes on bible paper. Those volumes, now in the Office of Historical Affairs, were among the hundreds of books Fidel read and studied during his imprisonment at the National Men's Prison on the Isle of Pines. These are the excerpts that Fidel underlined from the *Collected Works*.

...an earnest, solid, and imposing revolution, worthy of the participation of honest men.

Waiting is one way to win, but when our country calls one must answer.

Just as it is admirable to give one's life for a great ideal, it is contemptible to use a great ideal for personal ambitions of glory or power.

One has a right to give one's life only when it is given selflessly.

The highest degree of greatness is to show respect for a people that loves and puts its hopes in us.

I serve duty alone, and with that I shall always be sufficiently powerful.

We must proclaim to the country and consolidate with our efforts a program worthy of winning over the people, who will no longer follow the first person who uses a sacred name to proclaim himself their leader.

Our country is a thinking country, and we can do nothing without winning our people's minds.

Long service obliges one to continue serving.

The courage, prestige, pure aims, and exemplary martyrdom of revolutionaries abroad will be useless as long as they do not work together.

War cannot be waged if the country lacks faith in it and in those who begin or lead it.

All revolutionary work is in vain if it lacks the spirit of the country.

Now that we are able to create or destroy, let us create.

To rise above intrigue is to rise above a nest of vipers.

Governments may ignore us, but the peoples will always love and admire us.

In a revolution, the methods must be hidden, the aims made known.

We stand up for the country. To stand upon it is a crime.

I can offer no remuneration other than the pleasure of sacrifice.

...to create, with the collective efforts of all men of good will.

But Cubans, like a great strategist, know that nothing must be done that our enemies want us to do.

Only flowers planted in poor soil need to be watered daily.

The ambitions of a group will die; what the people want lives on.

A lazy soul kindles no fire.

It would be useless to ask the armed and imperious master to pass laws that would deprive him of prosperity and power.

...a republic is made through effort and work, not disputes and names.

...and if passion seeks revenge on the innocent for crimes committed by the defeated government, there will be many who will act to shield the innocent from vengeance.

...to build up a good and sincere nation with people who, should their honor ever come to an end, would wind up a ruined province of a sterile nation, a mere outpost, or a bridge for a disdainful neighbor.

The courage of the wronged is as great as the evident panic of the foe who wrongs him.

These are our people, who are only unwilling and invisible when they grieve or become indignant because they are not being served with true love or with the promptness and fullness their great poverty and neglect demand.

...a colony has only to free itself from such abuse in order to develop to the fullest the remarkable proven intelligence of its sons and daughters.

If the illness leads to death before the remedy can be prepared, what good is the remedy?

No one has the right to endanger the homeland by his indolence.

The homeland is sacred; all who love it unselfishly and unceasingly owe it the whole truth.

The noblest passions must yield to realities that make them untimely and fruitless.

Words are superfluous when they fail to create, attract, or contribute.

What is thinking but creating?

To think is to open the way, lay the foundations, and give the heart its watchword.

Hail the brave; hail them a hundred times, even when they have erred or belittled themselves!

Give what is just, and we will not be asked for what is unjust.

He who is afraid to be a man should hire himself out to the ambitious, who will use him, pay him and defend his breed or his ill-gotten gains.

We should do what is good for our people, sacrificing ourselves, and not what is good for ourselves, sacrificing our people.

The homeland needs sacrifice. It is an altar, not a pedestal, to be served, not used to serve oneself.

The strong plan ahead; second-rate men await the storm with arms crossed.

The youth go in silence to honor the graves of the heroes.

Sad must be the heart of he who helps oppress others.

The vain admire their names; honorable men, their homeland.

At the decisive moment, indecision is a crime.

Once again, in Cuba and Puerto Rico, there will be men who will die in purity, unstained by selfishness, defending the rights of men.

When courage is called for, cowardice is loathsome.

Roots give life to the tree, and the men who give life to the truth are those who die at its feet.

Those who do not want to sacrifice are the enemies of those who do.

He who resigns himself to evil is its accomplice.

Those who want a secure homeland must fight for it.

Cubans, the only homeland is the one you conquer by your own efforts.

In a people, as in a man, virtue is silent.

We are a carpet for our people to step on.

He who blames others for not creating must himself create.

...and for the opportunity, now nearly lost, for the enslaved Antilles to come and take its rightful place as a nation in the American world, before the disproportionate development of the most powerful part of

America turns these lands, which can still be a garden for their inhabitants and a standard for the world, into a scene of universal greed.

Glory is for those who look forward, not backward.

Let the cowards show respect; let the great move forward!

Every Cuban who dies is one more hymn; every Cuban who lives should be a temple to honor the dead.

It is better to die of one's wounds than to let the enemy see them.

Words must now be foundations and battle trenches.

When has a nation been created by begging for its rights?

The homeland is happiness for all, sorrow for all, and heaven for all — but no one's fief or estate.

True men are concerned not with how they can live better, but with where their duty lies.

Words that do not come from a unstained and pure heart are a dishonor.

Let us educate the simple and ignorant, instead of letting them follow our passions and envies like sheep.

We must reject, as ill-fated and unworthy of men, any sham and perfidious freedom that might be attained through settlement or payment.

I have faith that martyrdom will reign and heroism triumph.

To lead is to foresee.

Those who deny men the beautiful right to be moved and to show admiration are deluded.

Enthusiasm has never had gray hair.

Ardor induces ideas, strength, love, and a convinced soul, and it produces earnest, revolutionary aims and a cordial, constructive patriotism.

The homeland's honor — and dishonor — are shared by all.

The highest altar of honor is that of the bodies of our martyrs.

The only relief for acute pain is the joy of soothing the pain of others.

Tombs speak through the flowers of resurrection that grow on graves.

Some regret a necessary death; I believe in it as a place of rest, as leavening, as the triumph of life.

A people with bloodstained brow cannot enjoy freedom.

The tree with the sweetest fruit has a dead man buried at its roots.

Homeland means community of interests, unity of traditions and aims, a sweet and consoling fusion of love and hope.

Honesty is the vigor with which one defends one's beliefs.

Appendix 5

Amnesty Law

EXECUTIVE POWER
JUSTICE
Law No.2

I, FULGENCIO BATISTA Y ZALDIVAR, President of the Republic of Cuba, make known: that the Congress of the Republic has adopted, and I have approved, the following LAW:

Article 1. Amnesty is granted for the following offenses committed before April 15, 1955:

A. those in Part 2 of the Social Defense Code listed below:

1. all those in Chapter I of Section 1;

2. all those in Chapter IV of Section I except those connected with the offense described in Article 128;

3. all those contained in Chapters I, II, III, IV, and V of Section V;

4. those in Articles 468, 469, and 470;

B. all those contained in Law 5 of 1948, as modified by Legislative Decree 265 of 1952 and Legislative Decree 1052 of 1953;

C. that contained in Article 341 of the Social Defense Code, if the main offense involved is one of those listed in this article.

Article 2. Amnesty is granted for the following offenses committed before April 15, 1955, if they had political motivations or aims, or if they were committed in order to facilitate, repress, investigate, or prevent any of the offenses contained in the previous article:

Those included in Part 2 of the Social Defense Code, listed below:

1. all those in Chapters I, II, III, and IV of Section III;

2. all those in Chapters VI and VIII of Section V;

3. that described in Article 271;

4. all those in Chapter VIII of Section VI;

5. those included in Paragraphs A and B of Article 465, provided the property burned was an automobile or some other vehicle;

6. all those in Chapter IX of Section XIII.

Article 3. Benefits deriving from the above two articles will not be applicable, in any case, to offenses committed for the direct or indirect aim or purpose of expediting interventionist political action [sic] by international communism or facilitating its plans or projects.

Article 4. Amnesty is granted for all crimes and presumably criminal, fraudulent and culpable actions, as well as violations and misdemeanors committed by or imputed to members of the Army, Navy, National Police, Secret Police, Court Police, or other armed bodies belonging to a ministry or to any other national, provincial, or municipal state organization whose purpose prior to April 15, 1955, was to prevent and prosecute crimes or misdemeanors, regardless of the court, judge, or judicial authority charged with their cognizance. In addition, amnesty is granted for any infraction that may have been committed of the Social Defense Code or of any other legal ruling. Said amnesty includes both the main sentences and additional provisions thereof, no matter what form of criminal action may have been charged.

Benefits deriving from this article will be applicable only in the case of persons who are active members of the above-mentioned bodies, agencies, or organizations when this Law enters into effect.

Article 5. Benefits deriving from Articles II and III of Legislative Decree 1991 of January 27, 1955, will include all grounds for dismissal or disciplinary action with respect to officials, employees, aides, and subordinates in any of the state powers and their autonomous agencies.

Article 6. The provisions of Articles XV, XVI, XVII, and XX of Legislative Decree 1455 of June 3, 1954, will be followed in applying the benefits of this Law and determining whether to grant or deny such benefits.

Article 7. Prisoners serving a nonappealable sentence will not be released under the amnesty until its applicability has been determined by the courts.

Article 8. The granting of amnesty does not eliminate the civil obligations imposed by the verdicts in these cases.

TRANSITORY PROVISION

Those who, within 30 days after this Law enters into effect, turn over to the authorities or their agents all weapons, ammunition, equipment, and material that the authorities or their agents could legally confiscate without a warrant — excluding any weapon for which the owner has or intends to seek a permit (in the latter case, the weapon in question will be held for a maximum of one hundred and eighty days; at the end of this period, if the party in question has not yet claimed the weapon by showing the permit for its possession or use, it will be automatically confiscated) — will be considered free of criminal responsibility. All weapons, ammunition, equipment, and material turned over to the authorities or their agents will be held in custody, as indicated in the existing provisions on this matter.

If voluntary delivery to the authorities or their agents is effected between April 15, 1955, and the date this Law enters into effect, the crime of possessing weapons, ammunition, or explosives will be considered part of this amnesty.

FINAL PROVISION

All laws and other provisions inconsistent with the enforcement of this Law, which will enter into effect as of publication in the Republic's OFFICIAL GAZETTE, are hereby repealed.

Therefore: I order that this Law be fully complied with and enforced.

Decreed at the Presidential Palace, Havana, May 6, 1955
FULGENCIO BATISTA
Jorge García Montes, Prime Minister
César E. Camacho, Minister of Justice

Index